BOKO HARAM

VIRGINIA COMOLLI

Boko Haram

Nigeria's Islamist Insurgency

HURST & COMPANY, LONDON

First published in the United Kingdom in 2015 by
C. Hurst & Co. (Publishers) Ltd.,
41 Great Russell Street, London, WC1B 3PL
© Virginia Comolli, 2015
All rights reserved.
Printed in England

Distributed in the United States, Canada and Latin America by
Oxford University Press, 198 Madison Avenue, New York, NY 10016,
United States of America

The right of Virginia Comolli to be identified as the author
of this publication is asserted by her in accordance with the
Copyright, Designs and Patents Act, 1988.

A Cataloguing-in-Publication data record for this book
is available from the British Library.

ISBN: 978-184904-491-2

www.hurstpublishers.com

This book is printed using paper from registered sustainable
and managed sources.

CONTENTS

CONTENTS

ACKNOWLEDGMENTS

There are a number of individuals and organisations I owe a big thank you to. Many, unfortunately, I will not be able to acknowledge in writing to respect their wish to remain anonymous. First is my friend and colleague Raffaello Pantucci who gave me the impetus to write this book in the first place. I am grateful to Akali Omeni for his expert advice. I would like to thank Lucy Freedman and James Verini for sharing their contacts and those listed below for agreeing to being interviewed and generously sharing their knowledge with me: Admiral O. S. Ibrahim, Major General Chris Olukolade, Minister Abba Moro, Major General Sarkin Yaki Bello, Dr Fatima Akilu, Dr Ustaz Aminu Igwegbe, Reverend Musa Asake, Bishop Ronsome Bello, Professor Tijjani Bande, Hussaini Abdu, Muhammad Zubair, Dr Freedom Onoua, the staff at the Ministry of Foreign Affairs in Abuja, Borno state officials, the staff of the Nigeria Stability and Reconciliation Programme (NSRP), the British High Commission, the American Embassy and the European Union Delegation in Abuja, the Legal Defence and Assistance Project (LEDAP), the Cleen Foundation, the Foreign and Commonwealth Office (FCO) in London, Bala Mohammed Liman, and many Nigerian citizens who shared their often traumatic experiences with me.

My employers at The International Institute for Strategic Studies (IISS) deserve a special thank you for supporting my 'extra curricular' research and field work. I am indebted to the staff of GRM International for their hospitality in Kano and to Hurst Publishers for their flexibility.

Lastly, I owe a big thank you to Matteo for his support and patience throughout the project, especially during the numerous evenings and weekends I spent writing.

Nigeria

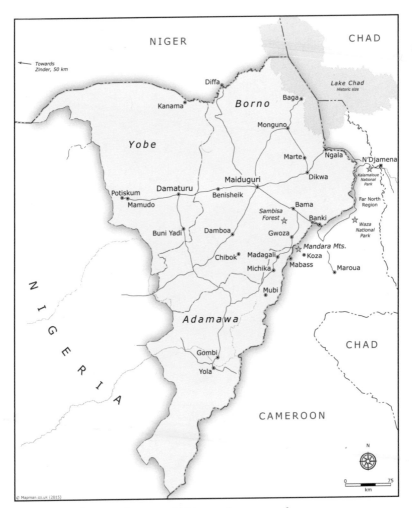

Adamawa, Borno and Yobe: under a state of emergency

1

INTRODUCTION

Neither the holy month of Ramadan nor the fact that it was Friday made any difference. Boko Haram militants had long stopped caring. Attacks had been launched day and night, on civilian and military targets, with Christians and Muslims alike killed with what seemed like relish. Friday, 18 July 2014 was no different.

When militants descended on Damboa, in Borno state, no mercy was shown to its people. Half of the buildings were torched, many bodies were left behind and the remaining inhabitants fled to neighbouring villages, leaving Damboa a ghost town.[1]

Boko Haram has been in existence in its current, more radical, form since 2009 but in the West policymakers are still struggling to get to grip with this phenomenon that has produced over 3,000 deaths between 2009 and 2013, during what can effectively be described as an insurgency campaign in northern and central Nigeria and that in autumn 2014 shows no signs of abating.[2] Indeed, by the end of July casualty levels were well beyond the 6,500 mark with over 3,200 people being killed by Boko Haram between January and July and over 4,300 militants and civilians estimated to having died at the hands of Nigerian security forces as part of the anti-Boko Haram counter-insurgency campaign in the same period.[3]

And it is not just deaths that were recorded. Around 3.3 million people have been displaced by the violence since 2010[4] and over

400,000 civilians were forced to flee their homes in north east Nigeria in the first seven months of 2014 alone according to the National Emergency Management Agency.[5]

As we will see later in the book, the local economy has also suffered significantly as a result of increasing violence in the north. Traders are afraid to open their shops or to man their market stalls; customers are too scared to visit them. In addition, temporary border closures to stem the movement of militants have had a negative impact on commercial activities across the border with Nigeria's neighbours as the free flow of goods and people has been curtailed in the name of security. Furthermore, much needed foreign investors—which have been crucial to Nigeria's economic diversification away from a model reliant on the energy sector and subsistence agriculture—have been deterred from sinking money into infrastructure and manufacturing operations in the north east as a result of the violence, growing instability and the now proven ability of Boko Haram to seize and control over parts of the territory.[6] Although Nigeria is considered a gain country capable of offering substantial returns, investing in the north is unlikely to be the preferred option of foreign investors in the context of almost certain disorder ahead of the presidential polls in spring 2015.

In the north of Nigeria, the north east in particular, are the states that desperately need such injections of capital given that they are desperately poor—in a country that appears to be running at two speeds. The continent's number one oil producer,[7] Nigeria became the richest nation in Sub-Saharan Africa,[8] in April 2014, replacing South Africa as its largest economy.[9] In spite of such wealth, life expectancy (54) is 16 years less than world's average (70),[10] and 60.9 per cent of the population—112.47 million—were living in absolute poverty in 2010, a paradoxical increase from 54.7 per cent in 2004. Moreover, the local picture shows great disparity in the redistribution of resources with poverty plaguing 27 per cent of southerners and an alarming 75, per cent of northerners,[11] which highlights the severity of underdevelopment afflicting northern states.[12] How and whether poverty feeds the insurgency is a delicate matter that will be covered in more detail in subsequent chapters.

Although it has been possible to compile some alarming statistics on fatalities and displacements and, to some extent, on financial losses, measuring the full impact of the insurgency and counter-insurgency campaigns can hardly be described as an exact science. And this is not simply the result of incomplete reporting or eagerness to attribute most violent acts and crimes to Boko Haram. Most of it is intangible.

As argued by former Supreme Court Justice George Oguntade, the crisis facing Nigeria today is one in which the social contract between the State and the people is broken. Voters, having surrendered some of their rights, agree to be ruled and are entitled to be protected by the state.[13] Protection, it seems, is not something the Nigerian system can fully ensure. What is more, government agents have themselves turned on the people they are supposed to serve and countless instances of human rights violations, amid an astonishingly widespread culture of impunity, have become one of the most infamous features of the anti-Boko Haram campaign. It should be noted that summary executions, intimidation, demanding bribes and pre-trial detentions that last years are not the exclusive preserve of the current insurgency. They are in fact recurrent fixtures of everyday life to which most citizens have resigned themselves, as some of the examples I recount later indicate. Neither are they the prerogatives of Nigeria alone. A recent book with the evocative title *The Locust Effect: Why the End of Poverty Requires the End of Violence* stresses that the threat of physical violence and the condition of helplessness in the face of state institutions or the rich are common denominators among the poor in places as varied as Peru, Kenya and India.[14] An additional weakness pertinent to the Nigerian case but shared by other former colonies relates to the British legacy of policing. The latter was introduced and designed to protect the colonial power's own interests and once colonialism ended what remained was a police force that had been structured around the provision of state security, and later the intimidation of political opponents, rather than the protection of the average Nigerian.[15]

As a result, today Nigerian civilians find themselves stuck between two brutal opponents—Boko Haram and the security forces—both of which have been accused of war crimes by human rights organisations and the media.[16] Thus a significant part of this book is devoted to understanding the government response to the insurgency (including its little reported successful aspects). Having observed the security and judicial response to the insurgency, it is fair to contend that the Boko Haram crisis—besides the killing of civilians and the widespread mayhem it has caused—has also brought out the worst in people. Extra-judicial killings and the targeting of innocent men and women by the military, the police or vigilantes are not dictated exclusively by evil or the mentality of the vengeful mob. Frustration at the judicial system's inability to deal effectively with terror suspects and the knowledge that it is often possible to bribe one's way out of prison play a role in driving those in uniform to commit such acts—in a perverse attempt to ensure justice is served. Furthermore, most of the political class has proved unable to offer an effective response to the violence, which has been in the main politicised, i.e. used by the President and the ruling party as well as by the opposition as a tool to discredit each other, to accuse one another of ineptitude or collusion, and all while, any progress made in the theatre of operations has been fairly easily reversed by Boko Haram's crescendo of attacks against an increasingly disgruntled soldiery on the ground. The latter have in fact resorted to mutiny[17] and even to shooting at the vehicle of one of their commanding officers to express their frustration at the lack of proper weaponry and leadership in spite of an ever-spiralling defence budget.[18]

The other hard to quantify, but certainly dramatic, impact of the violence is on education. Boko Haram has repeatedly attacked schools in the north, burning down buildings, slaughtering teachers and children and, increasingly, abducting young girls and boys to be forced into marriage or to be coerced into joining the militants in fighting or support roles. In some towns and villages schools have stayed closed for months on end and parents cannot be blamed for stopping their children from attending classes for fear of attacks. Repercussions are deep and long-term. Northern states were already battling with low levels of school attendance—among the lowest in the country—and the insurgency has made things worse. A 2011 survey indicates that in the state of Borno, Boko Haram's stronghold, 72 per cent of children had never been to school (in contrast to 4 per cent in the Federal Capital Territory).[19] In spite of new initiatives to increase security around schools and to build more of them (see below), these efforts appear insufficient to respond to the needs of millions of children who, without an education, will be able to provide only a limited contribution to the northern economy and public life, let alone increase northern representation at the federal level.

But children are paying for this insurgency in multiple ways. In a sickening turn of events, it became clear in 2014 that children had been selected by Boko Haram for suicide missions. The group had first introduced body-borne improvised explosive devices in 2011 at a time when many would have sworn that the concept of suicide attacks was foreign and completely un-Nigerian. They were proved wrong and the first such attack (Abuja, June 2011) sent a chilling message to the nation. The unthinkable had happened. Fast forward to 2014: teenage girls were responsible for suicide attacks in Kano and a ten-year-old girl was arrested in Katsina wearing a suicide vest. This happened only weeks after the very first female suicide attack (Gombe, June 2014).[20]

* * *

Nigeria is a complex and linguistically and culturally diverse[21] country and certainly a fascinating case study for those interested in not only security studies but also development. Notwithstanding all the internal challenges mentioned above, it retains a strategic status in the continent and is a key player within the Economic Community of West African States (ECOWAS) block and the African Union (AU). It is a major contributor to peacekeeping operations and possesses one of the most advanced and better-equipped armed forces in Africa.[22] How it uses them against the insurgency is the focus of chapter six.

The seriousness of the security, humanitarian and economic threats that accompany the current insurgency is one of the reasons I believe a book like this needed to be written. In spite of what some may have believed back in 2009–10, Boko Haram was not a glitch in the system, a small and poorly armed group of disenfranchised religious fanatics that could be easily contained or, even better, eradicated. What began as an isolated sect has grown into the perpetrator of death and destruction that today is undermining the social fabric of Nigeria, and exploiting ethnic kinship in neighbouring Chad, Niger and Cameroon to extend its reach, spreading insecurity and precipitating a humanitarian crisis among already desperately poor local populations. Meanwhile, over time Boko Haram has built and nurtured relations with al-Qaeda's affiliates and sympathisers primarily, but not exclusively, in the continent, raising concerns among Western government and security services that something bigger may be brewing, a threat that goes beyond Nigeria's national borders and may—as in fact it did—see Westerners and other foreigners become victims of kidnappings and killings.

The decision to embark on this project also stemmed from the realisation that even though some respected experts, both from Nigeria and internationally, had produced written analyses of Boko Haram, most of the available research tended to be fairly short and for this reason rather limited in scope. I hope that in the space of a book I will have the chance to adopt and develop a more comprehensive approach so that this volume can offer a robust basis upon which future research can be built, and a resource for a broader audience, including government practitioners, wishing better to understand the dynamics of religious extremism in Nigeria and the region, how ideology feeds on socio-economic marginalisation, and what this means in terms of designing effective responses that produce lasting solutions. Key to the achievement of the latter is the need to look at the current problem comprehensively and within a very specific historical and societal context so that measures address both the insurgency and its root causes and hopefully can prevent, or at a minimum limit, the recurrence of cyclical violence and the periodical re-emergence of extreme religious movements.

In order to fulfil this objective I conducted extensive desk and field based research in 2012, 2013 and part of 2014 (in addition to earlier work) interviewing a variety of individuals including Nigerian, American and British officials from government and the military, academics, international and non-governmental organisations, civil societies, and journalists, and I took advantage of every opportunity to speak to common Nigerian citizens, including those who had survived attacks.

The ensuing chapters follow a thematic rather than chronological order with some overlap being inevitable. The aim of chapter two is to provide an historical background recounting the roots of religious extremism touching upon some key phases in the history of Northern Nigeria, namely Usman Dan Fodio's Jihad and the Sokoto Caliphate, the impact of British colonial rule and the process of adoption of sharia law in northern states. Chapter three discusses the genesis of Islamist[23] groups looking at the processes of splintering, transformation, reform and formation. This brings us to 2002, when a small sect known as the Nigerian Taleban set up bases in Yobe state. The major protagonist of chapter four is Boko Haram itself. I discuss the origins of the group while navigating among the incongruences among the various historical accounts of the group's origins. The personalities of Mohammed Yusuf and Abubakar Shekau, the founding and current leader respectively, are also discussed. The chapter highlights the ideological framework in which the group evolved, especially during its early stages, and what influenced it. But overall it seeks to answer the question 'who are Boko Haram?' by describing the movement's social make-up, its funding streams, and support network. While the focus of this chapter will be domestic, chapter five will look at the internationalisation of Boko Haram's activities, especially its international connections both at the regional and sub-regional levels. This focus is merited by the escalation of the Malian crisis in 2012 and into 2013, and second, by Boko Haram's significant expansion in terms of cooperation with foreign groups, the number of its attacks and the geographical coverage of its offshoot Ansaru. Because of its broader international outlook, Ansaru deserves a prominent role in this chapter. Chapter six—on the response to the insurgency—tells the other side of the story: one of military crackdowns, denial, attempted dialogue, states of emergency, and alleged human rights abuses. But it is also a story in which Nigeria's foreign partners, namely the United Kingdom and the United States, have grown increasingly concerned about the country's fate—but also about their own commercial and political interests in West Africa. While they have started to signal their concerns by proscribing some members of Boko Haram and announcing awards for their capture, they still struggle fully to comprehend the nature of the insurgency and how best to deal with a partner nation that is not always transparent in its actions and statements. In the final chapter I set out my conclusions with an eye on the future.

Research challenges

Researching Boko Haram has not been without challenges. In the early phases of my work the published analyses publicly available were fairly limited and although a growing body of literature has since appeared, most, if not all, my fellow Boko Haram-watchers would agree that cross referencing information and obtaining accurate data remains the hardest part of our job. Moreover it is not uncommon that speculation, repeated often enough, becomes a "fact", even though it is clearly not, hence the need to exercise additional caution while conducting interviews and sifting through a myriad of (local) media reporting. Furthermore, there is an abundance of contrasting statements, usually surrounding sensitive developments as, for instance, was best exemplified in the immediate aftermath of the May 2013 state of emergency security offensive. Within a week the government declared that Boko Haram was in "disarray" and the military had made a major breakthrough including the destruction of camps and several arrests and killings of militants. Promptly Abubakar Shakau issued a video statement in which he claimed soldiers had been running away "like pigs". In the same video he also proudly showed military vehicles that had been left behind by Nigerian forces and then seized by the insurgents. Furthermore, as I will explain below, the mobile phone network was cut off for long periods during the operation in order to prevent militants from coordinating with one another, but, with mobile phones as the key means of communication in the country, this more or less translated into an information blackout, especially during the early days of the offensive.

Nor is the local media, although not always on the government's side, completely reliable either: newspapers and broadcasters in Nigeria often reprint statements verbatim from military officials. Added to that, some Nigerian journalists could only communicate with the outside world, including the rest of the country, and transmit their copy by phone, once outside Borno, Yobe and Adamawa states, causing inevitable delays in the way developments were reported.

As for foreign media reports, on 5 June 2013, just over three weeks after the declaration of state of emergency, several foreign journalists from AP, Reuters, AFP, and BBC were finally able to get near the affected areas, travelling with the army to Maiduguri and Marte, close to the Chadian border. By reading their reporting it was clear that the message Nigeria wanted publicised was that soldiers had removed the extremists. However the frustration of not being able to speak to the locals, and only being able to ask the officers and soldiers limited questions was self-evident, and several questions remained unanswered. For instance, previously the military had issued statements outlining quick advances and mass arrests, but they were still unwilling to talk about their own losses. Also they claimed that there had been no civilian fatalities even though they implied that soldiers would fire at will when their suspicions were aroused. Apparently 'hundreds' of people were being held in custody but no more details were given.

Although this was indeed a very special and delicate time in the history of the insurgency, it provides an insight into the difficulties observers had to overcome in order to assess what was happening—given that, owing to security restrictions, it was not possible to travel to the affected states at the height of the insurgency and military operation, and gather first-hand data.

Two final and more general difficulties to be borne in mind are that, first, given the nature of the subject it is not uncommon for officials and locals to be reluctant to talk about Boko Haram, for national security reasons, diplomatic sensitivities or fear of retaliation. For this reason, many of my interviewees are listed in this book as Anonymous Source #1, 2, 3, etc. Second, many violent attacks—not altogether uncommon in Nigeria—and crimes are automatically attributed to Boko Haram even when there is little or no evidence pointing to the Islamists' involvement, therefore distinguishing between real and fake Boko Haram actions is not always a straightforward endeavour.

Bearing these caveats in mind, it is now possible to embark on an examination of the historical backcloth against which today's insurgency has emerged and developed. Too often historical lessons fail (or appear to fail) to feature in the study of the Boko Haram phenomenon and the design of countermeasures. The ensuing chapter is my humble contribution to filling that gap.

2

ISLAM IN NIGERIA

HISTORICAL BACKGROUND

Although Boko Haram only made international headlines in the late 2000s–early 2010s, it is hardly Nigeria's first Islamist movement and while it has manifested almost unprecedented levels of brutality, religious violence is nothing new to northern Nigeria. The nature of the violence—motivated, albeit not exclusively, by religious belief—provides an additional challenge for the Nigerian security forces tasked with defeating a violent movement. In this regard, a study by Uppsala University (Sweden) that examined conflicts that occurred between 1989 and 2003, concludes that when religious demands are at stake, a negotiated settlement between the parties is unlikely, even when both sides belong to the same religious tradition.[1] This complication may sound familiar to the Nigerian authorities who have always dealt with religiously driven movements and groups in the north of the country through military means and, even when attempts have been made to negotiate, have seen their offers spurned—as in the case of Boko Haram's instant rejection of an amnesty when President Jonathan set up a Commission to explore its feasibility in April 2013.[2] Indeed, a 'just war' narrative justifying violence in response to Boko Haram's perceived persecution by the government and Christians has been resonating among the militants since 2009 with no sign of losing its appeal.[3]

This chapter provides an account of Islam in Nigeria from its origins in the fifteenth century until the present day. In particular, it highlights the crucial role of religion in shaping national identity and arms the reader with the necessary tools to better understand how historical legacies affect recent political, security and social developments in Nigeria and the north of the country in particular;[4] indeed, scholars have generally presumed that violent Islamist extremism is predicated on Nigeria's religious divide,[5] and given the influential role played by religion in Nigerian society any form of recurrent and religiously driven violence warrants careful attention.[6]

Religious violence in northern Nigeria has evolved over time to include elements that now are as much socio-economic and political as they are denominational. It is today an armed struggle arguably directed just as much against the state, and even the Islamic establishment to some degree, as it is against other faiths (or non-aligned, rival strains within Islam). Moreover the phenomenon today has been hijacked and arguably exploited by local politicians and other unscrupulous elements in society, as will be discussed in chapters three and four. The political implications, and indeed vested interests, involved in religious conflict in northern Nigeria today are difficult to ignore. Thus to classify the insurgency as one fixed along religious lines—without taking into account its complicated political context and ethnic dimension—would constitute an incomplete, and perhaps even an incorrect, reading of how the phenomenon evolved and, crucially, of how it might be addressed by the state.[7]

Insurgency and religious extremism in northern Nigeria has gathered significant academic interest in recent years. Whereas the Maitatsine riots of the 1980s, undeniably had grassroots support, among scholars and analysts there has been a marked shift to focus on more recent instances of this phenomenon, and in particular the role of Boko Haram in threatening the Federal Government and its interests in the north. To better understand the evolution and maturation of Boko Haram's insurgency one has to look back at how the history of Islamist fundamentalism, anti-establishment revivalism, and religious identity in northern Nigeria has influenced the emergence of violent contestation and insurgency.

ISLAM IN NIGERIA: HISTORICAL BACKGROUND

Usman Dan Fodio's jihad

Up until the nineteenth century the region now known as northern Nigeria was dominated by city-states and kingdoms whose leaders were largely drawn from the Hausa ethnic group. Internecine and internal wars were the norm as kings constantly tried to expand their dominions. Common features of these kingdoms were highly hierarchical and bureaucratic structures and a truly predatory nature, as exemplified by an extensive reliance on slaves, usually sourced from areas at the kingdoms' (and later the Fulani empire's) periphery, such as the central Nigerian plateau.[8]

Whereas Christianity and Islam today are by far the two most dominant faiths in Nigeria, Islam has a much older heritage in the region. In fact, the history of Islam in Nigeria dates back to the fifteenth century when the rulers of the Hausaland converted to Islam. The Sahel had long acted as a barrier to the spread of Islam in West Africa but the desire to control merchant routes across the desert prompted eleventh century rulers in today's Mali and Ghana and in northern Nigeria later, to offer protection to the isolated Muslim communities that Arab and Berber merchants had established along commercial routes. This practice exposed the elites to Islam, which was gradually adopted by the Hausa royalty. At a time when the majority of the population practised pagan and fertility cults, Islam remained the prerogative of the elites and of some upper-class followers living in urban areas.[9]

The Fulani preacher Usman Dan Fodio, considered to be the founder of Islam in Nigeria, made it possible for this "new" faith to spread across the northern part of Nigeria through his call to wage holy war against infidels in 1804. Even today he remains a highly revered figure in Nigeria and among Muslims in Africa, and a source of ideological inspiration for groups such as the Movement for Unity and Jihad in West Africa (MUJWA) in Mali who look to Fodio's teaching, rather than to that of modern-day Islamists', for spiritual direction. Further evidence of his legacy is to be found in an open letter from Boko Haram to the Governor of Kano Rabiu Musa Kwankwaso in August 2011:

> The reasons [for our attacks] are clear: 1. The Nigerian Government is a KUFUR [infidel] system serving BOTH UNITED NATION (UN) AND CHRISTIAN ASSOCIATION OF NIGERIA (CAN) 2. We the Jama'atu Ahlisunnah Lidda'awati Wal-Jihad are MUSLIMS and are from the NORTHERN part of the country who spent eight years agitating for

13

ISLAMIC STATE, STRIVING TO BRING BACK THE LOST GLORY OF UTHMAN DAN FODIO. WHAT IS WRONG WITH THAT? Is just to go back to the ways of our creator (ALLAH) where justice, discipline, good morals, love and care, peace and progress etc will prevails [sic].[10]

Fodio belonged to the Toronkawa clan of the Fulani—a nomadic ethnic group that had moved to Hausaland from present-day Senegal in the 1400s. There, the Fulanis had come in contact with Islamic culture and education and once in northern Nigeria reached influential positions at the courts of the local kings. Fodio was born in 1754 in Gobir, the most prominent of the seven original Hausa states. Since an early age his life was devoted to the study of the Qur'an and he was exposed to the teachings of one of the key preachers of the eighteenth century, the Berber El hadj Jibril b. Umar, whose message echoed Wahhabi rhetoric,[11] having come to know the latter during a pilgrimage to Mecca. His education exposed the young Fodio to the Sunni tradition and to the legal system of sharia within the Maliki school.[12] Furthermore, he learnt about Sufism, a mystic strand of Islam that promotes introspection and contemplation and is organised in brotherhoods, each devoted to a saint. Indeed, Usman Dan Fodio later became the first leader of the Qadiriyya Brotherhood which remained an influential force in the Fodio family well beyond Usman's death and in the Sokoto Caliphate.[13]

From the age of twenty he started touring his and other Hausa states preaching Sunni Islam and establishing himself as a respected theologian. In his travels he gained trust and support in current day Katsina, Kebbi, and Zamfara states and his fame became so great that he was invited to the Gobir court. Here he did not hesitate to question King Bawa on his treatment of fellow Muslims and managed to obtain a reduction in taxation and the liberty to preach to people of all ethnic groups.[14] Most notably, by raising the issue of taxation and by convincing the King not to excessively burden his subjects with taxes Fodio proved his commitment to greater social justice and effectiveness which, undoubtedly, helped consolidate his authority and support-base among the masses.[15] Through the rest of Bawa's reign, his son's and his rather weak successors', Fodio's power grew exponentially as did his followers, now counting several hundred, and his condemnation of the Gobir court's laxity and a system that did not follow the principles of sharia. His condemnation was recorded in many poems and writings he aimed primarily at a Fulani audience with the goal to promote religious purification.[16]

The 1790s saw increased restrictions placed on the Fulani and with the ascent of King Yunfa to the Gibir throne in 1801, things took a turn for the worse. Even though the king had been a pupil of Fodio in his youth, he tried to undermine the preacher, including through an attempted assassination, and started actively to persecute the Fulani. This led Fodio and the community of his followers to flee and set up their first stronghold in Gudu, near the western border of Gobir, in 1802.[17] The community attracted several new members and came to represent a pole of opposition to the king who decided, perhaps unwisely, to attack Fodio and his followers. It was at this time that Fodio was formally elected Commander of the Faithful (*Amir al-Mumiriin*)—a title that gave him both religious and political power. His jihad against Gobir, often described as the "warrior-scholars" rebellion, started in 1804 with the first battle ending in favour of Fodio's mujahedeen. The guerrilla warfare that followed resulted in thousands of casualties.[18]

Interestingly, Fodio and his followers made use of religion as an instrument with which to assert Fulani ethnic supremacy over the Hausa. Strategically, they capitalised on the growing resentment among the population—including peasants, merchants and even non-Muslim Fulani—towards despotic Hausa kings and mobilised criticism of the Hausa's corrupt system as a common denominator for grievances shared by people from different ethnic and social backgrounds. More specifically, Fodio stressed that the high level of taxation (especially cattle tax), oppression of the peasants, enslavement (of Muslims), the practice of cults, and the permissive environment where alcohol could be consumed freely and women were not required to wear the veil, went against sharia law. By doing so, he succeeded in portraying the kings as apostates, having moved away from the principles of Islam, hence making them legitimate targets of jihad. The pairing of religious zeal and social criticism proved effective and resulted in the ousting of the Hausa kings by the end of the five-year Fulani War: in 1809 Fodio conquered Gobir's capital Alkalawa, killed King Yunfa and founded the Sokoto Caliphate, of which he became the first Sultan (or *Shehu*, Hausa for Sheikh).[19] As of today, the Caliph of Sokoto, in spite of no longer having formal political powers, remains a leading figure in Nigerian society and someone whose support is sought by presidents.

Notwithstanding all the rhetoric about greater social justice and fairness, the Fulani families that were now in power did not dismantle the feudal system introduced by the Hausa leadership and indeed embraced their predecessors' despotism.[20] This led to revolts. The Fulani however managed to maintain power by re-directing the mounting internal aggression against infidels outside the empire.[21]

Throughout the nineteenth century Fodio's warrior-scholars travelled east, west and south bringing jihad and expanding the territory of the caliphate. They managed to conquer territories beyond Hausaland expanding to the east into Bauchi and south into the Nupe and Yoruba territories that evolved into emirates that were vassals of the Caliph of Sokoto. Fodio was now the leader of all Nigerian Muslims.[22]

Theocratic rule and the dissemination of Islamic rites were used to bind together the various peoples that now constituted the empire; however this did not mean equality for all who converted to Islam—converts occupied an inferior position in a highly stratified social system. Indeed the territories at the margins of their empire were regularly raided and plundered by the Fulani and slaves were taken. Slavery was indeed the indispensible engine behind the growth of the caliphate's urban prosperity, to the point that some of the conquered populations were forbidden from converting to Islam so that they could be more easily forced into slavery. These practices, which were common until the late 1850s, prompted many people to run away to the Middle Belt (in what is today central Nigeria), and generated high levels of insecurity especially on the empire's periphery. In the centre of the caliphate some forms of assimilation took place and those who had been subjugated adopted the culture and language of the largest ethnic group, the Hausa. Even the Fulani, in spite of their dominant position, followed suit.[23] Yet, great differences remained between the Fulani and the Hausa and it was religion that acted as a catalyst for the emergence of a form of shared identity—leading to what is now known as the Hausa-Fulani, the largest ethnic group in Nigeria, which accounts for nearly 30 per cent of the population.[24]

Through the second half of the nineteenth century there were a number of insurgencies against Islamic rule and religion was often used for political purposes, resulting in the replacement of one despot by another.[25] By the late nineteenth century life in the cities was very much influenced by Islam and the enforcement of sharia law, though not so much in rural areas and among the poor.

ISLAM IN NIGERIA: HISTORICAL BACKGROUND

The British colonial era

When the British subjugated northern Nigeria in 1902–3, in the process establishing the Northern Nigerian Protectorate (1900–14), they found it markedly different from the south coast and its hinterland. Very few signs of modernity were to be observed and the relatively few Christians present in the north led segregated lives and faced many limitations on their involvement in social and public life. Historical accounts reveal that the Muslim northerners generally despised the south which was considered "pagan" and "alien" and which "might well belong to another world".[26]

Mindful of their colonial experience in Sudan and the resistance to it offered by the Mahddist revolt,[27] and aware of the not inconsiderable power of local rulers to mobilise opposition to them along religious lines, Britain allowed the administrative system of the Fulani empire to persist, with sharia remaining the recognised legal system until the end of the colonial era—even in those regions of the empire where the majority of the population was pagan. By forging an alliance with the Fulani aristocracy, the British under Lord Lugard effectively established a system of "indirect rule" resulting in the Fulani being able to further expand their areas of influence to encompass tribes of peripheral lands who were now subjugated to Islamic authorities. Writing a confidential memo on the attitude of the Muslim Provinces of Nigeria During World War I, British Colonial Officer H. R. Palmer had no doubt this system had proved effective in preserving stability in the north (in spite of some skirmishes):

> The British Government has pursued a policy of retaining under the guidance of Residents the native rulers and their Muslim polity, shorn of abuses; so that the upper classes in Nigeria have everything to lose and nothing to gain by any kind of disorder—at least, most of them have.[28]

By upholding sharia provisions, the colonial administration institutionalised the inferior status of non-Muslims. They also banned from the emirates Christian missionaries who were only allowed to preach in "quiet places" till 1931. Christian teachings did however find followers among pagan minorities in the north.[29]

When Nigeria finally achieved independence in 1960, the isolation that had characterised the north for so long and the extremely low number of northern graduates meant that most official positions were given to southerners, predominantly Igbos. Historian Martin Meredith recalls

17

that out of over 1,000 students at University College of Ibadan, only fifty-seven came from northern states and nationally less than 1 per cent of high-level official positions were occupied by northerners.[30] This power shift in favour of the Christian south left the northern aristocracy worried that their traditional and highly conservative way of life would come under threat—a sentiment that is at the root of much of the inter-religious and inter-ethnic conflict that followed.

Nigeria's North-South and ethic divides were to pave the way for one of the darkest chapters in its history—the Biafran or Civil War of 1967–70—whose legacy remains alive today, as evidenced by a compensation claim for 2.4 million nairas demanded in summer 2014 for the devastation suffered by Igbos land during the conflict.[31]

* * *

Half of a Yellow Sun was expected to open in Nigerian cinemas in April 2014 but viewers had to wait until 1 August as censors had doubts that the screen adaptation of Chimamanda Ngozi Adichie's bestselling novel (premiered a year earlier at the Toronto International Film Festival) was fit for viewing.[32] Many people speculated that what lay behind the delay was concern that a movie that might have looked favourably at the separatist cause driving the Biafran conflict would, at a time of heightened tension and deadly Boko Haram violence, fuel ethnic divisions.[33] But debates about the Civil War's legacy were perhaps reawakened more directly when Chinua Achebe—one of Africa's most eminent authors—published his long awaited memoir in 2012, *There Was a Country: A Personal History of Biafra*.[34] Having written dozens of books, this was the very first time he decided to reopen an old and painful scar to publish on the conflict.

Following independence from Britain in 1960, Nigeria was fragmented along ethnic lines. In spite of the existence of a multitude of ethnic groups, the Hausa-Fulani in the north, the Yoruba in the south west and the Igbo in the south east emerged as the dominant ones, all with their distinct social, political and religious traditions and beliefs.[35] As already alluded to, Igbos dominated politics at the federal level.

The January 1966 attempted coup d'etat by a group of junior army officers resulted in the killing of two prominent northern leaders and in the head of the Nigerian Army, General Johnson Aguiyi-Ironsi, an Igbo, becoming president.[36] As the plotters were mainly Igbo, the coup was perceived to be benefiting the Igbo population giving rise to what some (wrongly) described as an Igbo conspiracy.[37] In the summer northern soldiers launched a counter coup. Their leader, Lieutenant-Colonel Yakubu Gowon, a Christian from the north, became the Supreme Commander of the Armed Forces. Ethnic tensions became more intense and Igbos living in the north fell victim to mass pogroms.[38]

On 30 May 1967 Colonel Odumegwu Ojukwu, the governor of the southeast, proclaimed the secession of eastern Nigeria and the establishment of a new and independent nation, the Republic of Biafra. In spite of several peace accords, the drumbeat of war became inevitable and hostilities broke out between the poorly equipped Biafran forces and those of the Federal Government of Nigeria, which had British backing.[39] An offensive by the latter to retake territory on 6 July 1967 marked the official beginning of the conflict. By 1968 it had reached a stalemate and it took till 15 January 1970 for the war to draw to an end following a major Nigerian offensive led by Colonel Olusegun Obasanjo—who later became president (twice)—in December 1969, which split Biafra into two areas, and a final offensive in January 1970 resulting in Biafra's surrender.[40]

Regrettably, one of the most infamous images of the Biafran War is one of starvation and malnourished children with swollen bellies—the by-product of Biafrans being besieged by Nigerian forces accused of using hunger as a weapon of war.[41] Many churches, NGOs and volunteers from around the world took part in a major airlift operation to provide relief to the starving Igbo population. Around two million Biafrans are believed to have died of malnutrition in spite of international humanitarian efforts.[42]

While the Biafran war had some religious connotations and had already highlighted the role of religious tensions in civil conflict (alongside ethnic and political rivalries), it was in the late 1970s that religious conflict intensified, and was manifested in intra-religious fights, i.e. among Muslims; inter-religious tensions, i.e. between Muslims and Christians; and conflict between the state and religious activism.[43] Meanwhile the Iranian Islamic revolution of 1979 inspired demands for the adoption of sharia law across Nigeria.[44]

The path to Sharia

Islamising Nigeria, in other words ensuring that it becomes a fully Islamic state governed by sharia law, is what appears to be Boko Haram's ultimate goal.[45] The group's spokesman Abu Qaqa confirmed as much in an interview in 2012:

> It's the secular state that is responsible for the woes we are seeing today. People should understand that we are not saying we have to rule Nigeria, but we have been motivated by the stark injustice in the land. People underrate us but we have our sights set on [bringing sharia to] the whole world, not just Nigeria.[46]

While Boko Haram's ability (and desire) to bring sharia to "the whole world" is debatable—I discuss in chapter 5, below, limitations to any expansionist plans Shakau may nurture—the issue of sharia implementation is certainly one worth exploring as it arguably is one of the fault-lines that threatens the Nigerian federation.

Beginning with Zamfara state, a total of twelve northern states had, to varying degrees, adopted sharia law by 2001. This trend had been accelerated by the influx of missionaries from countries such as Libya, Pakistan, Saudi Arabia and Sudan (benefiting from Saudi sponsorship) that descended on northern Nigeria in the 1990s to promote Wahhabism.[47]

An initial move in this direction had already started in 1977 when heated debates in the Constituent Assembly over the possible establishment of sharia courts of appeal at the federal level highlighted strong ethnic and religious divisions within society. Over a decade later, in 1988, a sharia-related debate in the Constituent Assembly brought the discussion of constitutional proposals for the Third Republic to a standstill, only to be resumed when the new president, General Ibrahim Badamasi Babangida, banned sharia as a matter for discussion.[48]

But it was in 1999 that the real impetus for broader sharia implementation became evident. This new drive came from Ahmed Sani, the new governor of Zamfara, who wanted Islamic law, up until that point applied in some 75 per cent of all penal cases, to be fully adopted, citing Saudi Arabia as a model. Criticism and condemnation from Christians around the country, especially through the Christian Association of Nigeria (CAN), reflected the fear that such a move would impact future developments. Deadly clashes in Kaduna, Jos and elsewhere did nothing to prevent the states of Bauchi, Borno, Gombe, Jigawa, Kaduna, Kano, Katsina, Kebbi, Niger, Sokoto and Yobe from following in Zamfara's footsteps.[49]

The new system involved the establishment of State Sharia Courts where Sharia Penal and Criminal Procedure Codes were applied. This was accompanied by a burgeoning of additional legislation aimed at ridding society of social vices and un-Islamic practices such as gambling, alcohol consumption and prostitution; and limiting interaction between unrelated men and women. In addition States established, among others, bodies for the collection of taxes, Hisba militias for the enforcement of sharia, and State Sharia Commissions and Councils of Ulama [Islamic scholars]. Kano and Zamfara also set up Public Complaints and Anti-Corruption Commissions.[50]

By 2003 thousands of people had been killed as a result of clashes between Christians and Muslims and stories such as that of Safiya Husaini—a woman from Sokoto state who was sentenced to death by stoning for adultery (and later pardoned)[51]—made international headlines. Meanwhile, President Obasanjo, a born-again Christian enjoying the support of Muslim voters, was criticised for not taking a firmer stance on sharia and the implementation of harsh punishments such as the severing of hands for convicted thieves.[52]

Some reflections on religious identity

Religious identity has been defined as a determinant of, among other factors: orientation towards authority; tendency to conflict; and the possibility of conflict resolution.[53] On a scale local to the north of Nigeria, religious identity has been associated more with local movements such as the Sufi brotherhoods or with orientation towards ideologies such as the anti-innovation legalists (the Yan Izala) or the anti-establishment syncretists.[54][55] Whereas on an individual scale, Islamic identity could mean the decisions made by locals to identify themselves as adherents of one ideology or another (within Islam), additionally, such decisions could indicate religious and political orientation: whether an individual is sympathetic to the state, to the established Sufi order, or to any of a number of sects or movements (some of which enjoy increased following within certain ethnic groups, compared to others) within the Muslim *ummah* [community] in northern Nigeria.

On a national scale however, Falola suggests religious identity as being defined more along the broader lines of faith and politics, and contributing to a deliberate attempt to impose sharia and "establish moral and political control through religious law".[56] Quoting an excerpt from a sermon by influential Muslim scholar Ibrahim Suleiman, he refers to the following as "a rallying cry among Muslim preachers, and scholars":

We will be betraying the cause of Islam and the integrity of the Muslim *ummah* if we fail to discharge our obligations as Muslims. These obligations entail, among other things, the establishment of Islam as a complete polity and the dismantling of all Western influences as they affect us.[57]

In truth, the Muslim *ummah* in Nigeria are as unified as the narrative suggests:

Indeed, the Islamist movement in Nigeria is made up of an assortment of groups that rarely, if at all ever, coordinate their actions. Their reluctance to do so hints at the profound differences that exist between both their respective agendas and approaches to pursuing them.[58]

To be sure, the position that Western influence is *haram* [not permissible, or forbidden], for instance, is one shared by at least some of the *ummah*. Yet, so far as violent contestation against the state and the incidence of insurgency is concerned, proponents of these views, with the willingness to act violently upon them, constitute a small minority and—as seen through the campaign and ideologies of Boko Haram—a radical extremist minority at that. Moreover, in so far as the influence of Westernisation relates to local education, popular feelings of mistrust or disapproval may be less about the divide between Western and Islamic education, and more about failures of the Western educational system itself, or increased accessibility and local acceptability and credibility of *Tsangaya* [Qur'anic schools].[59]

Similarly, G.K. Brown notes that rather than being by Muslim communities' choice, exclusion from the secular educational system could rather be a consequence of poorly-managed state policies.[60] These two views contrast somewhat with the established narrative by scholars such as Jarmon, which holds that secular education has been generally eschewed due to the rich history of Arabic education in northern Nigeria, already established in custom and practice.[61] Thus assumptions that local Muslims send their children to *Tsangaya*, or away to learn the *Qur'an* becoming *almaijirai*, due to perceptions of *karatun boko* [Western education] as *haram*, may preclude the real possibility that some people in Northern Nigeria simply see a reflection of state failure in *karatun boko*, and so default back to the traditional Islamic system which, in the view of some, has the added benefit of a sound religious upbringing.[62]

It is worth noting in relation to religious identity in northern Nigeria the following three points:

(1) That the Muslim *ummah* in Nigeria encapsulates a wide variety of ideologies, movements and orientations, which complicates the cultural space within which Boko Haram functions. Paden for instance highlights "cross-cutting tendencies" within the *ummah* as playing a major role in incidents of religiously-linked conflict in northern Nigeria.[63]

(2) That these various identities do not necessarily concur with, or even agree to disagree, on certain potentially volatile topics. For instance the quartet of anti-establishment syncretists, the *Ikhwan* (sometimes labelled as the Shiites), the Wahhabi sects, and the anti-innovation legalists (the *Izala*) all adopt a less tolerant stance on the role of Western influence and of coexistence with other faiths, than do Northern Nigeria's traditional Sufis.[64] On the other hand, Abubakar Gumi and his support base, "acting with Saudi Arabian support",[65] and adopting a "doctrine inspired by Wahhabi'ism",[66] founded the *Jamā'at Izālat al-Bid'a wa-Iqāmat as-Sunna* [the Association for the Eradication of the Innovation and the Establishment of the Sunna; in Hausa: Yan Izala] in 1978. The *Izala* stressed that Muslim women should be better educated, as well as enjoying a more prominent role in the political process—a case for which had not been made hitherto within the established order of Sufism and the *turuq* (Sufi Brotherhoods).[67] Yet attempts by the *Izala* to promote a correct interpretation of Islam did little to avert sectarian rifts among Muslims.[68]

(3) That the orientation of the local populace towards one ideology or the other may not be motivated by religious sentiment. Socio-economic deprivation and political considerations not necessarily related to Islam may also play a role here—for instance as seen in some locals' take on why they prefer Islamic education to *makarantun boko* [Western schools]. Another example is offered by Harnischfeger, who notes the view of a political scientist in Kano that "the majority of Muslims do not want Sharia", either in Kano, the biggest city of the North, or elsewhere, even though most observers had the impression that the Sharia campaign enjoyed widespread support.[69] This unpopularity is explained not by religious ideology but rather by how poorly the government had implemented Sharia.

As noted above, the history of Nigeria has been marred by ethic, intra- and inter-religious tensions, and the country's social landscape is very much influenced by its fragmented past and the broader yet nebulously defined schism between the country's North and South. It remains undeniable however[70] that the North and the South of the country have taken very different paths economically, politically and religiously, as exemplified by the decision of twelve northern states to adopt sharia law. This division is what, for far too long, has led many southerners to regard Boko Haram as a product and problem of the North, almost as if did not affect the nation as a whole. Regrettably, this ahistorical myopia affected the man and woman on the street as well as many senior bureaucrats and politicians alike.

3

THE GENESIS OF RADICAL GROUPS

It is against the historical, cultural and religious backdrop analysed in the previous chapter that a plethora of radical Islamist groups has over time emerged in northern Nigeria. The following pages discuss the emergence and evolution of the most radical movements, their ideology, influences and rivalries, as well as how they have instrumentalised religion as a political tool since their emergence. Also discussed is how Boko Haram fits into the broader picture or, in other words, to what extent today's militants represent a natural progression from earlier violent extreme movements active in Nigeria.

If many youth, either involved in delinquency or affected by the so-called "*almajiri* syndrome"[1] (discussed in the next chapter) are said to be the tactical-level drivers of the insurgency phenomenon in northern Nigeria,[2] then radical Islamist networks, at the operational level, constitute the vehicle by which the phenomenon becomes, or could potentially become, a threat to national security. These radical networks in northern Nigeria emerged through several processes, with the trinity of splintering, transformation and reform—or modernisation—being particularly relevant to our narrative.

Splintering

Commonalities between Islamic networks and radical extremist Islamist sects and movements in northern Nigeria have always existed due to their shared origins in Sunni Islam, and, relatively recently, Shiism. However the extent of shared practices, ideologies and alignments with the larger Islamic establishment—between groups viewed by some as "deviant" and the larger Muslim *ummah*—has arguably been sharply influenced by how strictly the main Islamic currents were interpreted in practice. For instance whereas Boko Haram's roots lie in Sunni Islam, its strict Salafi[3] interpretation of this particular branch of the religion—what some have referred to as "ultra-Salafism"—has been central to the establishment of an identity quite separate from that embraced by the broader *ummah*. The notion that these groups do not understand the Qur'an or that they are "misguided" may not be entirely true. Such groups simply have may have chosen to interpret it differently. As Moghadam notes, groups employing terrorism in the name of Islam do not necessarily represent "deviant sects", but are often guided by a radical interpretation of the religion.[4]

Roman Loimeier, taking the Sufi Brotherhoods as a case in point, notes that before conflicting views led to violent tensions between groups, they had in the past co-existed with and competed against each other.[5] Moreover, groups often adopt ideological elements from or employ similar strategies to other movements—of which they may or may not be a splinter.[6] Tensions may also be manifest within a network due to in-fighting and disagreements over ideological postures, over divergent tactical goals and *modus operandi*, or over a realisation that certain doctrinal practices, frowned upon by some members within the broader network, would not be changed by its leadership. Such tensions may well escalate post the emergence of an off-shoot network from the parent body, due either to ideological differences or to operational and tactical disagreements.

When such irreconcilable differences occur between senior members and their leader-mentors, such members may take a small band of loyalists and new groups may emerge: a phenomenon commonly known as "splintering". Indeed such splintering is already occurring within the context of the Boko Haram network, with at least one splinter, referred to as *Ansaru—Ansarul Muslimina Fi Biladis Sudan* [Vanguard for the Protection of Muslims in Black Africa]—led by a former Boko Haram commander, Khalid al-Barnawi. With regards to the divergence in operational and strategic objectives of Ansaru and Boko Haram, Zenn for instance notes that its leader, al-Barnawi, "may be only marginally committed to Boko Haram's goal for an Islamic State in northern Nigeria and revenge against the government for killing Boko Haram founder Mohammed Yusuf in 2009."[7]

Splintering among Islamic and Islamist sects and networks in northern Nigeria has a long and complex history and it arguably is as prevalent within the traditional Islamic establishment as it is among the Sufi Brotherhoods and even within more fundamentalist networks like the Yan Izala and the Shiites, as well as within even those networks at the far end of the extremist ideological spectrum. Within the religious environment in northern Nigeria today, Boko Haram may well be the outlier of this trend.

Just as al-Barnawi and his Ansaru network are an off-shoot of Boko Haram, Adesoji notes that Mohammed Yusuf, the leader of Boko Haram, was formerly a leader of the Jamâ'atul Tajdidi Islam (JTI) in Borno State; which in turn was a faction of the Kano-based JTI led by Abubakar Mujahid; and which in turn had broken away in the 1990s from the Shiites led by Ibrahim Zakzaky.[8] One report provides some additional insight here, noting that Abubakar Mujahid's decision to break away from the Shiites (the Islamic Movement of Nigeria, IMN) was precipitated by what he and many others perceived as a softening of Zakzaky's rhetoric over time, particularly with regards to his stance on Western influence and the status of the United States of America (whether or not they should be seen as the enemy of "the Islamic world").[9]

Specialists such as Hill have noted that that Zakzaky's increasing fascination with the Iranian model had a negative impact on many of his followers, who felt increasingly alienated by it.[10] However Hill acknowledges the influence that the parent IMN movement had on Ahl al-Sunnah wal-Jamâ'ah, Ja'amutu Tajidmul Islami (MIR), Mujahid's new network. Indeed, he points out that MIR retained several elements of the militant *hora* [guard] system used by the IMN; a vigilante-type group who, he states, "quickly developed a reputation for causing and exploiting street level violence".[11]

This is not to say that differences in ideologies would necessarily lead to in-fighting or splintering, or that splintered factions necessarily must differ in ideology from the parent network, or that splintered groups do not work, or coordinate efforts, with the former. Indeed, the IMN and MIR do cooperate on occasion. Referring to one such instance where the IMN and its splinter network, the MIR, worked together, Hill notes that they "collectively [were] referred to as the Muslim Brothers", and that "they became a formidable grass roots force" with a large base of popular support, the total potential support of which amounted to nearly half a million people in the streets, and which concerned the security agencies and authorities.[12]

With regard to Boko Haram-Ansaru cooperation, later in the book in a section on funding I describe instances of collaboration between Shekau and al-Bernawi. It is also believed that the kidnapping of a French family in Cameroon in February 2013, for which Boko Haram claimed responsibility, had in fact being facilitated, if not carried out, by Ansaru. According to a source on the ground, with AQIM coming under heavy attack in northern Mali, its ability to support its Nigerian sympathisers was markedly diminished. In addition, the French-led military intervention in Mali, Opération Serval, had forced the return of Boko Haram and Ansaru fighters to Nigeria where they found themselves operating in increasingly overlapping areas. Thus the two outfits had to resort to cooperation in order to ensure each other's survival.[13]

Some scholars, however, appear to take a different view. Jacob Zenn notes that Al-Barnawi reportedly favours negotiations with the government, while the main faction of Boko Haram led by Abu Shekau takes a more hardline approach towards talks. As a result of these differences, al-Barnawi may have provided the government with critical information that helped it to arrest Boko Haram leaders aligned with Shekau. Meanwhile, Shekau's faction reportedly tipped off Nigerian intelligence about Boko Haram members that have defied him and carried out kidnappings of foreigners instead of attacking the Nigerian government (which is largely seen as the modus operandi of Ansaru).[14]

Factors other than ideological differences *per se* may inform the decision to establish an offshoot. Loimeier argues that the influence of a religious scholar was, in a sense, a correlate of his following. As his following increased, the radical nature of rhetoric became more difficult to control, so long as it resonated with his followers enough to increase both their number and broader support.[15] Nor was this so much a purely religious phenomenon as it reflected the political dynamic of the times. As Loimeier puts it: "the more followers a *Shayk* [leader] has and the greater his network, the stronger his political weight becomes in elections, and consequently his bargaining power grows."[16]

Thus it may not be irreconcilable differences between factions in a network that precipitates splintering. Indeed, as was the case when

Malam Aminu d-Din Abubakar formed the fundamentalist Daawa [mission] movement, he did so despite having already reconciled with Abubakar Gumi and the Izala; with Loimeier pointing to the fact that "Abubakar's ambitions" were incompatible with the goals of Gumi and that Abubakar needed to expand his own following and sphere of political influence.[17]

Such alternate viewpoints regardless, splintering could nonetheless be due to marked differences in ideology, as well as political ambition and a quest for increased influence. This can be seen in the case of Mohammed Yusuf, the Boko Haram leader who first broke away from the JTI[18] and subsequently again broke away from his position as an Imam at Indimi mosque in Maiduguri, and, becoming "an avowed critic of his former colleagues", amassed a significant following consisting of "illiterates, indolent, the unemployed…including some educated persons who were reported to have torn up their preaching certificates as a means of attesting to their joining his group".[19] For this reason, coupled with the fact that "Yusuf was not a certified preacher",[20] both the Islamic Preaching Board and the Council of *ulama* in Borno were unsuccessful in attempts to curb his radical preaching.[21]

In looking at the specific case of Mohammed Yusuf and of how, in splintering from parent movements and umbrella affiliations more than once, he eventually shaped the Boko Haram network, it is worth asking why he chose to separate from these umbrella movements. Also worth probing further is whether said splintering contributed to the significant following and support that Yusuf's movement came to enjoy.

For the latter question, Mohammed provides a direct response: Yusuf's radical doctrine was embraced by the audience he courted—the urban and rural *talakawa* [commoners], who regarded some popular imams as being too soft towards the Nigerian state and as failing to address, or even clearly identify, the socio-economic and political discontent brought about by failing governance.[22] In this regard, the existing Sufi order, with its established core, could not accommodate the radical views necessary to address and challenge the perceived failures of the state. Yusuf, in splintering from this established order and building a following around his softened Salafist core ideologies, thus traded space for acceptance into the broader *ummah*. Within this space however, he afforded himself the freedom slowly to gravitate towards a more ultra-Salafist approach which, due to a festering anger within the *tal-*

akawa, saw him gain acceptance there and then gradually broaden his base to include the more affluent and politically influential, as his popularity grew. Loimeier offers an explanation. He argues that due to pressures to increase "bargaining power" and political influence, the role of religious scholars has assumed an added dimension over the decades. As he puts it, "not only were they [the religious scholars] now the spiritual leaders of their networks, but they also took over the political task of mobilizing their followers". Loimeier refers to this as the "politicisation of Islam".[23]

Although Loimeier, in making this argument, refers specifically to power struggles between the Sufi brotherhoods since the 1940s, a similar dynamic can be seen even beyond the brotherhoods, and as relevant to other splintered networks. Indeed, such "politicisation of Islam" seemed central to the strategy of Boko Haram. Led by Yusuf, the ranks of the movement swelled. Indeed, the popular support it enjoyed, under Yusuf, in the years before the battle of Maiduguri in 2009, would appear inordinate—particularly *vis-à-vis* what would have been possible had he stayed within the ambit of the existing traditional Islamic system. As Mohammed notes, "Yusuf's persistent penchant to attack anything western made him a hero and a role model. He was using Islamic knowledge to justify and articulate his mission to the admiration and acceptance of his followers."[24]

Mohammed makes an important observation here also, namely that the notion that Westernisation and Western education (*karatun boko*) were considered "Islamically prohibited" (*haram*) was "not new in northern Nigeria".[25] The implications of this comment, seeing how the Yusufiyya swelled in number as Yusuf ratcheted up his anti-*boko* rhetoric, are twofold: (1) Yusuf may well have realised that such rhetoric would not be tolerated had he stayed within the ambits of traditional Islamic preaching; and (2) the *talakawa* could be exploited if religion could be "politicised" and presented as a solution to a failed socio-economic system, brought about by *boko* influence. Of course it helped that Yusuf, in amassing this following, also helped his followers with economic assistance and even some forms of micro-finance. Indeed, with Yusuf being in charge of his own flock, and with primitive forms of social and economic control mechanisms *in situ*, mobilisation and indoctrination arguably became easier. Moreover the splintering from the established order also afforded Yusuf the space to influence his followers without fear of being shut down by the *ulama* and senior religious leadership (whom he had already begun threatening).[26] Such influence may have been considerably attenuated had Boko Haram been attached to a parent network.

Indeed Loiemeir argues that the opportunity for exerting political influence brought about by splintering could explain why this phenomenon within Islamic and Islamist movements in northern Nigeria has occurred fairly frequently over the decades, bequeathing to the region several competing and coexistent networks.[27]

Transformation

In some instances, although these appear to be fairly rare, a movement may undergo a transformation: adopting stances it hitherto had not, and being more receptive to certain ideologies and political strategies, or tactical options. Sometimes such transformation is positive, and is triggered by a general consensus within the movement itself (as opposed to being driven by an individual based on personal visions and ideologies). For example, Loimeier notes that the Tijâniyya branch of the Sufi brotherhoods underwent a transformation into a mass movement; one that was inspired by "reaffiliation among Tijâniyya scholars…in Kano",[28] as part of a process that took decades and that was very much membership-driven, rather than strictly leadership-driven. This is in sharp contrast to the nature of transformation seen in Boko Haram over the years, which has very much been driven by the leadership first of Mohammed Yusuf and then of Abubakar Shekau. Indeed, that the Tijâniyya (and shortly after, the Qâdiriyya in similar fashion) underwent a scholarly transformation of this nature[29] is arguably indicative of profound knowledge of Islamic scholarship within the collective body of the Sufi brotherhoods—a situation which makes it unlikely that radical ideologues[30] attempting to contort the Qur'an and *hadiths* in their preaching would not be found out and frowned upon.

Regarding Mohamed Yusuf and Boko Haram for instance, Mohammed notes that in the early days of his leadership—which, according to Mohammed, Ustaz Yusuf seized in a coup of sorts, from the original Boko Haram leader, Abubakar Lawan, who had left to further his Islamic studies in Saudi Arabia—Yusuf, after coercing support from senior clerics of the sect through "corruption allegations", "…began to reshape and re-mould the movement in line with his ideology of mulling the idea of waging a Jihad (religious war)".[31] This narrative is similar to that of Adesoji who notes that Yusuf seems to have "prepared himself for the leadership role which he played in the Boko Haram sect, with his membership of other fundamentalist groups", and who suggests that Yusuf's subsequent severing of ties from these other fundamentalist movements may have been brought about "by the desire to actualise his long-term dream of reform, which perhaps was being slowed down by those less passionate".[32]

Moreover, whereas Yusuf shaped Boko Haram's ideologies and stance against the state and the established Islamic order, it was arguably Abubakar Shekau who over the years truly transformed Boko Haram from a movement characterised by large gatherings of its supporters and mass confrontations with the authorities into a clandestine network, well-equipped for irregular warfare—as the Nigerian state has experienced to its cost.[33]

Reform (modernisation)

Paden uses the word "reform" to describe how the Sufi Brotherhoods evolved since the Second World War and "modernisers" to refer to the reformed version of these movements and "modernisations" to refer to some of the changes incorporated into the group during this process.[34] However some find Paden's use of the terms "reformed" versus "traditional" misleading in his description of the evolution of the Qâdiriyya and Tijâniyya Sufi Brotherhoods. Loimeier argues that neither the "traditional" nor "reformed" Sufi Brotherhoods are quite as "clear, quasi-monolithic" as Paden makes them out to be, and that their aim was not to present a "modern" take on Islam.[35] Rather Loimeier argues that deliberate attempts by Sufi scholars to revitalise and purify "a corrupted faith"[36] were in fact aimed more at popularising the *tajdîd* [revivalist, reform-oriented] movements—as pointed out by Hiskett.[37] Loimeier prefers to refer to this "popularisation" process as one entailing "transformation" rather than reform *per se*. Thus, by Loimeier's account, Paden's assertions suggest that "these movements introduced new things into a religion of Islam"—a notion which Loimeier argues "would be rejected outright" by the Sufis.[38]

Whereas debates about "modernisation" and "reform" have not been prevalent in the literature on the Maitatsine, these themes are discussed more often with regards to Boko Haram. To be sure, the fundamentalist view of the *'Yan Tatsine* was that modernisation, particularly within the context of Western influence—not just *karatun boko*—was *haram*.[39] This viewpoint also seemed central to the Yusufiyya.[40] However, in the case of the Yusufiyya, the movement itself has been very much "reformed" and "modernised" since its inception around 2002.

Higazi notes that Mohamed Yusuf, who many agree was the founder of Boko Haram, was made leader of Ahlus-Sunna, "a modernising group" that was opposed to certain positions adopted by the *ulama* in Maiduguri.[41] McGregor meanwhile refers to Boko Haram as a "modern radical Islamist movement in northern Nigeria".[42] "Modernising" in this context refers more to the aspirations of the group (particularly of Yusuf) in terms of what he saw society becoming, should his anti-*boko* preachings take root.[43] Somewhat ironically then, "modernising" was not about modernisation in the Western context; rather it was about reforming certain practices, ideologies, and assumptions regarding the role of the *ulama* in northern Nigeria.[44] Moreover, as Walker argues, "Boko Haram, as a group, clearly does not utterly reject the modern world out of hand. The group's use of mobile phones, video cameras [...] automatic weapons, and cars shows it is more than prepared to use the fruits of Western education when it suits them".[45]

Ahmed Salkida, a Maiduguri-based journalist, and of whom prominent northern Nigerian analyst Shehu Sani notes is "the most authoritative voice on Boko Haram today",[46] said in an interview that "Yusuf, the movement's founder, has based his teachings on the works of Ibn Taymiyya, after whom he named his *masjid* (mosque) in Maiduguri, and who has influenced other modern radical Islamist movements".[47] "Modern" again in this context refers more to ideological reform, than to tactics and operations. Rice also alludes to this "modernisation" of Boko Haram in the assertion that the face of the sect is "changing".[48]

Furthermore, with regards to tactics, operations, and the nature of its insurgency, Boko Haram certainly has shown a propensity for modernisation, sophistication and evolution over the years since its formation. Murray Last alludes to this in his argument that "significant changes" have occurred "in the tactics of the Muslim militant group *Jamâ'at ahl al-sunna li'l-daw'a wa'l-jihad* [the name by which Boko Haram is sometimes referred to]".[49]

The 2011 report to the US House of Representatives Committee on Homeland Security, by Representatives Patrick Meehan and Jackie

Speer, also highlights this increased modernisation and complexity on the part of Boko Haram, in its central argument that "Boko Haram's attacks [have] become more sophisticated, coordinated, and deadly".[50] More specifically, their report reveals that there has been (1) "a significant shift in Boko Haram's targets, tactics, and geographic reach"; (2) "an evolution in the capabilities of Boko Haram, beginning in the mid-2000s, from attacks with poisoned arrows and machetes to sophisticated car bombings"; (3) "increased sophistication of attacks executed by Boko Haram" arguably facilitated by training with al-Shabaab in Somalia and "Al Qaeda in the Lands of the Islamic Maghreb (AQIM)"; (4) "quick evolution in sophistication of targeting and bomb making" by Boko Haram; (5) "an elevation in the sophistication of Boko Haram's methods of communication", which the report takes as an indication that Boko Haram is now "an organisation which is far different from the local group fighting a tit-for-tat battle with the army and police in northern Nigeria" and is "now another beast, more international in its ambitions"; and (6) "increased use of internet forums" and social media, a situation which the reports argues as being "indicative of the growing sophistication and threat potential of Boko Haram".[51]

Consequently, Meehan and Speier conclude that "the sophistication of its tactics, use of the Internet, and its recent attack on the U.N. headquarters in Abuja all point to a dangerously evolving organisation".[52] Onuoha likewise alludes to this tactical "evolution" of Boko Haram where he notes that from merely posing a local disturbance and attempting to incite hate through their preaching, they "took up arms against security forces" late 2003.[53] Other have also noted that this effectively marked a tactical turning point in the sect's trajectory which hitherto had avoided any major confrontations with the security agencies, and with the Nigerian Army in particular.[54]

The evolution in Boko Haram's tactics and modus operandi will be explored in more detail in subsequent chapters. In summary, one of a number of deductions to be made from this narrative in the literature, and from the various field sources, is that Boko Haram arguably have undergone modernisation (reform) in two areas. First in terms of the group's ideologies, doctrine, and strategic objectives; but also in how it aims to achieve that strategy and espouse that ideology and doctrine—at operational and tactical levels.

Formation (creation)

Arguably, the creation of a new network is the most challenging of the four methods by which Islamic and Islamist networks emerge. An examination of the existing body of works by scholars such as Loimeier (1997), Paden (2002, 2005), Hiskett (1997) and Hill (2010), indicates that new networks may not indeed be new at all: not in the sense that they were established without prior affiliations. Rather, most networks are created due to divergent interests and ideological positions that may have changed over time (from those of the parent outfit). The examples that follow highlight this narrative.

Daawa

One historical example within the northern Nigerian religious environment of a group created that had strong prior affiliations to at least one other existing network is that of the Daawa movement. Daawa (mission) was a "fundamentalist" group whose leader, Aminu d-Din Abubakar was pro-Iranian initially and who "preached openly against the pro-Saudi positions of Abubakar Gumi".[55] After reconciling with Gumi in 1981, Abubakar went on to establish Daawa as a non-militant movement with "Wahhabi tendencies" in the mid-eighties.[56] As Loimeier notes, among the reasons why Abubakar established Daawa was because he sought to dissociate himself "from financial dependence from Gumi" and because "Abubakar's ambitions were not compatible with Gumi's claims to supreme authority within the [Izala] organisation"; with one commentator noting that "he [Aminu d-Din Abubakar] wants to lead himself".[57]

Ahl al-Sunnah wal-Jamâ'ah, Ja'amutu Tajidmul Islami/Islamic Movement of Nigeria[IMN][58]

Zakzaky's Islamic Movement of Nigeria (IMN) also arguably falls into this category of created movements; and is one which, by some accounts, is considered a more radical movement than the Izala—with Hill referring to both Zakzaky and his protégé, Majahid,[59] as "noisy supporters of al-Qaeda and Osama bin Laden".[60]

A fundamental difference between the IMN and the Izala is that whereas the Izala are Salafists who espouse Wahhabi ideologies and are supported by Saudi Arabia, the IMN is a Shiite organisation—with a militant system, *hora* [guards], modelled after the Iranian Revolutionary Guards.[61] The IMN, as Hill notes, is supported by Iran and is more inclined than the Izala to use violence in furtherance of the network's ambitions of a Sharia-driven revolution, similar to the 1979 Iran Islamic Revolution, through contestation with the secular authorities and the Sufi brotherhoods: the former because it is "not fit to hold power" and the latter for its links "to the northern establishment".[62] In fact IMN did not recognise the Nigerian state and engaged in violent clashes with government forces until 1999. Sheikh Zakzaky himself was jailed on numerous occasions.[63]

However, whereas this "embrace of Shiite Islam" won the IMN "influential backers in Tehran", Hill contends that it had a highlly negative impact on a large number of his Sufi followers on the ground in northern Nigeria—a situation that was subsequently exploited by Zakzaky's protege, Mujahid, in his formation of the MIR.[64]

Yan Izala[65]

Yan Izala, as earlier highlighted, was founded by Abubakar Gumi in 1978; though Loimeier notes that as far back as 1972, Gumi already had started a struggle against the *turuq* "on a dogmatic level", one aimed at the purification of the religion and the elimination of all *bid'a* [heresy].[66] To Gumi and the Yan Izala, the *turuq*—the face of which was the Sufi brotherhoods—were "actual bearers and propagandists of the *bid'a*".[67] This stance by the Yan Izala proved popular among many. Indeed, and somewhat ironically, some within the Sufi Brotherhoods (particularly within the Tijâniyya) would even help swell the ranks of the Izala. However, as one might have forecast, Gumi's accusations and radical preachings—a trend continued by his protégé Isma'ila Idris—would bring him and his supporters in direct conflict with the Sufi Brotherhoods and also with the authorities.[68] As the *turuq* formed an "organised resistance" against Gumi and his followers, and as disagreement gradually inched toward escalation and violence, Gumi and his supporters decided that they should form an organization of their own.

A protégé of Gumi, Malam Isma'ila Idris, is largely identified as the founder of the Izala. However Loimeier notes that Idris was rather its "organiser" and "nominal leader".[69] For instance, Gumi himself was not present at the official founding of the Jamâ'at Izâlat al-Bid'a [Movement for the Eradication of Innovation] in Jos, on 8 February 1978. However, Gumi—in a gesture of the power and influence he had over the group—sent his compliments and proposed the addition of *"wa Iqâmat as-Sunna"* ["and the establishment of the Sunna"][70] to the name of the new movement, something which was later accepted by the delegates. Loimeier also points out that the Izala movement flourished in the years that followed its formation—despite many cited instances of violent clashes with the authorities and with the Sufi Brotherhoods.[71]

That the Izala "thrived" despite its ongoing militant struggle was certainly helped by the financial support given to Gumi by donors from Saudi Arabia and Kuwait.[72] Paden, who refers to the Izala as "anti-innovation[73] legalists" is of a similar view—noting that many large mosques constructed during the rise of the Izala had been made possible thanks to donations from those two countries.[74] For the particular instance of the Yan Izala, however, this may not have been a clear-cut case of an independent movement created from scratch—the counter-argument could certainly be made that Gumi only went ahead with his decision to create a new movement when, as Loimeier notes, "it became evident to Gumi that the JNI [Movement for the Support of Islam][75] was no longer an adequate platform for his own efforts of *tajdîd* [reform]".[76] Nonetheless Loimeier notes that Yan Izala was "founded and inspired" by Shiekh Gumi; and that the Izala constituted "a new movement of *tajdîd* (renewal)" started in the 1970s.[77] However Loimeier suggests as well a political agenda on the part of Gumi in the creation of the movement. Specifically Loimeier states that Gumi had to resort to "personal patronage…by attempting to gain access to a broader public" in order to further his struggle against the *turuq*.[78] Indeed, he was told by Gumi himself, that the Yan Izala was formed as a counter to Fityân al-Islâm; a conservative Sufi organization with the strong support of the *malamai* [clerics].[79]

The radical nature of Yan Izala's agenda is suggested where Loimeier notes that in laying "a foundation for a mass movement of his own", Gumi would have gained the requisite fame and popularity required "to shift the struggle against the *turuq* from a mere scholarly dispute between the *malamai* to a struggle at grassroots level".[80] With regard to the ever-growing membership of the Yan Izala, with a deliberate expansionist thrust Gumi built an organizational structure that rapidly gained ground across northern Nigeria".[81] In this same period, violent clashes with the Sufi brotherhoods became common, particularly so because the Yan Izala tried to bring "as many mosques as possible under their control".[82] Kaduna, Kano and Sokoto bore the brunt of the violence.

I acknowledge that many "new" networks within the northern Nigerian religious environment inherit enough elements from existing and competing networks to suggest that they may not indeed be new *per se*. Furthermore, as McCormack notes, several other networks were created in the years that followed the creation of the Izala.[83] This was due in part to the enabling environment at the time and the growing resentment of some against the existing Sufi order. Nonetheless, there are relatively few instances wherein such movements could be described as new constructs, rather than off-shoot networks.

Within this context, the Izala probably constitutes one of the better examples within northern Nigeria's religious environment, for two prime reasons. First, was the lengthy period of time during which Gumi was technically no longer affiliated to the Sufi brotherhoods, prior to the creation of the Izala. Specifically this was when Gumi first began having major, but still "dogmatic", disagreements with the Sufi Brotherhoods (around 1972 according to Loimeier) and when he eventually created, or rather endorsed the creation of, the Izala movement in 1978. Second, was the particular novelty associated with such a clean break from the established Islamic order at that particular time. The creation of the Izala was the first time "in the history of Islam in Nigeria [that] a religious leader had turned explicitly against Sufism and the *turuq*".[84] Undoubtedly there are nuances and factors that must be considered in responding to those who argue that the Izala had an entirely different ideological set of influences (Salafism, with some Wahhabi influence), rather than being one formed through the "softening" of Sufi ideologies. Nonetheless there remains a case to be made for the Izala being an example of a created network within northern Nigeria's religious environment.

Maitatsine

Perhaps more than any of the other northern Nigerian religious movements discussed to date, Maitatsine, with its stark ideological and operational departure from the even more radical networks of the time (such as Izala), and given its founder's background (a Cameroonian who had been exiled for years prior to the group's establishment) presents a pertinent historical example of the creation of a new religious movement. Moreover Maitatsine was arguably the most widely cited religiously-motivated insurgency in Nigeria before the emergence of Boko Haram. Radical Islamist network creation (formation) as a precursor to violent insurgency is thus a consistent thematic fit for Maitatsine, if not necessarily for the other groups discussed. Furthermore, analysis of Maitatsine as a case study of a created movement, and in particular its surge in popularity relatively soon after its establishment, indicate several contributing factors that may in practice swell the ranks of a newly-created network as much as past or existing affiliations or inherited connections from their parent networks.

These contributing factors include: (1) ideology (West contends that "more radical Islam that can provide a fertile environment for terrorism")[85] (2) style of engagement with followers (both Isichei and Falola suggest that Marwa Maitatsine, the movement's founder, was a selectively and a manipulatively benevolent leader);[86] (3) "an atmosphere permeated with radical Islamic thought";[87] and (4) "an environment in which terrorists can be recruited and terrorism can thrive".[88] West refers to this final contributing factor as an enabling environment—one facilitated by "poverty, disaffection, and hopelessness" even though such discontents should not be necessarily seen as causative of terrorism and insurgency.[89]

As mentioned earlier, the surge in the popularity of the Maitatsine so soon after its establishment as a new network in what was now becoming a crowded religious "marketplace" in northern Nigeria in the 1970s, is indicative of the group's meteoric rise at the time. For instance Isichei notes that by 1972, Marwa Maitatsine had a large following already.[90] Falola likewise notes that Marwa had at least 1,000 followers by 1972, and that he built that support base after returning from forced exile to Cameroon in 1966, and 1972, when the first major clash between the Yan 'Tatsine [Maitatsine followers] and the Nigerian police occurred in Kano on 6 August.[91] Such hostilities would continue over the years, but particularly intensified between 1979 and 1980.

Enabling environment aside, it is worth trying to understand who Marwa Maitatsine was, and how he amassed such a large following willing to engage security forces in their thousands, despite being hopelessly outmatched.

Marwa, in attempting to be distinctive as a way of attracting a following, created a "highly individual doctrine" that marked a sharp departure from those of the Sufis, or even of the Izala.[92] Falola points out that Maitatsine was a mystic who "created a doctrine and an interpretation of his own", for which he became revered, in a cult-like fashion, much unlike what other movements' leaders enjoyed.[93] Danjibo helps corroborate this narrative in his account: "he [Marwa Maitatsine] rebelled against many popular opinions among Kano Islamic circles, denouncing certain parts of the Holy Qur'an and even criticising Prophet Muhammad".[94] Moreover, the extremely fundamentalist doctrine of the Maitatsine removed any moral reservations they may have had about killing "infidels" (essentially anyone who did not belong to the sect). Danjibo for instance quotes a *Guardian* newspaper article from March 1984 in which the reporter contends that "The Maitatsines [sic] preach a strong compulsion to kill. They believe that if they are able to kill 'Arnas' (infidels) who don't believe in Allah, they will go to heaven".[95]

It is this level of fanaticism associated within the sect, and the mystic aura with which Marwa surrounded himself, which may also have proved a draw to many and may have contributed to Marwa's mass following.[96] This was so much so that even when Marwa called himself an *anabi*, a prophet with a divine mandate, his followers were said to have begun "praying in his name"[97] and that his actions within the sect were not seen as blasphemous or out of the ordinary—such was the influence Marwa had come to wield over his followers. Consequently in the years just before the Maitatsine riots in 1980, the *Yan Tatsine* numbered almost 10,000—judging by the figures given of suspected adherents after the riots.[98] Moreover, as Falola notes:

By 1975 he [Marwa Maitatsine] had over two thousand followers. Five years later, he had tripled that figure in his home base of Kano alone, with sizeable followings as far away as Bauchi, Maiduguri and Yola. Estimates of the total number of Maitatsine range from eight to twelve thousand, and according to one of his wives, his following increased in 1980.[99]

Falola also flags "economic decline" of the time, rather than just Marwa's charisma, as being one of the reasons why so many *talakawa* flocked to the Maitatsine. This is similar to the account by Isichei (1987) who notes that up to 2,000 followers lived with Maitatsine; and that he provided support for them.[100] As for how he recruited such a large number of people for his campaign, Falola notes that Maitatsine "had mallams under him who worked to recruit other disciples far and wide",[101] a thing which she notes made him a figure of envy for many '*ulama*.[102]

Part of the doctrinal ideologies spread by Marwa's surrogates was that *karatun boko* [Western education] was *haram*; that anyone who sent their child to such schools was *kafir* [an infidel]; and that the *Yan Boko*, by virtue of their wealth, were also infidels.[103] It is worth noting at this juncture that the viewpoint that *karatun boko* was *haram*—fundamentally, was an ideological shared link between the Yusufiyya and the Yan 'Tatsine.[104] As both Falola and Mohammed note, however, such anti-*boko* rhetoric was not unusual. Indeed, many clerics spoke out against the corrupting influence of the West.[105] What proved different in the case of the *Maitatsine* was that the socio-economic situation at that time left many if not most people impoverished, while a small coterie of government officials and politicians lived in comfort. Thus, to the *talakawa* [commoners], Marwa's message was a particularly welcome one: they were told that he would help purify society,[106] and that killing *kafirai* [infidels] was a prerequisite to active participation in jihad.[107]

Furthermore, and perhaps crucially, Yan 'Tatsine were given a target to direct their anger against: the secular state, and the Sufis and more traditional establishments that either supported or were indifferent to the increasingly westernised state. As Harnischfeger puts it, the Christians were not the main target of the Maitatsine, rather they viewed as the chief enemy "the hypocritical Islamic dignitaries who pretended to be guardians of the faith while basking in Western luxury".[108] Despite his inflammatory anti-establishment rhetoric, however, Maitatsine was said to nonetheless have "cultivated relationships with segments of the establishments"; relationships that went all the way up to Kano State governor Rimi.[109] Yet it appears that just as the relationship between Boko Haram (via Commissioner of Religious Affairs, Alhaji Buju Foi) and Borno State Governor, Ali Modu Sherrif, soured as Boko Haram declared all-out war against the State in June 2009, so too did positive relations between the Yan 'Tatsine and the Kano State government deteriorate when the Maitatsine attempted to take over Kano's central mosque in December 1980. The resulting clashes occurred first with the local police, but then with the Nigerian Army, who were called in after Yan 'Tatsine's ranks swelled and its members dug in for a showdown. These clashes left over 4,000 people dead according to official statistics.[110]

After the initial showdown, and with hundreds of Yan 'Tatsine detained, it was also learned that Marwa Maitatsine himself had been killed. Marwa's demise notwithstanding, the violence did not abate entirely. Indeed, in the years that followed—in 1982, and between 1984 and 1985—there were sporadic clashes between the regrouped Yan 'Tatsine and security forces. These renewed hostilities led to the killing of thousands more sect members.[111] While 1985 saw the final clashes between the Yan 'Tatsine and the authorities, some scholars contend that the group still commands some level of following, even today; though they now go by the name Kala Kato.[112]

Conclusion

The aim of this chapter was to highlight the almost cyclical nature of extremist Islamic group formation in northern Nigeria. Such groups had different identities and objectives, these being predicated on the Shia-Sunni divide, though it is possible to identify some commonalities.

Common factors among militant groups have included vocal criticism of the country's leadership as corrupt, unjust and unable to deal with social and economic problems, and rejection of Western values that, in their view, caused society and some clerics to abandon the tenets of Islam and to embrace secularism. The sense of injustice, albeit not a frequent feature of Boko Haram's rhetoric, is nonetheless present in the group's statements as evidenced by my earlier reference to Abu Qaqa's declaration that "we have been motivated by the stark injustice in the land".[113] Given that the implementation of sharia law is often described as the solution to societal laxity and corruption—to mention two important issues—then Boko Haram's plan to Islamise Nigeria can be seen as part of a broader struggle to address society's ills.

One aspect worth emphasising is that the government response to the emergence of extremist groups did very little to calm inter-religious tensions or to contain (let alone eliminate) popular resentment towards the authorities. I will devote a whole chapter to this issue vis-à-vis Boko Haram but here it suffices to say that, historically, three responses have been adopted: first were attempts to manipulate religious sentiments, such as offering jobs based on the candidate's faith or the secret attempt to join the Organisation of the Islamic Conference in 1986; second was heavy-handed repression; third was the ostrich approach, simply hoping that the group and their demands would eventually fade away.[114] As one can imagine, all three approaches were at best temporary solutions and, for sure, backfired. Not least as military repression and arrests of group leaders only resulted in people feeling they were targeted as extremist Muslims and increased the perception that the government was un-Islamic.[115]

In 2012, the then Chief of Army Staff Lieutenant-General Azubuike Ihejirika appears to have grasped the risk of such groups' formation and re-emergence. Visiting the newly inaugurated Nigerian Army Training Centre (NATRAC) complex in Kontagora, Niger state, he warned army graduates that "[Nigerians] should not think of Boko Haram alone because when Boko Haram goes, another one [insurgency] may come."[116]

4

WHAT IS BOKO HARAM?

This chapter aims to shed light on how, building on the experience of earlier Islamist movements discussed in the previous chapter, Boko Haram came about. More specifically, in this section I trace Boko Haram's tactical and ideological evolution from an isolated, mostly peaceful, religious community, to a violent insurgency that embraces suicide attacks and hostage-taking. But understanding Boko Haram's trajectory is not a straightforward exercise. Over a decade since its inception, politicians, the military, academics, clerics, the media and common citizens are yet to agree on what Boko Haram stands for. During field research in Nigeria in spring 2013 I was struck by the degree of disagreement over what drives Boko Haram's insurgency campaign, not to mention various, more or less plausible, conspiracy theories regularly floating around. This general confusion is reflected in people's views of what constitutes the appropriate strategy to stop the violence and eradicate the group. Some of these arguments will be addressed later in the book. In order to do so, it is essential to explore the social make-up of the group and to get a better sense of its funding sources and support network, including from among Northern Nigeria's political elite.

Where it all started

While most media reports indicate 2002 as the founding year of Boko Haram, and Ustaz Mohammed Yusuf is commonly identified as the original leader of the group,[1] the reality is that even before the charismatic preacher Yusuf made his mark, at least two, if not three, other important figures emerged and should be given credit for what became known as the "Nigerian Taleban" and later Jama'atu Ahlis Sunnah Lidda'awati w'al Jihad [People Committed to the Propagation of the Prophet's Teachings and Jihad] a.k.a. Boko Haram.

According to the Nigerian security forces, the true origins of the group can be traced back to 1995 at the University of Maiduguri, Borno state, when the Ahlulsunna wal'jama'ah hijra [Muslim Youth Organisation][2] sect was set up by Abubakar Lawan. In its earlier years the sect could be described as a conservative non-violent Islamic movement. In 2002 Lawan left Nigeria to pursue further Islamic learning in Medina and Mecca and, in his absence, a committee of *shaykhs* appointed Mohammed Yusuf, an ethnic Kanuri for Girgir village in Yobe state, leader of the sect. Later he ousted the committee amidst allegations of corruption among its members. From around this time, many names were used to describe the sect—including Muhajirun, Yusufiyyah, and "Nigerian Taliban"—which increasingly showed signs of wanting to overthrow the Nigerian state and its secular ideology. Yusuf led the first spate of violence on Christmas Eve 2003 in Kanama and Geiam, Yobe state, when the sect attacked public buildings and police stations. The next year its members established a base in Kanama, named "Afghanistan" and it was then that their activities became more concerning. That same year several students in tertiary education abandoned their studies, destroyed their school certificates and joined the sect. On 21 September they staged attacks against police stations in Bama and Gwoza, Borno state, killing several officers and taking their weapons.[3]

A slightly different version of how Boko Haram originated is put forward by Andrew Walker. In 2002 some of the most radical young worshippers at the Alhaji Muhammadu Ndimi Mosque in Maiduguri became highly critical of the city administration but also of the local religious establishment which they believe to be corrupt and to have lost touch with true Islamic values. This sentiment prompted them to isolate themselves, replicating Prophet Mohammed's *hijra* when he left Mecca to retreat to Medina, and to move to Yobe state where they set up a base in Kanama, three kilometres from the Nigerian border, under the leadership of Mohammed Ali. The religious community established in Kanama, re-named "Afghanistan", was based on Salafi principles and the societal model of the Taleban—reports indicated that the Afghan flag was displayed in the community—and urged other Muslims to return to the true tenets of Islam. New members arrived from neighbouring Niger, Chad and Cameroon but despite its increasingly multi-national membership, the group only sought to exert influence within Nigeria, and its messages and anti-state criticism were targeted at Nigerian institutions. At the time they were believed to number around seventy members and to possess some weaponry, albeit only for defensive purposes. In December 2003, some members became involved in a local dispute over fishing rights and, as the police intervened, they managed to overpower some of the officers and steal their weapons. In response, the army mounted a siege on the local mosque which lasted until early 2004 when, during a major shootout, Mohamed Ali and most of his followers were killed and their Kanama base was destroyed. The survivors returned to Maiduguri to re-join their original youth group at the Alhaji Muhammadu Ndimi Mosque, now led by Mohammed Yusuf. Soon after, Yusuf established the Ibn Taimiyyah Masjid [mosque] specifically for the group, in the north of the town centre, on land owned by his father-in-law Baba Fugu Mohammed. From here they began to expand their reach into Bauchi, Yobe and Niger states, and establish something akin to a state within the state with independent religious police and a cabinet.[4]

At this point it is worth pausing to reflect on ideology. The naming of the group's mosque in honour of the thirteenth-century theologian Ibn Taymiyyah was not casual. As already introduced in the previous chapter, Ibn Taymiyyah inspired many ultra-Salafist movements and it is around his teachings that Mohamed Yusuf modelled his own preaching. Salafism (sometimes referred to as Wahhabism, or closely aligned to Wahhabism, although true Salafists find the association with Wahhabism derogatory) is a movement within Sunni Islam that is characterised by being literalist and puritanical in its interpretation of the Qur'an and *hadiths*. Their study, i.e. the study of the basic source of Islam, is at the core of Salafism and a way of ridding Islam from external/non-Muslim influences.[5] Furthermore there is a strong propensity among its followers to clash with the state due to the three tenets of Ibn Taymiyyah. This is not to say that Salafists are de facto violent. Rather, that ultra-Salafism—which is an even stricter form of Salafism and is fiercely anti-innovation in its ideology—and Salafi-Jihadism are what are particularly problematic but also violent. What is undeniable is that Salafism and its more radical interpretations are fundamentalist in their ideology and thus do not promote co-existence with other religions and even other more moderate strains of Islam in the same state.

Yusuf's preachings were undeniably ultra-Salafist. In an interview for the BBC Yusuf explained:

> the present Western-style education is mixed with issues that run contrary to our beliefs in Islam…Like rain. We believe it is a creation of God rather than an evaporation caused by the sun that condenses and becomes rain… Like saying the world is a sphere. If it runs contrary to the teachings of Allah, we reject it. We also reject the theory of Darwinism.[6]

Nevertheless, he was educated at graduate level, spoke fluent English and, reportedly, drove a Mercedes-Benz, as well as enjoying a "lavish" lifestyle.[7]

Other accounts indicate that before 2000 a man called Aminu Tashen Ilimi inspired a group of students to leave the University of Maiduguri and to follow the teachings of a foreign preacher who argued that Western education was contrary to Islam. The group began to influence Mohamed Yusuf, who was then preaching at the popular Alhaji Muhammadu Ndimi Mosque in Maiduguri, and who, as a result, left the Indimi mosque in 2000 to set up his own teaching structure in Anguwan Doki, using a building owned by his father-in-law Alhaji Bapur. Here, from 2002, Yusuf's teaching began to attract growing numbers of pupils but also criticism from Aminu Tashen Ilimi, Mola Umar and others who accused him of promoting an ideology they deemed too liberal. Hence they broke away from him in October 2003 and moved to Yobe state where they set up a new base outside Kanama—"Afghanistan"—from which they aimed to establish an independent territory; they spoke almost exclusively Arabic (which is very unusual) and led a life secluded from the rest of the population. According to this version, in January 2004 members attacked police stations in Kanama and Damaturo provoking military retaliation resulting in a two-day battle at the end of which dozens of their followers had been killed and about fifty members were arrested. In September, an affiliated group attacked and destroyed the local police headquarters in Bama, also in Borno state, killing officers including the Assistant Commissioner (a Muslim). Similar attacks were staged in Gwoza. This time the response came from the Federal Government in the form of a military deployment and after two days of fighting in the Mandara hills twenty-eight members were killed and the group was forced under-ground until May 2007.[8]

A final version of how Boko Haram came about sees Mohamed Yusuf establish the sect in the early 1990s under the name of *ahl al-sunna wa-l-jama'a wa-lhijra*. Roman Loimeier described Yusuf as a student of prominent cleric Sheikh Ja'far Mahmud Adam in Kano but from whom he distanced himself in 2003 and with whom, until 2007, Yusuf engaged in a heated theological debate through sermons, CDs, and pamphlets in which the teacher criticised Yusuf's rejection of Western education. The latter was believed by Adam to be necessary in the longer term in order to fight Western enemies. Adam also discouraged military actions against the Nigerian state while Yusuf fiercely opposed the secular educational system and Nigerian institutions as well as modern Islamic teaching such as the Yan Izala's, and refused to accept the Sultan of Sokoto as the "nominal head of all Nigerian Muslims".[9] The latter, in particular, is highly significant in that it reinforces the concept of irreconcilable differences between Yusuf and the religious establishment.

Just before the 2007 presidential elections, Adam, who was a regular preacher at the Ndimi mosque in Maiduguri but at the time was in Kano where he administered a mosque, was assassinated. It is believed that the killing had been ordered by Yusuf and, as a result, it became clear that any form of reconciliation between the sect and the religious establishment in northern Nigeria was now unattainable.[10] In December 2003 clashes erupted between Yusuf's followers and the security forces in Kanama and in January around 200 members attacked several police stations. In September more attacks took place in Borno state and twenty-seven members were allegedly killed while many escaped to Cameroon.[11] The last attack in this initial phase of Boko Haram's history took place on 10 October when a convoy of sixty police personnel came under fire at Kala-Balge on Lake Chad. Twelve officers were taken hostage, their fates unknown.[12]

All competing, albeit somewhat overlapping, accounts of the early years of the sect are plausible and, for the sake of producing a comprehensive history of Boko Haram's evolution, are worth recording. However, all these versions converge on Yusuf entering the scene and marking a defining moment for the group. Through his charismatic personality he became a magnet for its members and the recognised leader or at least main front-man of the sect. Also widely agreed upon is the understanding that the name "Boko Haram" was used by the media and by the group's neighbours in Maiduguri. The name, which is Hausa for "Western education is sinful" reflected the sect's rejection of what it believed to be un-Islamic Western values, but was never adopted by group members themselves who, in fact, prefer Jama'atu Ahlis Sunnah Lidda'awati w'al Jihad.[13] In 2009, after Yusuf's death, the then acting leader Mallam Sanni Umaru shed light on the meaning of the sect clarifying that was not *education* per se but Western *civilisation* they rejected:

> Boko Haram does not in any way mean "Western education is a sin" as the infidel media continue to portray us. Boko Haram actually means "western civilisation" is forbidden. The difference is that while the first gives the impression that we are opposed to formal education coming from the West, that is Europe, which is not true, the second affirms our belief in the supremacy of Islamic culture (not education), for culture is broader; it includes education but not determined by western education. In this case, we are talking of western ways of life which include: constitutional provision as it relates to, for instance, the rights and privileges of women, the idea of homo-sexualism, lesbianism, sanctions in cases of terrible crimes like drug trafficking, molestation of infants, multi-party democracy in an overwhelmingly Islamic country like Nigeria, blue films, prostitution, drinking beer and alcohol and many others that are opposed to Islamic civilisation.[14]

More recently the current leader Abubakar Shekau reconfirmed their preferred name in a leaflet circulated in Kano following a series of explosions that had killed over 170 people in January 2012:

> In the name of Allah, Peace and Mercy! We are the group called 'forbidden' that is Boko Haram but we love to call ourselves *Jama'atu Ahlissunnah Liddaawati wal Jihad*…Message from Leader Jama'atu Ahlissunnah Liddaawati wal Jihad. Imam Abu Muhammad Abubakar Bin Muhammad (Shekau).[15]

As also indicated by David Cook, it remains unclear what truly triggered violence in 2003 beyond the fight over fishing rights recalled by Walker. As Cook himself admits, the political climate of 2003 may have been a contributing factor with President Obasanjo—a Christian—being re-elected for his second term and widespread speculation that the election results had been fixed. If this theory were true, it could have ignited the latent belief among some Muslims that they had to take up arms to protect their interests.[16]

* * *

The sect goes underground

As evidenced by the different accounts presented above, some inconsistencies exist regarding the events up to 2004 but all versions point to a more or less "dormant" phase between late 2004 and 2008 when, in spite of some sporadic hit-and-run attacks in parts of Yobe and Borno, especially against security forces, the group remained largely inactive.

Worth nothing was a violent parenthesis in 2007 when the group re-appeared in Kano and attacked the office of the Federal Road Safety Corps in Sharada, the Panshekara police station and exchanged fire with the military. In the midst of this violence Yusuf was frequently questioned by the authorities, especially by the State Security Service (SSS), but he always declared that those responsible for the attacks had broken away from him and no longer listened to his teachings and that he had lost control of them.[17]

But in spite of being a quiet period in terms of militant activities, it was not an insignificant one in the development of the sect, its ideology, recruitment drive and shoring up of resources. Some senior Boko Haram members are in fact believed to have travelled to Pakistan to obtain funding from al-Qaeda to carry out attacks against American targets in Nigeria. Albeit hard to confirm with absolute certainty, a number of court cases show that this is a possibility that should not be discounted. Mallam Mohammed Ashafa, a suspected Nigerian Taleban member from Kano, was arrested in 2006 on charges of receiving funds from two al-Qaeda operatives at the Tabligh headquarters in Lahore, Pakistan, to attack Americans in Nigeria, and of recruiting twenty-one fighters sent to be trained with the Algerian Salifist Group for Combat and Preaching (al-Qaeda in the Islamic Maghreb's forerunner) at a camp in Agwan, Niger. As of June 2013 the trial continued with the defendant claiming his innocence and denouncing physical abuse on the part of the SSS and being prevented from speaking to his lawyer.[18] According to the retired head of the SSS' anti-terrorism department Ashafa had been sent to Pakistan by the Resident Chief of the al-Qaeda network in West Africa, Mallam Adnan Ibrahim, who resided in Kano at the time.[19] In a separate case, a Boko Haram member involved in the 2009 uprising, Abdulrasheed Abubakar, confessed to having spent three months in Afghanistan, at Yusuf's request, to train as a bomb specialist with the plan to return to Nigeria and pass on his newly acquired expertise to five fellow group members.[20]

The dispersion of the group in this period led to Yusuf's self-exile to Saudi Arabia. As indicated by Loimeier, Yusuf had been strongly influenced by Saudi scholars, particularly the Wahhabi Abubakar b. 'Abdallah whose text *al-madaris al-'alamiyya al-ajnabiyya al-isti'mariyya: ta'rikhuha wa-makhatiruha* (The Secular, Foreign and Colonialist Schools: Their History and Dangers) provided theological backing for Yusuf's rejection of evolution theory and Western science.[21]

Upon his return to Nigeria he continued his preaching quite openly in Yobe and Borno states and by 2007 had already amassed a significant following due to his seductive rhetoric and the resonance of ultra-Salafist puritanical and anti-innovation ideologies among the *talakawa* [commoners]. This period of 'recruitment' would see Yusuf use a combination of preaching and social incentives—both innovative and effective—as ways to attract and familiarise many *talakawa* to what Boko Haram represented. Shrewdly, he made available a system of informal social welfare through micro-financing to help his followers set up small businesses and also arranged marriages—all measures that helped increase his popularity. Many of the local commoners came to see Yusuf not only as a preacher, but as a provider. This continued until 2009, when the infamous Battle of Maiduguri occurred, between Yusuf and his Boko Haram and Nigerian security forces.

Because of his ability to mobilise the youth he was seen as a useful political tool, especially in Maiduguri. Both governors of Yobe and Borno states approached Yusuf and while some obstacles limited the extent of Yusuf's involvement with the former, Ali Modu Sheriff of Borno appointed Buju Foi, an influential Boko Haram member, as Commissioner of Islamic Affairs in 2007, in a committee of which Yusuf was also part and that was responsible for selecting those who would go on the *Hajj*, or pilgrimage to Mecca.[22] This is probably the most explicit example of how the sect, in spite of officially rejecting state authority, managed to exert influence over local politics as a result of its growing popularity. However the relationship was short-lived. The government's failure to put in place an effective mechanism for the implementation of sharia law (officially adopted in 2000)[23] precipitated a falling out and the resignation of Foi and Yusuf from their political positions.

WHAT IS BOKO HARAM?

The 2009 turning point

For current Boko Haram members, as well as for those studying the movement, 2009 marked a key point in the evolution of the group that continues to resonate today. The extra-judicial killing of Yusuf—whose importance and charisma have been amply highlighted earlier in this chapter—not only left the group thirsty for revenge but also paved the way for a change in leadership, embodied by second-in-command turned supreme leader Abubakar Shekau. The latter altered the nature of the movement which, from this point on, took a more radical and violent turn becoming the fully-fledged insurgency Boko Haram has become known as.

But let us take a step back and understand how from a state of inactivity events suddenly accelerated so dramatically. First, I shall spell out what prompted Boko Haram's re-emergence in 2009.

Tensions were already at a high level in June 2009 during a confrontation between sect members and officers belonging to "Operation Flush", the latter having been established a year earlier in Borno state as a joint effort between the police and the military to tackle robberies. Operation Flush was also later tasked with enforcing new legislation introduced in the state in 2009 imposing the wearing of helmets by motorcyclists. As Isa Umar Gusau recalls, security forces felt that Boko Haram's defiance of this latest piece of legislation was a sign that the group refused to recognise the authority and legitimacy of the government. For this reason Operation Flush vigorously enforced the law often seizing the motorbikes of those failing to comply.[24]

On 11 June, Boko Haram members on motorbikes were on a procession to bury a fellow member who had died in a car crash on the Biu-Maiduguri road. Officers stopped the procession requesting the riders to wear helmets. The refusal to do so led to a confrontation during which some (possibly seventeen) Boko Haram members were wounded. There are conflicting reports as to whether anyone died but some of the injured were taken to University of Maiduguri Teaching Hospital (UMTH).[25] Also unclear is whether the checkpoint was actually prompted by the lack of helmets or was the result of a tip-off suggesting that Boko Haram was about to bury a member they themselves had killed.[26] Three days later Yusuf threatened a reprisal:

> What I said previously that we are going to be attacked by the authorities

had manifested itself...therefore, we will not agree with this kind of humili-ation, we are ready to die together with our brothers.[27]

I will not go into a detailed chronology of what happened in the fol-lowing days as it has already been amply recorded by others.[28] However, the ensuing weeks saw arrests of Boko Haram members, the recovery of weapons and explosives, and the death of a Boko Haram bomb-maker, Hassan Sani Badami in an explosion at his house. The security forces paraded before the media some of those who had been captured.

Violence broke out on 26 July when sixty sect members attacked Dutsen police station in Bauchi. Fifty people are believed to have died in this incident. The police retaliated by cracking down on the group's base around the Bauchi airstrip. In Bauchi, the local government reported that five wells had been contaminated with cyanide and phos-phorous—chemicals believed to have been used by Boko Haram to build explosive devices.[29]

By the next day violence had spread to Borno, Kano, Katsina and Yobe producing more than 100 casualties in the course of attacks against police stations and government buildings. In the chaos that ensued, a number of prisoners were freed by Boko Haram. Arrests of suspected group members were carried out in Kaduna, Sokoto and Gombe states although there had been no outbreak of violence in those areas.[30]

An official statement was issued by President Yar'adua's spokesman directing the security forces to spare no effort in "identifying, arresting and prosecuting leaders and members of the extremist sect involved in the attack".[31] Following a presidential order, the next day hundreds of soldiers from the Army's 3rd Armoured Division, accompanied by six light armoured tanks and police elements descended on Maiduguri to crush Boko Haram's headquarters. In particular, they aimed at regaining control of Maiduguri, Galadima, Kasuwan Shanu and Low Coast, all of which Boko Haram had taken since Sunday 26 July. Meanwhile the violence had displaced thousands of locals who had to seek refuge in military and police buildings although many could not escape being caught in the crossfire and were subjected to road blocks and checks by the sect.[32] Three days of intense confrontation followed resulting in the death of between 700 and 800 sect members, including one of the group's main financiers, Buji Foi, and Yusuf's father-in-law, seventy-two-year-old Baba Fugu Mohammed. Several were arrested, including on 30 July Mohamed Yusuf July and his deputy Abubakar Shekau.[33] The

Ibn Taymiyyah Masjid—the mosque established specifically for Yusuf's followers in Maiduguri—was also destroyed during what became known as the Battle of Maiduguri.

Dead or alive?

The question of what happened following the apprehension of Yusuf has caused much debate and controversy. At first police claimed on national television that he had tried to escape and was then killed attempting to do so.[34] Later it emerged that the military had handed him over unharmed (with the exception of an old wound on his arm) to the police for questioning after the man had given himself up "peacefully"— as indicated by Colonel Ben Ahanotu, who was leading the operation and made the arrest.[35] Quickly rumours, and then images and videos, started to leak. They showed Boko Haram's leader being interrogated by the police, and then a series of gruesome pictures of his "bullet ridden" body began to circulate. Rights groups started to call for an investigation into the extrajudicial killing of Yusuf.[36]

I had the opportunity to interview a civilian who was at the scene on 30 July and who had seen Yusuf's body and had pictures of it. According to this source, by the time Yusuf reached the police station, officers were extremely angry, having suffered a number of casualties including the loss of a Mobile Police Commissioner. "When Yusuf went into custody it was chaos", he recalled.[37] This account is compatible with a video showing police officers dancing around the body with one, as a way of justifying what had just happened, claiming that had Yusuf gone to trial he would have been "let off the hook".[38] The lack of confidence in the judicial process is not an inconsequential matter, even more so as this feeling remains very much alive among security forces. Indeed, it has become evident vis-à-vis subsequent extra-judicial killings that became the focus of campaigns by international human rights organisations.

Another source reminded me that Yusuf's killing had not been the only extra-judicial execution that took place that day at the police station. Many Boko Haram members suffered the same fate which, according to the interviewee, was a reflection of the police's anger and frustration and even, the source argues, corruption.[39] A video obtained by Al Jazeera in February 2010—and still available online for those who can stomach it—showed alleged Boko Haram members and, most likely, innocent civilians being required by army officers to lie on the ground before being shot. The same footage included the body of Yusuf, covered in blood, with his hands in handcuffs.[40] Shekau however had a lucky escape. He claimed that a "true Muslim" had set him free following his arrest.[41]

The army, before handing Yusuf to the police, had the chance to video record a brief interview in Hausa. Needless to say, we could have learnt much more about the sect, Yusuf's beliefs and his personality had we had more than just a 5 minute 43 second exchange with the man. I report the transcript below.

> Military: We went to your house yesterday and we saw a lot of animals, syringes and materials used for making bombs, what were you keeping all that for?
>
> Yusuf: Like I told you, to protect myself…
>
> Military: (Cuts in)…to protect yourself how? Isn't there the authorities, the law enforcement agencies?
>
> Yusuf: The authorities, the law enforcement agents are the same people fighting me…
>
> Military: What did you do?
>
> Yusuf: I don't know what I did… I am only propagating my religion Islam.
>
> Military: But I am also a Muslim…
>
> Yusuf: I don't know why you refuse to accept my own (Islam)
>
> Military: Why should you say Boko is Haram (sinful)?
>
> Yusuf: Of course it is Haram
>
> Military: Why did you say that?
>
> Yusuf: The reasons are so many…
>
> Military: The trouser you are wearing…
>
> Yusuf: (cuts in)…it is pure cotton and cotton belongs to Allah
>
> Military: But Allah said in the Qur'an iqra (read), that people should seek knowledge…
>
> Yusuf: That's correct, but not the knowledge that contravenes the teachings of Islam. All knowledge that contradicts Islam is prohibited by the Almighty…sihiri (sorcery or magic) is knowledge, but Allah hath forbidden it; shirk (Polytheism or sharing or associating partners to Allah) is knowledge, but Allah has forbidden it; astronomy is knowledge, but Allah has forbidden it…
>
> Military: At your place we found computers, syringes…are all that no products of knowledge?

Yusuf: They are purely technological things, not Boko…and westernization is different.

Military: How comes you are eating good food—look at you, looking healthy—you are driving good cars, and wearing good clothes while you are forcing your followers to sell their belongings and live mostly on dabino (dates) and water?

Yusuf: That is not true. Everybody is living according to his means. Even you are different. Whoever you see driving good cars is because he can afford them, and whoever you see living in want also means he doesn't have the wherewithal.

Military: Why did you abandon your mosque and your compound?

Yusuf: Because you went and opened fire there…

Military: But you sent your people there to die in the fire?

Yusuf: No my people have left the place.

Military: What about those who came to fight for you…where and where do you have followers?

Yusuf: You have chased all of them away.

Military: Apart from Maiduguri…

Yusuf: There are some in Bauchi but police chased them away even before now; there are some in Gombe, police went to their house and chased away; there are some in Yola, Adamawa, police attacked them, same with those in Jalingo, Taraba State. It was after chasing them away that they turned to us here in Maiduguri.

Military: What happened to your hand?

Yusuf: I fell

Military: In this town (Maiduguri), how many areas do you have?

Yusuf: The headquarters is right here.

Military: What about other branches?

Yusuf: We have in Gwange, Bulunkutu…

Military: Where they intercepted weapons the other day, right?

Yusuf: (Laughs) Intercepted weapons?

Military: What about your 2IC (second in command)…because they said you have soldiers, police, etc?

Yusuf: That is not true…

Military: But don't you have a 2IC, who acts in your absence?

Yusuf: I have…

Military: What is his name?

Yusuf: Malam Abubakar Shakau

Military: Where is he now?

Yusuf: I don't know.

Military: Who and who escaped with you?

Yusuf: I did not run with anybody

Military: Who are your sponsors, here at home or abroad?

Yusuf: No body

Military: No, tell us the truth...

Yusuf: Insha Allah, I won't lie to you...

Military: You have a farm around Benishek?

Yusuf: yes

Military: Now you have made us kill people that are innocent. What do you have to say?

Yusuf: You bear responsibility on all those you killed.

Military: What about those killed by your followers?

Yusuf: My followers did not kill anybody

Military: What about those killed among your followers?

Yusuf: Those killed among my followers, whoever killed them are those who committed crime.

Military: Where are you from originally?

Yusuf: I hail from Yobe State.

Military: Where in Yobe State?

Yusuf: Jakusko

Military: What about your father?

Yusuf: He is also from Jakusko.

Military: What about your mother?

Yusuf: She is from Gashua

Military: Have you ever travelled abroad?

Yusuf: Only Hajj (Pilgrimage)

Military: What year was that?

Yusuf: 2003 and 2004.[42]

Post-Yusuf

In July 2009, following the killing of Yusuf, a spokesman for the National Police, while acknowledging that some pockets of violence remained in the north, dismissed the idea that the sect could carry on much longer: "This group operates under a charismatic leader. They will no more have any aspiration…The leader who they thought was invincible and immortal has now been proved otherwise".[43] The official in question may have not thought much of speculation that only became publicly available a couple of years later and according to which senior security chiefs had pointed to the factionalisation of Boko Haram in the immediate aftermath of Yusuf's demise. Based on the story reported by the media, three splinters, led respectively by Abubakar Shekau, Mamaan Nur and an unknown leader, had replaced the more unified Boko Haram movement that had been in existence until summer 2009 and were primarily the product of tensions between Shekau—popular among the younger generations—and more moderate members who found Nur's openness to dialogue a more appealing approach for the future of the movement.[44] Interesting to note is that in spite of his earlier reputation as a more moderate chief, Nur is wanted for the attack against the UN building in Abuja in August 2011 and his al-Qaeda connections—more on this later—and some analysts including Jacob Zenn believe his faction may have been responsible for the killing of Yusuf's brother-in-law, Babakura Fugu, in September 2011 just after the man had met with security officials in an attempt to facilitate dialogue with Boko Haram.[45]

Although in his last interview Yusuf had indicated Shekau as his second in command, and the latter indeed announced the group's comeback under his leadership with a video on April 2010, some questions remain regarding the identity of the person who took over as interim leader in the immediate aftermath of Yusuf's demise while Shakau was recovering from injuries. Some experts argue that Mamman Nur could have been the one temporarily leading the group,[46] however there appears to be stronger evidence in favour of Sanni Umaru, as per his statement quoted earlier in this chapter and interviews with a number of sources.[47]

Either way, establishing with absolute certainly the identity of who led the group in that brief period is not essential to understanding Boko Haram's trajectory. What is noticeable is that between August 2009 and April 2010 the group was believed extinct, with many members having been killed, arrested or having fled into neighbouring countries as a result of the July 2009 crackdown.

The Shakau era—the beginning of the insurgency

When Shakau, an ethnic Kanuri from Yobe state, took over the leadership in 2010, Boko Haram assumed a new, more violent identity. Nonetheless, it is worth highlighting that that in spite of Yusuf's main characterisation as a preacher he favoured violence more than was often depicted. Indeed, some believe that he was simply waiting for the "perfect time" to embark on an asymmetric campaign.

The radical turn under Shakau was evident from his personality which contrasted markedly from Yusuf's. Those who met him described him as a coarse individual, an avid hashish user and "somehow more feared than Yusuf"—as recalled by one of the few journalists who have had direct access to members of the sect, Ahmad Salkida.[48] In fact, since the change of leadership it has become increasingly difficult to reach out to the group. I met with a journalist who had been at Yusuf's house in Maiduguri and had the opportunity to interview him and to regularly interact with his spokesperson. He described Yusuf as "softly spoken, moderate and unassuming". The preacher was adamant he had no links to the Afghan Taleban although he supported their cause and opposed government authority. His admiration for the Taleban was so well known that some of his followers would refer to him as "Yusuf Taleban". He also added that he was constantly trying to dissuade some of the most hard-core members from committing violence since he felt the time for jihad was yet to come. In spite of some fractures caused by ideological differences he eventually had to reconcile with the hardliners, as he needed their support.[49] Salkida also stressed how Yusuf's rejection of Western values went beyond merely the Western-inspired education system—as it is often reflected in the translation of "Boko Haram" as "Western education is sinful". In fact, democracy (as something that had no place within Islamic society) was a major issue for Yusuf. From this, one could infer, as Salkida does, that had it not been for the failing governance system characterising Nigeria at the time (which I argue still continues today), Boko Haram's violence would have lacked a catalyst and an important recruitment drive in the form of deep-seated disaffection towards the government.[50]

Gathering this level of insight into Shekau's mind-set and thinking is much more complicated in spite of the several video messages he has issued over time—usually wearing a *keffiyeh* and sitting next to an AK-47. What is known is that he does not deal directly with most of his followers, let alone the media, and prefers to give orders, and distribute or collect money through his lieutenants. He also seems to have the last word on all decisions in spite of the existence of a Shura Council consisting of thirty senior members who, from across Nigeria and neighbouring countries, form Boko Haram's decision-making body running what has become a cell-based organisation.[51]

From several accounts it has emerged that Shekau was a dedicated theology student who moved to Maiduguri in 1990 and settled with a local Islamic cleric in the area of Mafoni. Later he married one of the cleric's daughters who died during childbirth. This event possibly triggered some existing but hitherto repressed psychiatric problems: he became so violent that it was necessary to put him in chains.[52] He married one of Yusuf's four wives and adopted his children following his death.[53]

He was introduced to Yusuf by Mamman Nur in, possibly, the late 1990s and among the three he was no doubt the one holding the most radical beliefs to the point that he even criticised Yusuf for being too "liberal". Moreover, his religious drive was such that it won him the nickname of *Darul Tawheed*, i.e. specialist in Tawheed, or Islamic doctrine.[54] His extreme views were reflected in some of his messages. In one of the most infamous ones, following the death of over 180 people in Kano in January 2012 he confessed "I enjoy killing anyone that God commands me to kill the way I enjoy killing chickens and rams".[55] What I would also describe as a fundamental shift introduced by the Shekau leadership was the attempt to link the group, perhaps more rhetorically than in practical terms, to the struggle of foreign jihadist groups—but I will leave the "foreign" dimension for the next chapter. This is such a critical aspect—of interest to many including the American, British and Canadian governments—that devoting a whole chapter to its study is mandatory.

On several occasions over the course of the years Shakau was declared dead by the Nigerian security forces only for him to release video or audio messages days later, effectively ridiculing the government effort. I grew very sceptical at every report of his demise. The only time I almost believed such claims was in August 2013 after the following statement was issued by JTF spokesman Lt Col Sagir Musa:

> Intelligence report available to the Joint Task Force, JTF, Operation Restore Order revealed that Abubakar Shekau, the most dreaded and wanted terrorist leader may have died. He died of gunshots wounds received in an encounter with the JTF in one of their camps in Sambisa Forest on June 30,

2013. Shekau was mortally wounded in the encounter and was sneaked into Amitchide—a border community in Cameroon for treatment from which he never recovered.[56]

Lt Col Musa also added that the man appearing in a video released by the group only days earlier was not Shekau himself but rather an impersonator. Admitting the leader's death would have weakened the fighters' morale and surely would have grown the confidence of the security forces.[57] In addition, details emerged of the killing of Yusuf's second in command Momodu Bama, *aka* Abu Saad, in Bama, alongside his father Abatcha Flatari, believed to be one of the "spiritual mentors of Boko Haram terrorists in charge of indoctrinating child foot soldiers who are mainly abducted children".[58]

Unlike previous instances, a message of refutation from the group did not follow. And for a few weeks analysts and security specialists debated whether the killing of Shekau was real and, if so, what the future held for Boko Haram. Would a third generation of its leadership be able to hold the movement together? If not, how long would the fight continue before Boko Haram was dismantled? These were some of the questions floating around among Boko Haram-watcher circles—at least till late September 2013 when Shakau himself reappeared in a video reminding the world he was alive:

> Here I am, alive, hale and hearty. Sagir Musa should bury himself in shame, President Jonathan should bury himself in shame, President Obama should bury himself in shame, and President Francois Hollande should bury himself in shame, Queen Elizabeth should bury herself in shame…They said I am dead, but here I am. The world should know that I am alive and will only die at the appointed time. Everybody should be judged according to the dictates of his conscience. What I am doing is written in the Holy Qur'an and the Hadith and I will not stop. I challenge all the clerics of the world to question my deeds. Those underrating my capacity should have a re-think. I will never allow democracy to thrive…The concept of Government of the people by the people for the people will never be possible and will never exist. Democracy shall be replaced only by the government of Allah, from Allah and for Allah.[59]

Press coverage of the attacks, abductions, prison escapes, video releases, and related activities that marked the Boko Haram insurgency campaign from its inception in 2010 to date are abundant, and a simple Google search will confirm as much. For this reason the rest of the chapter in treated thematically, rather than chronologically. Specifically

I have identified some key developments and trends that merit attention as indicating a new, more sophisticated tactical trajectory adopted by Shekau's outfit.

As in Yusuf's case, Shekau's rejection of democracy is evident and it is one element, together with religious fundamentalism, that continues to define the movement. In this context attempts to bomb political rallies (March 2011), attacks on polling stations (April 2011), the bombing of the Independent National Electoral Commission in Maiduguri (April 2011) and the assassination of various political figures and candidates should came as no surprise.[60] Democracy is in fact perceived by the group as a foreign imposition and a challenge to God's sovereignty.

With Boko Haram back to Maiduguri in mid-2010, a campaign of targeted assassinations, usually carried out on motorbikes, was underway. However those were not the only targets of drive-by shootings, bombings, armed assaults and assassinations. In fact 2011, saw the broadening of targets beyond the 'favourite' police stations and military barracks. Schools (guilty of spreading Western education), hospitals, bars, Muslim clerics who had dared to criticise the sect, mosques, local village heads, markets and average citizens all became legitimate targets. Andrew Walker recalls a 2011 incident in which a pharmacist in Maiduguri was shot and money and supplies were stolen from his shop.[61] And the area of operation, over time, expanded too. From the original states of Yobe and Borno, Bauchi, Adamawa, Kaduna, Niger, Plateau, Abuja and Katsina all witnessed some violence, later followed by Kano, Jigawa, Gombe, Taraba, and even Sokoto and Kogi in 2012. The latter is particularly revealing since it demonstrates the group's ability to stage attacks in areas where it is less likely to find a strong support network, including those where the ethnic composition of the inhabitants is very different from that of Borno or other northern states.[62] Those in Kogi were in fact the farthest south attacks carried out, to date, by Boko Haram. As indicated by Jacob Zenn and others, the state is "considered a staging point for attacking the south"[63] given its proximity to the Niger Delta region. A number of arrests have been executed in Lagos—Nigeria's financial hub—in the course of 2013,[64] and an alleged plan to attack Lagos international airport was uncovered in the spring.[65]

In addition, and starting early in the post-Yusuf era, prison escapes became a trademark of the group, beginning with a fifty-strong attack on Bauchi Prison on 7 September 2010 when over 700 inmates were freed, including at least 100 Boko Haram members.[66] Similar incidents were repeated elsewhere including, among others, in Adamawa (2011),[67] Yobe (2012),[68] and Borno (2013).[69]

Churches also came under attack starting as early as 2010 and the trend continues to date. The US Commission on International Religious Freedom released a report in August 2013 highlighting the extent of "religious targeting" by Boko Haram. Since 1 January 2012, states the report, attacks have included "50 churches that either were bombed, burned, or attacked, killing at least 366 persons; 31 separate attacks on Christians or southerners perceived to be Christian, killing at least 166 persons; 23 targeted attacks on clerics or senior Islamic figures critical of Boko Haram, killing at least 60 persons; and 21 attacks on 'un-Islamic' institutions or persons engaged in 'un-Islamic' behaviour, killing at least 74."[70] Most infamous were the attacks on and around Christmas Day, such as the multiple attacks in Jos, capital of Plateau state, on Christmas Eve 2010,[71] followed by similar incidents involving multiple bombings targetting worshippers in Abuja, Jos and Yobe state in 2011,[72] and in Yobe and Borno in 2012.[73] The mastermind of the suicide bombing of St Theresa's Catholic Church on 25 December 2011 in Niger state, Kabiru Umar, commonly known as Kabiru Sokoto, was at the centre of one of the most high profile Boko Haram trials to date. He was sentenced to life imprisonment in December 2013.[74]

As already alluded to in the introductory chapter, Nigeria's Middle Belt, and parts of Plateau state in particular, have suffered from outbursts of violence since the mid-1990s and then with greater intensity from the early 2000s as a result of ethno-religious tensions between indigenes and settlers, further inflamed by the introduction of sharia law in northern states. The latter prompted Muslim Hausa-Fulani to demand that sharia law be adopted in Plateau state, and small incidents spiralled in a wave of violence resulting in over 1,000 deaths in 2001.[75] Renewed and persistent violence forced the president to declare a state of emergency in three local government authorities in Jos in December 2011, in an attempt that "appeared to place Plateau state in the same category as parts of the north at the sharp end of the Boko Haram insurgency, notably Yobe and Borno states, portions of which were also placed under emergency rule", as maintained by Adam Higazi.[76] Boko Haram's staging of attacks in the Middle Belt, albeit not driven by the same animosity pitting the mainly Christian Berom against the majority

Muslim Hausa and Fulani, added to the local discourse prevailing among the Berom leadership who argued that an Islamic jihad was being waged in the state. Some of these claims included the belief that if Plateau were to be Islamised, that would cause the demise of Christianity across the entire Middle Belt.[77] While I find this scenario unlikely Andrew Walker is adamant that Boko Haram will continue its attacks against soft targets and increase its involvement in the Jos crisis by attempting to effectively scare away Christians, with possibly detrimental repercussions for nationwide stability.[78]

Splintering, factionalisation and kidnappings

Boko Haram is not a uniform movement and I have already alluded to factionalisation, especially in the post-Yusuf phase. The most obvious and concerning example of this phenomenon was the emergence of an off-shoot, Jama'atu Ansaril Muslimina fi Biladis Sudan [Supporters of the Muslims in Black Africa], normally simply referred to as Ansaru.

Following the infamous Boko Haram attacks in Kano on 20 January 2012 when over 200 people, mainly civilians, were killed, the new group published leaflets on 26 January condemning the killing of Muslims as "inhuman" and formally announcing its existence:

> For the first time, we are glad to announce to the public the formation of this group that has genuine basis. We will have dispassionate look into everything, to encourage what is good and see to its spread and to discourage evil and try to eliminate it.[79]

In June the same year the alleged leader of the group, Abu Usamatul Ansar (aka Abu Ussamata al-Ansary—possibly a pseudonym for Khalid al-Barnawi) released a video in Arabic, then translated in Hausa and English, in which he stressed that "Islam forbids killing of innocent people including non-Muslims. This is our belief and we stand for it". He condemned the killing of "innocent security operatives" but confirmed Ansaru's readiness to fight "any group of religion [sic] that attack Islam and Muslims."[80]

Starting from the name—which makes reference to Muslims in black Africa, not just Nigerians—and moving on to its critique of Boko Haram's indiscriminate targeting, the elements of disagreement between the two groups become apparent. My interviews about the group have helped to clarify some of the dynamics leading to the split as well as the relationship that has continued to date.

From information relayed by Boko Haram members, after the post-2009 crackdown, many fighters escaped to Algeria, Niger, Mali, Chad, Somalia, Sudan and Afghanistan. This experience, and especially the interaction with AQIM, exposed these men to the concept of global jihad and more sophisticated ideology. Upon their return to Nigeria, those who had trained in Algeria with AQIM were code-named "*yan Sahara*", the Hausa language for "Sahara men". It was these fighters who began to realise that the movement to which they belonged was led by a "madman" and that if their struggle were to be successful, a more sophisticated approach had to be adopted.[81] One of them was Adam Kambar, later designated by the United States as a global terrorist in June 2012. Confusingly, at a press briefing in June 2013 the Nigerian military—describing Kambar as the "main link with AQIM and al-Shabaab"—announced that he had been killed a year earlier, a claim the US government is yet to publicly confirm.[82] This timeline however corroborates the details I gathered on the ground according to which Kambar was to be Ansaru's leader but his death during a raid in Kano on 15 August 2012 created the opportunity for another AQIM-linked, US-designated terrorist, Khalid al-Barnawi, to take over the leadership. According to my source, al-Barnawi is "the most sophisticated extremist in Nigeria".[83] In addition, he is believed to have been closely involved in the kidnapping of a British surveyor, Chris McManus, and an Italian engineer, Franco Lamolinara, in Kebbi state in May 2011.[84] This event took many by surprise: Boko Haram had never carried out a kidnapping of foreigners; and Kebbi state, in the north-west of the country bordering Niger and Benin, was beyond Boko Haram's area of operation. To compound the air of uncertainty, in December 2011 a new group calling itself "al-Qaida in the land beyond the Sahel" claimed responsibility for the abduction. Sadly both hostages were killed during a failed rescue operation by the British Royal Navy's Special Boat Service in March 2012.[85] Later the British government proscribed Ansaru as a foreign terrorist organisation owing to its links to al-Qaeda and because it was believed to be responsible for the murders of the two men kidnapped in Kebbi.[86]

But it was no coincidence that al-Barnawi was involved in the abduction. He had gained kidnapping experience working alongside AQIM and was involved in the taking of French nationals in the Sahel.

Moreover it was indeed disagreement over the redistribution of ransom monies that caused a split between him and Shekau. It is believed that following the payment of 11 million euros to AQIM in ransom money, al-Barnawi received a 50 million naira fee (approximately €228,000; £189,000; US$312,000). As a result, he donated 40 million naira to Boko Haram, and here the controversy begun. Shakau wanted the money to be distributed among members while others argued that it should be used to compensate the families of killed fighters. Furthermore, Shekau refused to inform al-Barnawi on how the sum had been disbursed. From this point onwards an unofficial agreement was put in place that capitalised on each group's strengths: Shekau had the manpower to provide cover for operations and al-Barnawi had the expertise in the kidnapping of Westerners. Ransoms would then be shared and help fund Boko Haram.[87]

All these details support the thesis that although Ansaru broke away from Boko Haram, the two continue to cooperate—being, in Ansaru's words, like "al-Qaeda and the Taliban, pursuing similar objectives and engaging in the same struggle, but with different leaders"—in spite of areas of disagreement in terms of tactics (high profile targeting vs more indiscriminate killings), viciousness (al-Barnawi does not have such a strong, radical ideology as Shekau, his approach is more Messianic vowing to protect all Muslims in Africa),[88] areas of operation (regional vs national) and, possibly of some ethnic tensions. I elaborate further on this point later, but many analysts have put forward the thesis that Boko Haram is Kanuri-driven. The heartland of Boko Haram in Borno state is indeed ethnically dominated by the Kanuri. Shekau and Mohammed Yusuf both belong to the same ethnic group. There is speculation that the Hausa-Fulani—the second largest ethnic group among Boko Haram ranks—resent the fact that no Kanuri has ever been sent on a suicide mission and Kanuri in general are less likely to be arrested.[89] However these claims are hard to confirm. Dr Freedom Onuoha from the National Defence College in Abuja, an expert on Boko Haram, is sceptical. There is no national identity system in Nigeria and verifying the identity and ethnicity of a suicide bomber is no easy task. Many fighters, Dr Onuoha believes, may even come from abroad.[90]

Nevertheless, during interrogation following his arrest in 2012, the group's spokesman—a man going by the name Abu Qaqa—indicated similar ethnic tensions. Qaqa claimed that Kanuri members were seldom arrested while Hausa-Fulani were the usual targets of the security forces, raising doubts as to whether Kanuri elements were betraying their fellow militants and selling them off to the JTF.[91]

Like many extreme Islamist groups across West Africa, Boko Haram and Ansaru have fluid memberships and it appears that, based on my discussions with military and security practitioners on the ground, at the middle and lower ranks fighters change hats frequently, as and when it is convenient. Some even argue that the kidnapping of a French family in Cameroon in early 2013 and attributed to Boko Haram—the first kidnapping by the group and outside Nigeria—was facilitated by Ansaru as the two groups had to cooperate to ensure each other's survival following the pressure their funder AQIM had come under in Northern Mali following the French-led military operation Serval to expel the Islamists that had taken control of the northern part of the country.[92]

In another notable attack in November 2012, one which also fed suspicions that the two insurgent groups continued to cooperate, Ansaru targeted the headquarters of the Special Anti-Robbery Squad (SARS) in Abuja, from which scores of alleged Boko Haram members detained at the site escaped.[93]

A source within the defence establishment also indicated that there could be several other factions whose names have not become public. The source mentioned Mohamed Mohaan and Abu Mohamed Adu Aziz as possible heads of factions.[94] Another possible splinter group was represented by the now silent Yusufiya Islamic Movement which in 2011 circulated leaflets in Maiduguri concerned that:

> some people with evil motives have infiltrated our genuine struggle with a false Holy War that is outright un-Islamic…We therefore distance our group from all the bombings targeted at civilians and other establishments and equally condemn them and pray that Allah exposes those who perpetrated them and attributed them to us…This is necessary in the light of genuine concern by individuals and groups to the mass suffering of innocent citizens caught in the crossfire between our members and the Nigerian troops.[95]

A final name that was suggested to me as a factional leader was al-Jasawi,[96] but again this is very difficult to corroborate.

Research conducted by the International Crisis Group indicated a total of six factions: Shekau's; Kalid al-Barnawi's Ansaru (although this is better characterised as a splinter group); Mamman Nur's (albeit controlled by Shekau); Aminu Tashen-Ilimi's in Kaduna which I mentioned earlier in the chapter vis-a-vis pre-2000 Boko Haram; Abdullahi Damasak's (aka Mohammed Marwan); and Abubakar Shehu's (aka Abu Sumayya) in Bauchi.[97]

I believe it is safe to assume that a number of smaller factions exist although identifying the key figures may not be possible at present. Of all these factions Ansaru is no doubt the most threatening owing to the number of kidnappings of foreigners it has conducted, its closer cooperation with AQIM and other non-Nigerian Islamists, and its more international agenda. The latter was exemplified by the attacks against Nigerian troops en route to Mali in Kogi state on 19 January 2013.[98]

While kidnapping foreigners was a new trend introduced by Ansaru, Boko Haram was not completely new to this practice. The kidnapping of high value Nigerians to send a political message and/or to extort ransom is not anathema to Shekau, as I explain below in the context of fundraising.[99] There have also been reports of abductions and forced marriages "which locals call 'Auren Markas' (literally 'Markas marriage', named after Markas, the first headquarters of [Boko Haram] destroyed by the military in 2009)"[100] at the time when Boko Haram had taken control of some territory in Borno state, which prompted a large military operation in May 2013 under a state of emergency. These women were most likely used to prepare meals for the fighters living in the camps. At times, the "bride's" family was paid between 2,000 and 3,000 naira per girl—the equivalent of $12 to $31.[101] Yet the kidnapping of women and children was first reported as early as 2009 when abductions by a cleric named Mohammed Sani were traced back to Maiduguri and the Boko Haram enclave. On other occasions it was the husbands who, upon joining the movement, forced their wives and children to suddenly relocate to unknown destinations and prevented them from contacting relatives. Some of these women were later freed by the security forces.[102]

Suicide attacks

I have already alluded to a major development in Boko Haram tactics—suicide attacks, the asymmetric threat *par excellence*. We have seen this tactic used in many theatres around the world but until summer 2011 most security officials discounted the possibility of witnessing a suicide attack in the country as it something considered to be "un-Nigerian". The rude awakening came on 16 June 2011 when a car full of explosives rammed the Police Headquarters in Abuja where it detonated, killing seven people. On 26 August an even more spectacular attack was staged against the United Nations compound, also in Abuja, killing twenty-four people—this second incident was attributed to Mamman Nur's faction and was followed by the release of a martyrdom video made by the bomber.[103] All of a sudden, Boko Haram had hit the international headlines and although one could interpret the attack against the UN as one not necessarily aimed at an international target (if we consider that Boko Haram sees the UN as aligned to the Nigerian government and Western values—this is debatable), no one could deny that the summer of 2011 saw a change in trajectory, and a significant acceleration in the group's modus operandi. But why did this happen? Perhaps it was simply the realisation that other means had not been sufficiently successful. Or, was it also the by-product of foreign influences, namely of the al-Qaeda variety? This seems to me to be the most likely explantion. From this point on, improvised explosive devices (IEDs) mounted on vehicles, motorcycles, or strapped on soon-to-be martyrs, at times wearing stolen army uniforms, became a common challenge that only increased during 2012.[104] As noted by many, however, the first half of 2013 saw a decrease in suicide attacks and the re-emergence of less-sophisticated weapons such as knives and machetes. This shift was prompted, possibly, by the adoption of protective measures such as barricades and fences around government and security buildings as well as churches, and the increased state of alert on the part of the security forces. Others believe that the discovery of a bomb-making factory in December 2012 may have (temporarily) incapacitated Boko Haram's ability to carry out such attacks or that the emergence of Ansaru and the latter's aversion towards indiscriminate killing may have inhibited Boko Haram.[105]

As we know, things changed again dramatically with the declaration of a state of emergency in Borno, Yobe and Adamawa in May 2013 and the corresponding military deployment. The more robust government response that followed had a severe impact on Boko Haram and shaped the group's trajectory, making it easier than hitherto to trace an action/reaction dynamic between the two sides. Much of the discussion of this factor will be included in a later chapter that looks at the government's response. It suffices to say here that while for the ensuing months Boko Haram's efforts were concentrated on fighting the military, suicide attacks eventually resumed. The most recent was claimed on 14 January 2014, in Maiduguri.[106]

Who are these men?

In earlier sections, in trying to understand what motivates (usually young) men to join Boko Haram and Ansaru, the religious element, anti-Western feeling, including aversion for its modernisation and democracy, and the role played by Yusuf's welfare system in attracting followers have all been addressed. Even today some may still join the ranks of Ansaru and Boko Haram to vindicate the death of Mohamed Yusuf or of relatives who had been killed by the security forces. Others, including migrants from neighbouring countries, may be attracted by the prospect of financial reward. And some may be the product of the often-cited uneducated northern youths or boys attending Qur'anic schools (*almajiri*). These children are often stigmatised as the main recruitment pool for Boko Haram, in spite of very limited concrete evidence supporting that claim.

Nigeria has the highest number of non-attending school children in the world. The most recently available data shows that in 2010, there were 10.5 million children—one in three—out of school roaming the streets with the greatest concentration in northern states—where 70 per cent of the population is illiterate[107]—and with girls constituting the majority.[108] A crucial characteristic of the northern education system is that there are more Islamic than government primary schools and that the former are neither supervised not recognised by the state. These boarding schools, comparable to Central and South Asian *madrassas*, are aimed at boys from families too poor to properly support them, and are known as *almajirai* (plural of *almajiri*). No national totals are available but the 2006 census indicated that in Kano state alone there were about 1.6 million *almajirai*, some as young as four or five.[109] UNICEF estimates that 60 per cent of these boys will never return to their families.[110]

Arriving from rural areas in Nigeria and across West Africa, these children receive no education in English or Hausa. They do not learn any skills conducive to future employment and even if the teachings are in Arabic, they normally tend to simply memorise Qur'anic *surah*s without understanding their meaning or learning the language. For these reasons the rate of movement into formal education is very low. Anecdotal evidence indicates that a few lucky individuals manage to find job as fixers of one sort or another. Others become *mallam* [teachers] in the same Islamic schools. But the vast majority remains on the streets as they grow older. Local politicians are known to hire *almajirai* as thugs to intimidate political rivals and commit crime and it is easy to imagine how these boys could become recruits for Boko Haram.[111] To this effect, evidence that emerged in May–June 2013 pointed at fourteen *almajirai* between the ages of nine and fifteen, mostly arrested in Maiduguri and Bama in Borno and Damaturu in Yobe state, who had been paid by Boko Haram to set some schools ablaze.[112]

Plans to open properly run day and boarding schools for these boys have been piloted in Sokoto, but there is no equivalent in other states.[113] In addition, the Sokoto initative excludes girls who, are the least likely to receive any form of education, especially in large families where parents have to decide which children are "worth the investment" of being sent to school. But in a part of the world where there is no law on minimum age for marriage and where it is not uncommon for twelve-year-old girls to be given as brides to 50 year-old men (and there is no concept of paedophilia either, hence no protection of vulnerable children), giving girls an education would mean that they would get married and start to have children of their own at an older age which, in turn, usually leads to less numerous families.[114] And the smaller the family the lower the likelihood of the children becoming *almajirai*.

The issue of *almajirai* is a very sensitive one given that, first, the majority of the foot soldiers killed or captured by the police and army since the Boko Haram insurgency began, fall into the male youth demographic. Second, there is a well-established body of literature that breathlessly identifies the *almajirai* as the critical mass behind social disturbances, be they Maitatsine or Boko Haram. Third, it appears that a more nuanced understanding of the *almajirici*[115] system indicates that, perhaps, some of the negative connotations attached to these boys may be unjustified.

But first let us consider what the critics say. Isichei, pointing to "militant Islam" as one of a number of enablers of the Maitatsine insurgency, contends that "the Maitatsine movement was greatly aided by the *almajiri* system".[116] Danjibo is similarly critical of the role of the *almijirai* in the insurgency in the northern axis. Danjibo cites the Justice Aniagolua commission report that referred to the *almajirai* as a "contingent of armed disciples" in the Maitatsine insurgency and posits the *almajirai* role as one which was "very obvious" in the radical movement.[117] Moreover Danjibo also attempts to create a causal link between socio-economic challenges of the *almajirai*, and their tendency for recruitment by fundamentalist networks. Specifically, Marwa Maitatsine exploited the worsening economic situation and thus the *almajirai* system attracted many followers from among the commoners [*talakawa*] who, unable to afford the basic necessities of life, became die-hard supporters of the sect and of Marwa himself.[118]

Danjibo thus contends the *almajirai*, "a large army of unemployed vagabonds", are vulnerable to "social vices" and thus are "a ready-made army that can be recruited to perpetrate violence".[119] Nor is this perception limited to the literature. The stigma attached to the *almajirai* was very much what emerged from my own conversations with Nigerian officials as well as citizens, especially in Kano.[120]

Some experts, however, unlike others who broadly classify unemployed young men as being "*almajirai*", have attempted to distinguish between (1) those who come to study the Qur'an (*almajirai*); (2) those who simply migrate to avoid the hardship of the rural areas during the dry season and attempt to exploit the urban centres' increased potential economic earnings (*yan-ci-rani*); and (3) those who may not be seasonal migrants, but who nonetheless are street hustlers—amateur performers such as snake charmers and the like—in urban centres and who could be as ubiquitous as the former two categories, dependent on the town; this final category are called *gardawa* (plural: *gardi*) or *gaddawa*, although there are different connotations to this word in particular.[121] Hiskett's findings for instance indicate that whereas in some parts of northern Nigeria, *gardawa* and *almajrai* "may be regarded as, to some degree, interchangeable", in other parts, they could mean things that are "quite different".[122]

However, some may find such distinctions problematic. Mohammed for instance prefers to define *gardi* (he refers to the plural as "*Gangaran*" rather than as *Gardawa* or *Gaddawa*) as students over the age of twenty who have graduated from learning under an "*Alarammah*" [teacher] or "*alim*" (singular of *Ulama*) in a Qura'nic school, and who have "committed the sixty chapters of the Qur'an to their memories".[123] Mohammed however notes that *Gardi*, alongside *Kolo* (students aged from four to fourteen) and *Titibiri* (students aged from fifteen to twenty) all fall under the category of *almajirai*. Specifically, Mohammed contends that "the common name for all these categories is *almajirai* because they have migrated from their locality to another environment in search of knowledge".[124]

Contrast this with the argument of Hiskett, who suggests a distinction between *almajirai* and *gardi* where he notes that a typical *gardi* is positioned between an "*almajiri*, the beginner in elementary Qur'an studies" and "a fully-fledged malam".[125] Indeed, Hiskett chooses to define the *almajirai* as:

> Usually, although not invariably, young boys, are students at elementary Qur'an schools who come in from the countryside to study during the dry season and return to their villages at harvest time. They live by begging…but they also perform many of the crafts that Lubeck attributes to *gardawa*.[126]

However, there certainly is a common thread of thought between these two narratives as Hiskett acknowledges that *gardawa* are "grown-up disciples"; suggesting that *gardawa* are then effectively (and quite similar to the position of Mohammed) at an advanced stage in their studies within the "*Tsangaya*" Qur'anic schools. He also adds that such young men are no longer "seasonal migrants" presumably because at this point, after over a decade of Qur'anic study in an urban centre, it is likely that most of them would have taken root there and chosen to remain after their *Sauka* [graduation] from the "*Tsangaya*" Qur'anic school.[127]

What this analysis of the *almajirai* indicates is that there exist several social (in terms of class and strata) economic and religious variables within the youth sociology of northern Nigeria. *Almajirai* may well feature prominently within this demographic; but other intersecting or separate groups as the *gardi, yan-ci-rani, Yan Banga, Yan Tauri and Yan Daba* and others may all be of some significance here. Indeed, the youth system and demographic in northern Nigeria may well be the one of the country's more complex, least-studied, and over-generalised ones. This complexity of attempting to oversimplify who and what the *almajirai* consist of is partially captured by Hiskett where he notes that

> While both *almajirai* and *gardawa* may be expected to be substantially of Hausa origin…and are certainly exclusively Muslim, 'yan-ci-rani may [or may not] be Muslim Hausas. Such people, as well as being much less respected than *almajirai* and *gardawa*, are also certainly less cultured in the Islamic way, less obedient to Islamic morality and less conformist to the norms of Hausa Muslim society.[128]

This suggests that simply referring to as "*almajirai*" the young men who are often killed or detained in their hundreds, in armed confrontations during insurgency, may be an over-simplification of what the *almajiri* system entails, or a failure to understand who and what an *"almajiri"* truly is. As Hoechner notes however, such easy and neat characterisations of the issue result in *"almajiri"* now being seen as the problem, rather than as victims within a broken and failed socio-economic youth sub-system in northern Nigeria.[129]

Still within this narrative, other accounts regarding the role of the *almajirai* in violent insurgency more broadly, and in swelling the lower ranks of Boko Haram in particular, sometimes assume a more bombastic tone. Nobel Prize laureate Wole Soyinka for instance, whilst conceding the role that socio-economic hopelessness has played in shaping the *almajirai*, contends that the madrassas—the Qur'anic institutions where these young men are educated and for which reason any true *"almajiri"* makes the journey from countryside to urban Qur'anic centre—are in effect breeding grounds for the *almajirai* as "foot soldiers...to be unleashed on society".[130] Soyinka, making the case that the *almajirai* are today an instrument for Boko Haram, contends that they [the *almajirai*] have over time graduated "from knives, machetes, bows and poisoned arrows" to "AK-47s, homemade bombs and explosive-packed vehicles".[131] This final assertion alludes to an allegation that the *almajirai* are used as suicide bombers for Vehicle Borne Improvised Explosive Devices (VBIEDs): an allegation that is extremely difficult even for specialist security forces to verify.

Hoechner however disputes the validity of such claims, and asks for supporting evidence for how the *almajirai* and *almajirci* (the process of being an almajiri) have come to be so closely associated with social violence, insurgency and political thuggery in northern Nigeria.[132] In the author's paper, 'Fair Game for Unfair Accusations', Hoechner, who conducted ethnographic studies over a thirteen-month period with a group of *almajirai* in Kano state notes that narratives on the role of the *almajirai* in conflict often are taken to the extreme.[133] She is critical of a number of causal assumptions; and questions the existence of "systematic evidence" for this established narrative. She writes that, "To assume that violence results mechanically from some inherent feature of traditional Qur'anic education aborts prematurely the search for more meaningful explanations of violent behaviour".[134]

As mentioned in the paragraph above, part of the existing narrative creates a causal link between the socio-economic hopelessness of the *"almajirai"*—many of whom may in fact be *yan-ci-rani*, as Adesoji

75

(2011) notes—and the high participation of delinquent young men in conflicts in northern Nigeria (Adesoji, 2011; Isichei 1987; Danjibo 2009). Here too, Hoechner attempts to address this train of thought. She acknowledges the "putative refusal" of the *almajirai* "to acquire modern skills and knowledge" but counters by noting that these young men are hardly the only ones within their age and social demographic who lack such skills.[135] This assertion is strengthened in the distinctions made by Adesoji, between *Almajirai, Yan Tauri, Yan Daba, Yan Banga,* and *Yan Dauka Amarya.*[136]

Hoechner furthermore refers to as "problematic" assumptions of this seemingly causal relationship between the failure of the *almajirai* to integrate effectively into the economy and the high incidence of youth involvement in conflict in northern Nigeria: "If educational disadvantage and opposition to modern developments constitute the causal link between young people and violence" she notes in interview, "then we have little reason to conclude that our concern should focus merely on the *almajirai*".[137]

An especially important point made by Hoechner is that *almajirci,* and the hardship associated with it—including the street hawking, alms begging and hiring out for menial services—may in fact be a deliberate mechanism, within the *almajiri* system, to teach the young boys humility and to keep them firmly grounded in their Qur'anic studies.[138]

* * *

During the research for this book I had hoped to interview some detained Boko Haram members in order to interact with them directly (or at least through an interpreter). Unfortunately I was not granted access to the prison where they are held. The next best option that was suggested to me was to attend the debrief of a senior security officer who had recently interviewed eight alleged members of Boko Haram in Maiduguri prison in spring 2013. The passage that follows is based on information given to a security official by men behind bars and the official may have purposely omitted some details in my presence, so the usual caveats apply.

The interviewees ranged between the ages of seventeen and twenty-five with the sad exception of one ten-year-old boy. They all seemed to emphasise the monetary expectations of being members of the group, such as the rewards that would follow from a bank robbery, or the fact that they would be given wives without the need for an expensive wedding—thereby absolving them from a major preoccupation for young and unemployed males. One of the inmates, before his arrest, had been designated for a suicide mission. He claimed to have been content with his fate: his superiors had in fact settled all his debts and given his wife some money. Interestingly, one of the men was remorseful for his actions and wished the government had helped him set up a small business through a loan. The inmates also disclosed that often the training consisted of no more than two days (in a rented compound, rather than in the forest as claimed by others) and that disabled people were often used in suicide missions because they were less likely to attract attention.

Of course, the ideological component was also there. The officer who conducted the interviews had the impression that the men had been brainwashed and had great fear of and respect for Abubakar Shekau in spite of the fact that most members had not seen him since 2009. The cult-like attitude was also evident in the claim that leaving the group was not an option as it would undoubtedly result in death.[139]

In February 2013 former US President Bill Clinton pointed his finger at the alleged economic drivers of the violence:

> You have to somehow bring economic opportunity to the people who don't have it. You have all these political problems—and now violence problems—that appear to be rooted in religious differences and all the rhetoric of the Boko Harams and others. But the truth is the poverty rate in the north is three times of what it is in Lagos.[140]

The rebuttal from President Goodluck Jonathan did not take long: "Boko Haram is not as a result of misrule; definitely not… And sometimes people feel like it is a result of poverty; definitely not. Boko Haram is a local terror group."[141]

I report those statements here because, although I partly disagree with both, they are indicative of the types of conflicting explanations that are embraced by those seeking to explain why an individual joins a violent extremist group.

I do not like to sit on the fence but my answer is "all of the above". Like any insurgency, what we are observing in Nigeria and which goes by the name of Boko Haram or Ansaru is not a monolithic homogeneous grouping. Extreme religious ideology may well be the overarching driver and the most commonly used identifying characteristic of both outfits. But under the broader religious umbrella, financial, criminal, personal and political interests may drive the violence at the individual level. Does every unemployed Afghan peasant who joins the Taleban fully embrace their ideology? I (and then US Secretary of Defence Robert Gates) do not think so but believe that if joining a terrorist outfit is the only option to make ends meet then it becomes rather appealing.[142] If, on top of financial gain, the ideology is also attractive, all the better. I do not see the situation in Nigeria, or elsewhere for that matter, being much different. Surely it is more productive to move away from debates in which the parties claim to hold the ultimate truth and instead acknowledge the heterogeneous nature of the groups' memberships? From this realisation it is then possible to address or target different elements, i.e. criminal and religious hard-liners, in different ways, including identifying with which elements it is worth attempting engagement and, possibly, negotiation.

Funding

Insurgents and terrorists are unlikely to file tax returns so unveiling their sources of funding is usually a complicated job, even for professional investigators. Tracing Boko Haram's funding streams is no exception. Nevertheless, based on arrests and other reporting, albeit fragmented and often impossible to verify with absolute certainty, a fairly diversified pool of funds can be identified. These have evolved over time to meet the group's changing needs as well as in response to an altered environment, including new opportunities.

In the very early stages of the Nigerian Taleban, members were involved in subsistence agriculture in Yobe while some carried out some small trading activities. As already alluded to earlier in the text, through micro-financing support from Yusuf, some of his followers were able to set up small businesses including car and motorcycle taxis (allegedly purchased by Yusuf himself—many vehicles were found at his home after he died). Part of the income generated through those business activities was channelled into the sect and represented a major funding source in the early years.[143] In addition, while Mohamed Yusuf was alive, he would expect to receive daily membership fees of 100 Naira (approximately US$0.8 or £0.5) from each member. This may not seem much however, according to some estimates, he counted thousands of members who would have given him significant revenues boosting his already healthy finances.[144] It is hard to establish whether the collection of membership fees has continued following Yusuf's death but it is a possibility not to be discounted. Work conducted by The Inter-Governmental Action Group against Money Laundering in West Africa (GIABA) and Financial Action Task Force (FATF) indicates that at least until 2012 compulsory donations were expected of militants in addition to voluntary ones.[145] Another way the group obtains money from its own members is by buying and selling items to fighters in other locations at inflated prices.[146]

It was also during this earlier phase that the sect benefited from donations from local financiers. Indeed, it could be argued that some northern politicians supported the group in the hope of using it to attack its political rivals but soon lost control of what had in fact become a monster[147] or, to put it in Soyinka's words, "[r]ather than act in defence of Nigeria's Constitution, past rulers have cosseted the aggressors for short-term political gains. However, those who have tweaked the religious chord are discovering that they have conjured up a Frankenstein".[148]

These dynamics should be understood in the context of Nigerian politics where it is not unusual, especially ahead of elections, for politicians to hire local thugs to intimidate opponents. The most high-profile sponsorship came from a highly placed politician in Borno, who is believed to have continued sponsoring Boko Haram until around 2007, or possibly even 2009, together with other north-eastern governors.[149] His involvement was also confirmed by US government officials.[150]

One should not oversimplify and fall victim to the poverty-equals-extremism rhetoric: while many early members of the sect were young unemployed and former *almajiris*,[151] several well educated professionals and businessmen also filled the ranks of Boko Haram. Such wealthy members doubled as financiers. The influential Buju Foi is believed to be among those able to provide significant financial support especially once he was appointed Commissioner of Islamic affairs in 2007 as well as having twice held the position of Chairman of the Kaga Local Council in Borno. Given his position and the widespread lack of accountability that characterises political life, it is not unthinkable than in addition to his own funds, he may have used public finances to support the activities of the sect.[152] Arrests in late 2011 pointed at other politicians allegedly involved with Boko Haram, namely Senator Mohammed Ali Ndume representing Borno South Senatorial District, and former Ambassador to Sao Tome and Principe, the late Saidu

Pindar, even though the level of financial support they offered to the groups is unclear.[153]

Government funding of a completely different nature may also fund Boko Haram and Ansaru, namely when local authorities allegedly reach an agreement with the sects, effectively buying peace. Kano state is the most significant example of this sort. According to Muhammad Zubair, Director of the Human Rights Research and Advocacy Centre in Kano, in late 2009–early 2010 several Boko Haram members were driven to Kano state from Maiduguri having come under great pressure from security forces in Borno state. This flow of fighters continued through to 2012 as Kano, in this period, offered a permissive environment where anyone could take up residency and buy land and property without the need for identification or registration. In addition, it has been alleged that between 2009 and 2012 the ruling ANPP, worried by the Boko Haram inflow especially in the area around Wudil (40 kilometres from the city of Kano), agreed to issue monthly payments to Boko Haram so as to avoid attacks in the state. In addition, magistrates would not prosecute suspected Boko Haram members. Again, this was done in order to avoid retaliation.[154] These allegations, never confirmed, were taken further by Nigerian media claiming that from initial monthly payments of N5 million in 2004, Boko Haram had managed to extort up to double that amount each month by 2009.[155] Such claims have been consistently denied by then Kano Governor Ibrahim Shekarau.[156] Similar allegations have been made against Bauchi Governor Isa Yuguda upon his appointment in 2008 which, according to the same unconfirmed claims, included the assurance that Boko Haram members would not be arrested within the state and that, on the contrary, would be granted training grounds in the mountains.[157]

Besides financing from political figures, the sect benefited from the support of businessmen, notably an individual from Borno, arrested in 2011, and Mohammed Zakaria, killed in the same year. The latter was responsible for sourcing weapons from Cameroon and Chad. As pointed out by Freedom Onouha from the Nigerian National Defence College, the paucity of information regarding alleged financiers is often due to their extrajudicial killings and lack of thorough investigations.[158] Besides those two cases, the trial of Muhammed Bello Damagun in 2007, who ultimately was not convicted, brought to light a broader, international, dimension of Boko Haram's funding. Damagun was the director of the media group Media Trust, which owns several newspapers including the ever-popular *Daily Trust*. He was accused of allegedly transferring US$300,000 from al-Qaeda in Sudan to an account at a bank in London with the purpose of carrying out terrorist activities. The transfer had allegedly taken place in 2002.[159] While he was not convicted, there were widespread allegations at the trial about board members of the *Daily Trust* supporting Boko Haram.

But Damagun's trial is not the only alleged evidence of al-Qaeda's financing. In January 2011 the FBI, jointly investigating the recent New Year's Eve explosion at the Mogadishu Cantonment barracks in Abuja, concluded that building the bombs had been made possible thanks to al-Qaeda's technical and financial support. In addition, the incident shed light on the problem posed by the many fictitious bank accounts used to transfer large amounts of money believed to be destined for terrorist activities.[160] Later that year, the arrest of Somali and Sudanese Boko Haram members indicated the presence of those nationalities among the group's ranks with funding possibly coming from those two countries and from Iran.[161] C. Nna-Emeka Okereke cites unconfirmed reports indicating that arrested sect members had been found in possession of 170,000 euros which included some marked banknotes that had been paid in ransom to AQIM.[162] This, if true, would represent an additional piece of evidence vis-à-vis al-Qaeda funding for Boko Haram.

In spring 2012 the media cited an intelligence report presented to the president indicating that Boko Haram had recently received 40 million nairas from an unnamed 'Algerian sect'. The report, resulting from investigations conducted in Sokoto and Kano, concluded that the payment was only believed to be the first in a series of instalments.[163] Although no further details were provided on the origin of the money, one can only speculate that the "Algerian sect" in question was in fact AQIM.

The security crisis that erupted in Mali in January 2012 created an ideal opportunity for cooperation between both Boko Haram and its offshoot Ansaru and al-Qaeda affiliated groups fighting in northern Mali—namely AQIM, Ansar al-Din and MUJWA. This closer relationship is likely to have increased the financial flows among the groups. More details about this relationship are discussed in the next chapter but, with regard to funding, it was no doubt a lucrative interaction. Ansaru, and its leader al-Barnawi, had been involved in the kidnapping of French nationals led by AQIM. Similarly, for several years there has been speculation over links between Nigerian Islamist extremists and

Somalia's al-Shabaab. At the time of writing it remains unclear, albeit not implausible, that such links may involve funding.

In the context of kidnapping of foreign nationals, the release of a French family abducted in Cameroon in 2013 is believed to have been made possible following the alleged payment of a $3 million ransom. Later the same year a French priest was victim of the same fate and although both Boko Haram and the French government deny that any ransom was paid, it remains a possibility.[164] Kidnap for ransoms of high-profile Nigerian nationals has also become a more common practice and in 2014 the US administration estimated that Boko Haram earned, on average, $1 million for every (wealthy) Nigerian kidnap victim.[165] Most notable was the abduction of Dr Alli Shettima Monguno in May 2013 in order to extort money from the Borno state government. Monguno is a former Petroleum Minister and former head of the Organisation of Petroleum Exploiting Countries (OPEC).[166] He was held for four days and then released following an alleged multi-million naira ransom payment.[167]

Funds are also extorted in the form of protection money with payments expected from almost anyone, from villagers in rural areas to businessmen and local civil servants who receive calls and text messages with requests for specific sums of money, failing which violence will follow.[168] Reports indicate that similar practices take place in Cameroon.[169]

Bank robberies are no doubt a less glamorous but certainly lucrative funding source. Furthermore they possibly represented the key revenue stream until 2012 with dozens being carried out in 2011 and 2012 alone. Arrested spokesman Abu Qaqa has provided an insight on how the looted money would normally be redistributed, among the robbers, the widows of martyred jihadists, the poor, *zakat* [charity], and Boko Haram's leadership. However he also highlighted Shekau's propensity to appropriate large portions of the cash—a practice nobody dared question even though the issue of some unaccounted 41 million naira had, as mentioned in the preceding chapter, created some tensions among the membership.[170] More details emerged during my own field research. According to arrested Boko Haram fighters, proceeds from bank robberies would be sent to a trusted agent of Shekau's who would then collect the money but also travel widely distributing between 20,000 and 100,000 naira to the various cell members. I also noted that there was the tendency to trust Shekau's judgement and not to question how funds would be allocated.[171]

Other forms of criminal activities attributed to Boko Haram are the collection of passage fees from migrants and people traffickers,[172] and taxation in the local government areas it controlled before the imposition of the state of emergency in May 2013;[173] numerous car-thefts, which seems to have continued beyond May;[174] weapons smuggling across the Nigerian border;[175] begging (using *almajiris*, the elderly and disabled);[176] and possible involvement in drug trafficking. The latter, in particular, has raised some serious concerns. In spring 2013 the National Drug Law Enforcement Agency (NDLEA) launched an investigation to ascertain the likelihood of drug proceeds being channelled into Boko Haram, though to date no direct link has been registered.[177] This followed a report released earlier in 2013, which was heavily manipulated by the media, to indicate some direct connection between Boko Haram/ Ansaru and Latin American drug barons—something that the report itself does not claim.[178]

At this point it is worth adding that although robberies and other criminal acts are indeed against Islamic preaching, they have been justified by Boko Haram, as well as other Islamists groups around the world, as a means to wage jihad. The case of bank robberies in particular is often explained by claiming that the interest charged by banks is against Islam or by claiming that the banking system is run by Jews (thereby becoming a legitimate target in the eyes of extremists).

In March 2013 it was made public that a number of Nigerian charities and financial institutions were being monitored by the Nigeria Financial Intelligence Unit (NFIU). Banks are often reluctant to file Suspicious Transaction Report (STRs) which makes them an ideal, albeit unwitting, vehicle for Boko Haram funding.[179] Again, the paucity of details makes it very difficult to establish with any certainty the degree to which such cases belong to the realm of reality or remain mere speculation—as in the case of stories indicating that Saudi charities possibly support Nigeria's insurgency.[180]

Other have speculated that funds could reach Boko Haram's chest via *hawala*, the Islamic model of financing, and through internet scams where members start romantic relationships online until they obtain compromising pictures from the victims that can be used for blackmail.[181] However, little detail is available to corroborate these two possible funding streams. Similarly, claims by a retired member of the American military that Boko Haram had amassed around $70 million in the 2008–11 period are hard to substantiate.[182]

Boko Haram has transformed itself over the last decade, as this chapter has attempted to show. This evolution has included an ideological shift, the diversification of attacks in terms of tactics, targets and geography, the splintering of the group, and the diversification of its funding sources. Next we turn to an overview and assessment of Boko Haram and Ansaru's connections, operations and ambitions beyond Nigeria's borders. Exploring the latter is now a concern of many regional and international partners who are watching the deteriorating security situation in West Africa and the Sahel with growing apprehension.

5

THE INTERNATIONALISATION OF BOKO HARAM

For most of the preceding pages I have characterised Boko Haram as an inward-looking group feeding on local grievances and with a national agenda driven by the goal of Islamising Nigeria. Nevertheless, as with many contemporary violent groups that, like Boko Haram, have domestic priorities, Shekau's organisation has established links with foreign jihadists and carries out activities outside Nigeria in the immediate neighbourhood and, more recently, farther afield within West Africa. Partly because of necessity, partly because of convenience and partly because of ideological affinities, these relations and foreign activities have intensified over the years, most noticeably since 2010. The appearance of Ansaru has further highlighted the process of internationalisation as Boko Haram's offshoot appears to be the group enjoying the closest connection to AQIM and its affiliates and the one with greatest propensity for attacking foreign targets.

This chapter explores the nature and extent of Boko Haram's operations in neighbouring countries, especially in the borderlands with Niger, Chad and Cameroon, where the group has been able to exploit cultural, ethnic and religious ties with northern Nigeria. These territories have proved ideal areas in which fighters could seek refuge from Nigerian security forces and recruit new members.

The security crisis in Mali in 2012–13 brought to the fore the extent of Boko Haram and Ansaru's regional reach raising alarm over the possible establishment of an "arc of insurgency" in the making that connects northern Nigeria and northern Mali via Niger, and with the possibility of a spillover effect into neighbouring countries. In this context I investigate the tactical implications resulting from Nigerian groups' exposure to more internationalised and sophisticated groups, spelling out how external influences have affected their modus operandi.

Borderlands

Upon his return from an ECOWAS summit in March 2012, Nigeria's Chief of the General Staff Oluseyl Petinrin had no doubt that Boko Haram was no longer a problem for Nigeria alone: "we [Nigeria, Chad, Niger and Cameroon] must join forces so as to regain control over the situation as quickly as possible".[1]

Undeniably, Boko Haram has exploited the cultural, ethnic and religious ties that Chad, Niger and Cameroon share with northern Nigeria—not to mention the Protocol on the Free Movement of Persons of ECOWAS—for its own purposes, namely smuggling weapons, recruiting fighters, and allowing personnel flows between Boko Haram in Nigeria and their Hausa, Kanuri, and Muslim kin in Niger, Chad and Cameroon. At the same time, Boko Haram's presence has added a layer of complication in countries already facing a number of problems, be it the spillover effect of the conflict in the Central African Republic felt in Cameroon and Chad starting in 2013, or structural fragility and the presence of AQIM and its sympathisers in the case of Niger.

Nigeria's immediate neighbours have played an important role in the history of Boko Haram from the very early days of the sect when new recruits from Niger, Chad, and Cameroon would travel to Nigeria to listen to Mohamed Yusuf's preaching and when members would hide from Nigerian security forces beyond the national borders, or would undertake training, most famously at the Salafist Group for Preaching and Combat (GSPC)'s camp in Agwan, Niger.[2] Moreover, Yusuf controlled *amirs* [leaders] based in Niger and Chad who would report directly to him.[3] And when in December 2003 he set up a new base in the village of Kanama, following their removal from Zagi-Biriri, the choice of location was not casual; the 3,000-inhabitant village is in Yunusari Local Government Area of Yobe state—a very remote part of the country only seven kilometres from the border with Niger.[4]

Jacob Zenn and I argued in an earlier paper that it is at the sub-regional level that Boko Haram's external connections have proved more established and it is in those countries where the group managed to exert greater ideological influence although, operationally, Shekau has assumed a stance towards the governments of Niger, Chad and Cameroon that is in the main a non-confrontational one, with the exception perhaps of more recent developments in Cameroon.[5] For their part, neighbouring governments have been reluctant to launch a major crackdown possibly for fear of retaliation and, more concretely, owing to their limited capabilities. In spite of their contribution to the Multinational JTF, it was only in 2014 that a more concerted effort was actually embraced.

Cameroon

Starting in 2012–13, northern Cameroon's role as Boko Haram's rear base has expanded considerably, especially the Far North region, not least as the stage of a number of kidnappings of foreign nationals, but also for the number of clashes, arrests of suspected Boko Haram and the seizure of weapons destined for the sect. As early as 2004, attacks on security forces had been launched along the Cameroonian-Nigerian border and there was speculation—refuted by Shakau—that the leader had received medical treatment in Cameroon in the summer of 2013.[6]

In 2011 reporting of Boko Haram infiltration into Cameroon became more frequent. In places such as Lagdo, locals sighted strangers wearing "bizarre dressing, long beards and red or black headscarves" who would easily stand out for their appearance but also for their openly anti-Western sermons. In addition, and somewhat reminiscent of Mohamed Yusuf's offers of financial support as an incentive for new recruits, these preachers would offer large amounts of money to those willing to embrace their ideals. Other worrying indicators were the circulation of Boko Haram CDs and leaflets in Cameroonian villages and a growing numbers of reports related to extreme preaching in Cameroonian mosques—one such mosque in Limbe was closed for fear that Boko Haram had been successful in making inroads and gaining influence.[7]

The governors of the North region and of the Far North region of Cameroon had also warned of Boko Haram infiltration. The latter, in particular, announced the deployment of 600 Cameroonian soldiers along the border to prevent further incursions in early 2012. Troops from the 32nd Motorised Infantry Battalion in Mora, together with a contingent from the 4th Joint Military Region in Maroua, were sent to gather intelligence, monitor the flow of people and apprehend suspects following a number of arrests and interrogations pointing to a Boko Haram presence in the country. Moreover, the seizing of laptops and mobile phones belonging to self-declared preachers from an Islamic organisation called Daawa Islamiya provided evidence of links with the Nigerian militants. At the same time Abuja temporarily closed its borders with Cameroon.[8] Throughout 2012, Cameroonian authorities arrested several suspects trying to enter the country from Nigeria, and border towns such as Banki witnessed Boko Haram attacks.[9]

The real turning point for Cameroon, however, came with the kidnapping of seven French family members in Dabanga, in the Far North region, on 19 February 2013. As mentioned in the preceding chapter, collaboration between Boko Haram and Ansaru is suspected in this incident. A few days later, Boko Haram posted a video on YouTube showing the unharmed family, threatening the Cameroonian, Nigerian and French governments, and making it clear that the abduction had been conducted in retaliation for Paris' intervention in Mali, which had begun a month earlier.[10] In March the sect released a new video. Again, Shekau asked for a prisoner exchange involving both Boko Haram fighters and the wives and children held by Nigerian security forces.[11] Notably, and in line with other hostage situations in which Boko Haram has been responsible and which I discuss in other chapters, using hostages as bargaining chips to secure the release of militants or their family members appeared to be a higher priority for the sect than ransom payments. Nevertheless, rumours indicate that together with the release of sixteen militants held in Cameroon, a $3 million ransom was paid following negotiations between the Cameroonian government and Shekau which resulted in the French hostages' release.[12] France had however earlier denied that it would consider any form of negotiation with the group.[13]

Sadly, this was the first of a series of foreign kidnappings in Cameroon. It was followed by the abduction of a French priest on 13 November, 30 kilometres from the Nigerian border, who was released seven weeks later (again there were rumours of a ransom payment),[14] and the taking of two Italian priests and a Canadian nun in April 2014 in the northern district of Maroua. All three were freed nearly two months later.[15] In May, Boko Haram attacked a construction camp in

Waza, also near the border with Nigeria. Ten Chinese workers were abducted and one killed, alongside a soldier, in spite of the camp being normally guarded by troops from Cameroon's Rapid Intervention Battalion.[16] In early June, six arrests, including of three Nigerians, were made in connection with the incident.[17]

In December 2013 the Nigerian Defence Headquarters confirmed that the army barracks in Bama, Borno State had come under attack by suspected Boko Haram militants who reportedly came from cells located in Cameroon that had most likely relocated there and in the borderlands of Gwoza hills following the military offensive that, beginning in May 2103, had displaced several fighters from the North East, not to mention thousands of Nigerian civilians escaping the violence.[18] From this point, and throughout the first half of 2014, it became clear that Boko Haram's infiltration into Cameroon had reached a new high requiring the deployment of extra military units, guards and border patrols especially in the Far North region. In addition, in January the Ministry of Defence announced a new recruitment drive to expand its military and establish new units to fight Boko Haram and to contain spillover violence from the crisis in the Central African Republic. This included 6,850 men who joined the National Police, the military and the Presidential Guard.[19] It was a move welcomed by the Nigerian government which had often criticised Yaoundé for not doing enough to combat the spread of violent extremism in its territory, which is possibly one of the reasons Boko Haram had found in Cameroon a convenient area to where it could retreat and regroup. Following the occurrence of nearly daily attacks, in March 2014 Cameroon deployed 700 extra troops as part of the regional force established by the Lake Chad Basin Commission, and in May 1,000 additional soldiers were sent to beef up security along the border.[20]

Niger

The proximity of Boko Haram's original base in Yobe to Niger has already been mentioned, and Niger is the country that connects Nigeria to Mali and therefore is part of that arc of insurgency that worries so many analysts. The predominantly Kanuri towns of Diffa and Zinder have often been in the news, locally at least, as the stage of Boko Haram activities.

The first official confirmation came in September 2012 when Nigerien forces uncovered a five-member cell in Zinder, approximately

100 kilometres from the border with Nigeria's Kano state. The Zinder area was seen as a natural conduit for militants moving between Northern Mali and Northern Nigeria but also, increased activity in that part of the country coincided with a number of military operations in northern Nigerian states, including one resulting in the death of several senior Boko Haram commanders that likely prompted fighters to escape into Nigerien territory.[21] Also in 2013 and according to General Seyni Garba, head of the Nigerien military, Mali-trained Boko Haram militants had been arrested as they transited through the country with "the orders to lie low" in Madaoua, a town approximately 50 kilometres North of Sokoto state in Nigeria, and nearly 500 kilometres west of Zinder, presumably as a result of growing military pressure exerted by the French-led operation taking place in Northern Mali.[22]

This was not the first time the country had been used as retreat point. Earlier, Niger had witnessed the presence of the Izala movement in the 1990s, spreading from Nigeria, and likely had given refuge to Maitatsine fleeing the military crackdown in Nigeria.[23] Hence it was easy to believe unconfirmed reports from locals in Yobe state claiming that at the time of the state of emergency operations in Yobe in May 2013, 200 trucks carrying alleged Boko Haram militants were seen crossing into Niger ahead of the military's arrival.[24]

In the South East, the town of Diffa, very close to Borno state, is described by local officials as Niger's "frontline" in the Boko Haram insurgency and an area where there is virtually no state presence; instead, a very porous border allows for the free movement of people (and weapons) between the two countries in spite of attempts to prevent it through increased border patrols.[25] Luckily, so far there have been only small-scale skirmishes with Boko Haram on Nigerien territory and the government has avoided taking more substantial action for fear of retaliation. Nevertheless, Niger is "another weak link in the Sahel", to borrow the words of the International Crisis Group.[26] Therefore the decision to host the 2014 edition of the Flintlock[27] multinational counter-terrorism exercise in the country probably indicates a mounting concern at the level of Islamist infiltration faced by Niger, especially along the borders with Mali, Libya and Nigeria. Possibly in the same vein was the transfer to Niger of ten Toyota trucks and two Cessna planes under the US-led Trans-Sahara Counter-Terrorism Partnership (TSCTP) to boost border security in July 2013.[28] More specifically, the UNHCR had warned that the influx of refugees from Nigeria into the Diffa region might offer cover for Boko Haram penetration. Nor should one forget that beyond the challenge posed by Boko Haram, Niger had been the scene of terrorist activities at the hand of other groups. Most notably two suicide car-bombs hit Niger in May 2013—one on the Agadez military base and the other on the French-operated Somair uranium mine in Arlit. The coordinated attacks were carried out by Al-Mulathameen, a faction of the AQIM's breakaway group the Masked Battalion, and required the intervention of French Special Forces to rescue Nigerien cadets taken hostage by the Islamists in Agadez. Al-Mourabitoun, resulting from the merging of MUJWA and Al-Mulathameen, is now one of the most active Islamist groups in the Sahel, responsible for issuing threatening statements against France, and appears to be mostly operating in Niger and Libya.[29] In August the same year, local authorities uncovered a MUJWA sleeper cell in the east of the country.[30]

Chad

Chad does not share a land border with Nigeria and the two countries are separated (or united) by Lake Chad. In spite of cultural affinities among the people living around the lake, the topography has somewhat protected Chad from Boko Haram infiltration on the scale witnessed in Niger or Cameroon. Nevertheless border security to prevent a spillover from the Nigerian insurgency is a priority for the government in N'Djamena as indicated by the several cordon and search operations carried out in 2013 in the Lake Chad region down to the capital to stop the movement of fighters crossing from North Eastern Nigeria into Northern Cameroon and then Chad.[31]

A few arrests corroborate the existence of a Chadian connection. In January 2012 the Nigerian police arrested a Chadian national in Niger state who confessed to have joined Boko Haram after he had been protesting against a beauty pageant, which led to his expulsion from school.[32] Large groups of foreigners from Chad but also Sudan, Niger and Mali were apprehended in 2011 and 2012, en route to Abuja and in Benue state respectively, as suspected Boko Haram members.[33] However, I would caution against drawing conclusions based on reporting of large-scale arrests. Although in this specific case the context of their movements was rather suspicious (they were travelling at night and some carrying weapons), at other times Nigerian authorities have used the Boko Haram card to harass foreigners. In March 2013, for instance, 500 people resident in Lagos but originally from Chad, Niger and Mali (including children and women) were rounded up and interrogated. This operation was allegedly carried out to tackle possible Boko Haram infiltration.[34]

In recent years Chad and its neighbours have come together to jointly address the issue of border control through bilateral agreements such as those with Niger and by calling for a "joint deterrence force" under the banner of the Lake Chad Basin Commission to fight Boko Haram in 2012.[35] A further step was taken in May 2014 when Chad and Cameroon agreed to allow each other's forces to enter their territory to pursue Boko Haram suspects.[36]

But this is a two-way flow. Whereas refugees and some militants may enter Chad, in late 2013 the head of police division at the governor's office in the Far North Region of Cameroon spoke of an increase in arms trafficking coming from Chad and destined for Nigeria.[37]

Human security implications

Although attacks have been relatively rare, the populations of neighbouring countries have suffered indirectly from Boko Haram's presence and the exacerbation of violence that resulted from the declaration of the state of emergency on Adamawa, Borno and Yobe states. Statistics released in January 2014 indicated that up to 37,000 people from Niger and Nigeria had fled the violence since early 2012, most of whom had sought refuge with relatives in Niger. Here, in one of the poorest countries on earth and one often affected by food crises, communities are struggling to meet this emergency. Efforts by aid agencies, including the International Committee of the Red Cross (ICRC) and the UN High Commissioner for Refugees (UNHCR), have had only a limited impact owing, primarily, to the fact that most of those displaced have relocated to remote villages and are therefore difficult to reach. Job opportunities are also almost non-existent here.[38] But while many of those who had arrived in Niger "felt at home" owing to family ties and ethnic affinity (most of the displaced are Kanuri, as are the receiving communities in Niger),[39] those who escaped into northern Cameroon experienced a different fate. Around 8,000 Nigerians relocated to Cameroon in the latter part of 2013, a number of whom were forcibly removed from the Far North region of Cameroon into Adamawa state in Nigeria, prompting UNHCR to raise the alarm, given that the lives of those repatriated could be at risk due to the ongoing Boko Haram insurgency.[40] Nevertheless the displacement into Cameroon has not stopped. On 24 January 2014 the UN indicated that more than 4,000 people had reached the country since mid-January, primarily in Logone-et-Chari area of Far North region, bringing the total of refugees in Cameroon to 12,428.[41]

Chad, albeit to a lesser extent, has also received refugees from the violence in Nigeria. Reports in spring 2012 indicated the presence of approximately 1,000 Chadian migrants having returned to Chad, most of whom were children from Qur'anic schools separated from their families. New arrivals were registered on a daily basis. On arrival in N'Gbouboua in the Lac region (western Chad) migrants had been provided some support by the International Organisation for Migration (IOM) to help them return to their villages of origin but food appeared the most pressing priority.[42] As of summer 2014, many Nigerian refugees in Chad remained in urgent need of food, medical care, shelter and water.[43]

Besides the influx of displaced Nigerians, Cameroon has also suffered from additional economic repercussions on account of the instability. In fact, along the border with Nigeria commodity prices have increased dramatically owing to stricter border controls. Such measures had been put in place as a result of intelligence pointing at the use of northern Cameroon as a recruitment pool by Boko Haram. In an area where imported goods amount to nearly 80 per cent of basic commodities, restrictive measures and the fact that traders are afraid to travel to Nigeria to purchase supplies, translate into locals having to pay an extra 30 per cent for staple items such as palm oil in spite of government claims that bulk imports had been made to help those in need, according to 2012 data[44]

With the intensification of the insurgency, economic challenges remained. In 2014 locals of Cameroonian border towns lamented that foodstuffs such as sugar now cost 50 per cent more than before while others were no longer available.[45]

* * *

While discussing the Boko Haram threat with government officials but also with Nigerians in the street I did find a tendency to externalise problem. In other words, I was reminded, perhaps too many times, that several militants were not actually Nigerian nationals but rather they came from Chad or Niger or Cameroon, or even Sudan. One interviewee indeed claimed that "most" members were from abroad.[46] While I have no doubt the group has an international membership, I wonder whether the international aspect is overblown in order, first, to pass, at least partially, the blame on to other governments and, second, to make it an "international" problem hence more likely to attract attention and support.

But there is no denying that porous borders and cultural and ethnic links have turned Boko Haram into a cross-border issue and joint initiatives involving the countries around Lake Chad are certainly welcome. Nigeria's immediate neighbours contributed to the Multinational Joint Task Force (M-JTF) in support of JTF-ORO in the North East (more in the next chapter) and, as noted by Nigerian Interior Minister Abba Moro when I spoke to him in 2013, there was cooperation among the four countries as part of the Lake Chad Basin Commission, which included the monitoring of migrants beyond Boko Haram-driven displacement.[47] Joint patrol agreements are in place with Niger and Chad, and bilateral agreements with N'Djamena, Niamey and Yaoundé.[48] My interviews with senior officers at the Defence Headquarters and with the Ministry of Foreign Relations confirmed that there were ongoing diplomatic relations between Nigeria and its neighbours. However, while the cooperation was "easy", there was also the realisation on the Nigerian part that neighbouring countries had more limited capabilities to deal with the problem caused by Boko Haram and that the challenge itself was less of a priority there (owing to its smaller scale) than for Nigeria.[49]

These efforts were significantly stepped up in March 2014 when the Directors-General of External Intelligence Services of Nigeria, Benin,[50] Cameroon, Chad and Niger, alongside France, signed a deal to increase border policing coordination and intelligence sharing.[51] The possibility of forming a Joint Multinational Task Force was also discussed, with Baga, in Nigeria's Borno state, being indicated as a possible headquarters for the task force.[52]

A wild card: the Central African Republic (CAR)

From late 2012 onwards the already politically and economically fragile Central African Republic witnessed a total state collapse culminating in a coup d'état by predominantly Muslim Seleka rebels in March 2013.

The latter event prompted France, the former colonial ruler, to deploy a military contingent.[53] Since then, the country has descended into chaos and hundreds of thousands of people—20 per cent of the population—have been displaced. Although later in the year rebel-turned-President Michel Djotodia formally dismantled the Seleka, they were replaced by several armed groups that, at the time of writing, are fighting Christian self-defence groups.[54] The United Nations has expressed fears of a sectarian genocide.[55]

Observing the level of anarchy and complete lack of a working government in 2013 made it easy to draw comparisons between CAR and Northern Mali a year earlier. And this context of lawlessness and violence is arguably a possible magnet for foreign extremists. This proposition was put forward by Edmond Mulet, the UN Assistant Secretary-General for Peacekeeping Operations, who in November 2013 claimed:

> I don't think about al-Shabaab, but certainly Boko Haram we have some indications that there is some kind of a presence here...In different places, different elements are really already trying to get hold of some presence in the country.[56]

Yet, evidence of this presence is difficult to come by as little information is available. Jacob Zenn argues that given the use of Cameroon as a rear base for both Ansaru and Boko Haram in the north and the Seleka and other militants from the CAR conflict in the east, some interaction might take place. This might in part explain the sighting of alleged Boko Haram members in western CAR who, Zenn suggests, might have been Arabic-speaking Ansaru fighters from Cameroon.[57]

However, for the time being, this narrative seems to be driven by too much conjecture. In the case of Boko Haram, one may wonder what purpose stretching the group's resources into CAR would serve towards fulfilling its objectives—which are of a national rather than regional nature. In addition, even if the intention were not to become embroiled in the local conflict but to simply use CAR as a refuge, the central African state is too far from Boko Haram's area of operation. With regard to Ansaru, which does have a broader outlook than its parent organisation, the hypothesis seems more plausible, however it would be unwise to jump to conclusions till hard evidence emerges. While Christian and Muslim militias are fighting one another in CAR, I believe one should not conclude that this state of conflict amounts to jihad.

*Changing al-Qaeda patterns and Boko Haram's position
in the broader Islamist environment*

The post-Osama bin Laden era has seen the weakening of al-Qaeda Central and many counter-terrorism experts argue that the era of global jihad has ended. Furthermore some statistics indicate that global terrorist attacks have reached the lowest incidence level in years, more or less pointing to the demise of global jihad phenomenon. Or at least this was the view put forward in 2012 when the United States government's National Counterterrorism Centre (NCTC) released its *2011 Report on Terrorism*.[58]

What global trends fail to represent is that while the al-Qaeda leadership has been severely affected by counter-terrorism operations (primarily in Afghanistan and Pakistan) there are regional pockets of extreme ideology—accompanied by violent activities—reminding us that this threat has not gone away; if anything quite the contrary.[59] In addition, more recent data published in late 2013 by the US-based National Consortium for the Study of Terrorism and Responses to Terrorism (START) indicates that total terrorism incidents have registered an increase in the developing world during the past decade while there have been only a few attacks in the West.[60] With this in mind, the surge of violent Islamist activity across West Africa and the western Sahel confirms this trend. Here, both new and established armed groups are destabilising fragile states, creating a regional security threat, and undermining democratic governance.

The recent emergence of religiously motivated groups is symptomatic of a phenomenon that can be described as the regionalisation—or fragmentation—of jihad whereby groups are the by-product of very localised sets of circumstances and grievances and define their agenda, and targets, based on local priorities, such as the adoption of strict Islamic rule in a given country, and may or may not adopt a global jihadist rhetoric. This, does not stop some of these groups from broadening their ambitions as they become stronger and seek to establish links with foreign groups. Until the establishment of the so-called Islamic State in Syria and Iraq in June 2014,[61] terrorism analysts argued that the death of Osama bin Laden had weakened the concept and possibly the likelihood of fighting for the achievement of a Global Caliphate.[62] Noteworthy is a 2012 Pew survey carried out on the anniversary of bin

Laden's death. The data showed a marked decline in people's support for al-Qaeda and bin Laden with the most astonishing variation registered in Jordan where support went from 61 per cent in 2005 to 13 per cent in 2011.[63] Moreover, groups that until 2014 had indicated their support for al-Qaeda's ideology (either as formal branches of the al-Qaeda franchise or as simple 'admirers') have been drawing inspiration from the Islamic State, also known as the Islamic State of Iraq and al-Sham (ISIS) (in Arabic, *Da'esh*). In Nigeria, Boko Haram leader Abubakar Shekau had first stated support for ISIS's self-appointed *Caliph* Abu Bakr al-Baghdadi in a July 2014 video[64] and proceeded to declare his own caliphate in Gwoza, Borno state, in August,[65] in a series of events suggesting that ISIS's successes in Iraq and Syria may have catalysed this shift (although there are no links between the two groups).

What we have seen in Africa since 9/11 and more so in the post-bin Laden era is the convergence of three factors. First, American and Western counter-terrorism efforts as a whole have devoted little attention to the continent, the expectation being that key threats would emanate from Central and South Asia and the Middle East and North Africa, which has resulted in limited resources being spent in Sub-Saharan Africa irrespective of the establishment of the US African Command (AFRICOM) in 2008. This approach, however, should not be criticised too eagerly. After all, in spite of having lived in Sudan, bin Laden himself had demonstrated a limited understanding of Sub-Saharan African dynamics which has limited al-Qaeda penetration in the continent. Second, Algerian and American efforts against al-Qaeda in the Islamic Maghreb (AQIM) had pushed Islamists southwards to seek refuge in more permissive environments such as the desert areas of Niger and Mali, countries with less developed intelligence and security capabilities. Here, and more broadly across West Africa, they have become the common denominator among a host of local movements that are, to varying degrees, connected to AQIM.[66][67] Third, the voice of local movements, in the main disconnected from the larger jihadi community, has become louder, and the feeling of discontent resulting from growing inequality, lack of political representation, and general disenfranchisement has been manipulated by charismatic group leaders who advocate religious revival—to be pursued through violent means if necessary—as the solution. The influx of weapons and mercenaries from post-Gaddafi' Libya has boosted the size, capabilities and confidence of non-state actors in West Africa and the Sahel and has allowed the regrouping and revival of underground outfits, such as the Tuareg Movement for the National Liberation of Azawad (MNLA), and the formation of new ones. Among those, the 2012 security crisis in Mali has brought to the fore Ansar al-Dine, an Islamist group featuring both Tuareg and former AQIM components; and the Movement for Unity and Jihad in West Africa (MUJWA), an AQIM splinter group, heavily involved in criminal activities, that draws its ideology from historical figures in West African Islam such as Seku Amadou and Usman Dan Fodio as indicated in statements and videos released by the group.[68] Both groups are Mali- and regionally-focused.

But the group that best exemplifies the trend is Nigeria's Boko Haram—the most active, longest running and so far deadliest local Islamist group of the sub-region. A number of references to external connections have been made in the earlier chapters as avoiding overlaps has proved harder than planned. Below I look more closely at the relationship between the Nigerians and AQIM, which is arguably the most significant.

> There are reported communications, training, and weapons links between Boko Haram, al-Qaida in the Lands of the Islamic Maghreb (AQIM), al-Shabaab, and al-Qaida in the Arabian Peninsula, which may strengthen Boko Haram's capacity to conduct terrorist attacks.[69]

This is one of the issues that was raised by the US State Department when it announced in the summer of 2013 that up to $7 million would be paid as reward for information bringing Abubakar Shekau to justice.[70]

General Carter Ham, Commander of US AFRICOM was one of the first senior foreign officials to raise the alarm over a possible connection between Boko Haram and foreign, more established, groups. As early as August 2011 he declared it was likely that Boko Haram had established contacts with AQIM and, more loosely, with al-Shabaab. He described this as, if confirmed, "the most dangerous thing to happen not only to the Africans, but to us as well"[71] and believed that there were intentions on the part of Boko Haram and AQIM to coordinate their efforts even if they may not have yet been in the position to do so.[72]

His statement was preceded by one from AQIM leader Droukdel who, following the death of Mohamed Yusuf, offered his "Salafist brothers" in Nigeria "men, weapons, and ammunition to gain revenge on Nigeria's ruling Christian minority".[73] In October of the same year posters appeared on key road intersections in Northern Nigeria in which Boko Haram warned locals against assisting police in apprehending members of the sect. Each poster bore the signature of AQIM and warned that "any Muslim that goes against the establishment of Sharia law will be attacked and killed."[74] The significance of episodes like this, however, should not be overblown. I wonder whether the decision to use AQIM's signature was more of a publicity stunt, i.e. a way of increasing Boko Haram's profile and instilling greater fear, than the result of a clear directive by AQIM allowing the Nigerians to use their name. After all, the various statements issued by the groups since the beginning of Shekau's leadership indicate a clear attempt on the part of the new, more radical leader to emphasise the connection to mujahideen further afield.

To date, Boko Haram has not been recognised by the al-Qaeda core but many experts would agree that the rapid evolution in Boko Haram's tactics proves that the group has benefited from exposure to more sophisticated outfits such as AQIM and al-Shabaab that would have allowed the Nigerians quickly to graduate from machetes and small arms to drive-by shootings and IEDs, to more complex bombings and assassinations, and even to carry out the first ever suicide bombing in the history of Nigeria. Not to mention that the adoption of beheadings, and the filming of such executions, is also reminiscent of al-Qaeda's modus operandi.[75]

This cooperation, which in the main is of a tactical nature, belongs to a certain pattern featuring in the region. In fact, Islamist groups currently operating in West Africa and the Sahel all seem to share a link with AQIM. Previously known as the Salafist Group for Preaching and Combat (GSPC), it had earlier split off from Algeria's Armed Islamic Group and re-branded itself in 2006. Each group's degree of engagement with AQIM is different. Though many have broadly espoused Salafism (the Algerian version of which remains the most dominant in Africa), their specific goals may vary.[76]

Although AQIM seems to act as a sponsor, providing weapons, training, funding and ideological guidance, it has itself benefited from the regional proliferation of Salafist movements. As the erstwhile GSPC, Algerian and American counter-terrorism efforts had greatly diminished its ability to conduct attacks and had forced it to relocate to more remote parts of the Sahel, particularly in Mali and Niger. In order to survive, it has relied increasingly on the proceeds from criminal activities, such as trafficking and kidnappings for ransom—activities that run counter to al-Qaeda's ideology. Thus, the emergence of groups sharing a similar ideological drive—that are prepared to spread jihadist propaganda and fight abroad—helps AQIM by reinforcing its message and standing.[77]

Some early interactions between Boko Haram, including Mohamed Yusuf personally, and al-Qaeda were explored in the previous chapter, including the incident involving Mohammed Ashafa, a man arrested in 2006 on charges of receiving funds from al-Qaeda operatives at the Tabligh headquarters in Lahore, Pakistan, to attack Americans in Nigeria, and of recruiting twenty-one fighters sent to be trained with the GSPC at a camp in Agwan, Niger. Foreign trips in the period between the death of Yusuf in July 2009 and the Bauchi prison escape in September 2010 have been highlighted already. Militants are also believed to have trained in Algerian camps and in Mauritania.[78] Details of the latter were provided in an interview by Aliyu Tishau, believed to be Boko Haram's man in Gombe, Bauchi and Plateau state in 2011. Tishau, who managed to vanish from custody, causing considerable embarrassment for the Nigerian security apparatus,[79] declared that through contacts in Mauritania Boko Haram made its first entry in North Africa. According to his account, following the fall of the government in Nouakchott in 2004, Mauritanian warlords approached Mohamed Yusuf as they wanted to recruit mercenaries from the ranks of Boko Haram under the guise of providing advanced religious studies in Mauritania. Although Yusuf refused the deal on the basis that he did not wish to turn his movement into a band of mercenaries, some senior elements within the sect resented their leader's decision and did indeed travel to Mauritania. Furthermore, Tishu claimed that among those who had returned from training, there were three bomb-making specialists, which explained the escalation of bomb attacks in Nigeria.[80] Additional reporting appears to lend credibility to the practice of sending young members to Mauritania for training in order "to harden them so that when they come back, they would have been conditioned to be full of bitterness for the Nigeria's [sic] socio-economic and political situation. The training of these youths, who are said to be about ten years old, was to orientate them to be capable of inhuman responses to issues".[81] As mentioned in an earlier chapter, those who had trained in Mauritania (often at the Ummul Qurah camp), and even more so in the case of those who had been to Algeria, were nicknamed *yan Sahara* ("Sahara man" in Hausa).[82]

Boko Haram's al-Qaeda ties went beyond the African continent. The group's spokesman Abu Qaqa boasted in a 2012 interview:

> Al-Qaida are our elder brothers. During the lesser Hajj [last August], our leader travelled to Saudi Arabia and met al-Qaida there. We enjoy financial and technical support from them. Anything we want from them we ask them.[83]

These claims were later confirmed by documents found in Abbottabad, Pakistan, in the compound where bin Laden was killed in 2011, according to which al-Qaeda leaders had had direct or indirect contacts with Boko Haram in the preceding eighteen months.[84] Overall, however, the exchanges with AQIM are far more significant for Boko Haram than those with any other foreign jihadi outfit, both in terms of training and funding, and in spite of the drawbacks suffered by AQIM and its affiliates in Mali in 2013. The latter is in fact a special case. All the foreign linkages discussed so far have been aimed at boosting Boko Haram's capabilities in order to pursue its domestic operations. Nevertheless, the security crisis in Mali seems to have started to affect and alter Boko Haram's inward looking, Nigeria-focused stance.

The 2012–13 Malian civil conflict

Mali suddenly became the focus of global attention when a Tuareg uprising led by the Movement for the National Liberation of the Azawad (MNLA)—reinvigorated by the flow of returnees from Libya—erupted in January 2012 seeking independence for the northern region of Azawad. The military coup that took place in March deposing President Amadou Toumani Touré's government added to the chaos then engulfing the country and presented the ideal opportunity for the Salafist Ansar al-Dine to join forces with the MNLA to promote its own agenda and impose rigid Islamic law across Mali. The partnership between MNLA and Ansar al-Dine, which even included an attempted merger, was short lived. Tensions led to the Battle of Gao in June 2012, resulting in the Salafists gaining control over the key Azawad cities of Gao, Timbuktu and Kidal and de facto taking charge of most of northern Mali. Here they were joined by the Movement for Unity and Jihad in West Africa (MUJWA), a AQIM splinter group that had emerged in mid-2011 and that in November was responsible for kidnapping a French national in Diema. MNLA, now completely side-lined by the Islamists, announced in July that it no longer aspired to establishing an independent Tuareg state but instead wished to obtain "Quebec-style autonomy".[85]

France launched *Operation Serval* in January 2013 which was made necessary owing to the deteriorating security situation in northern Mali and delays in the deployment of an African-led International Support Mission in Mali (AFISMA), later replaced by a 13,000 strong UN peacekeeping force, the United Nations Multidimensional Integrated Stabilization Mission in Mali (MINUSMA). Following a premature declaration by President François Hollande that the Islamists had been defeated in September 2013, Paris had to deploy special forces and reverse plans to reduce troops on the ground from 3,200 to 1,000. Although Mali has returned to civilian rule following the coup d'état in 2012 and the resulting civil war in the north, the country is yet to see stability. Inability to reach a compromise with local armed groups and continuing attacks by both Islamists and Tuareg (as of May 2014) hinder successful peace talks.[86]

Nigerian (including the Chief of Defence Staff at the time of my interview with him), Nigerien, Algerian, French and Malian officials have been pointing at cooperation between Boko Haram and AQIM in northern Mali and, as alluded to earlier, Nigerien officials have confirmed that Boko Haram had been transiting from Nigeria to Mali via Niger.[87] More specifically, there was evidence of around 100 fighters fighting in the Battle for Gao alongside MUJWA and being responsible, with Ansar al-Dine and MUJWA, for the attack against the Algerian Consulate in Gao in April 2012 in which seven Algerian diplomats were taken hostage (an action later claimed by MUJWA).[88] A Malian official had no doubt: Boko Haram "were in a majority among those who attacked the Algerian consulate" in Gao, adding that the militants "had black skin".[89] Another was equally sure of Nigerian presence in the area: "They're not hiding. Some are even able to speak in the local tongue, explaining that they are Boko Haram."[90] It was also reported that Nigerian preachers were involved, under the lead of Ansar al-Dine, in delivering sermons on the benefits of Islam to the local population in Timbuktu.[91]

In November 2012 Boko Haram was also believed to be present in the Malian town of Menaka (Gao's region) together with AQIM and

MUJWA where they had taken fortified positions and used locals as human shields during clashes with the Tuareg.[92] In January 2013 Boko Haram joined forces with MUJWA, AQIM and Ansar al-Dine in the attack to take control over the town of Konna (Mopti region).[93] There were even speculations that Abubakar Shakau could himself have been present in Gao recovering from an gun wound[94] before possibly fleeing to Niger as a result of the French military operation in January 2013.[95]

While most of the foregoing discussion of Mali referred to Boko Haram, it is very likely that Ansaru, rather than Boko Haram proper, had the largest presence in the Sahelian country. Ansaru appeared to be more closely aligned to al-Qaeda ideology and willing to become involved in kidnapping foreigners—a practice that was only adopted by Boko Haram in 2013. The propensity for kidnappings was the aspect that made Ansaru appear to foreign governments as the number one threat, as indicated by the early proscription by the British government and the assessment shared with the author by American security officials. When talking to several Nigerian government and military officials in the spring of 2013, Ansaru only came up in conversation when prompted by my direct question on the subject. For their part, Nigerian officials saw Ansaru and Boko Haram as part of the same problem, hence requiring the same response. To their credit, a year later Ansaru is no longer making headlines and we can only speculate about the fate of the group. In the wake of Operation Serval in Mali, as many Islamists were displaced and sought refuge in remoter areas of, possibly, Mali itself, Niger and Mauritania, Ansaru and Boko Haram retreated back to Nigeria with their areas of operation now more or less coterminous. I believe this is possible also owing to the fact that while Ansaru splintered from Boko Haram, the two were never real enemies and cooperation has been and is taking place, particularly when it comes to kidnappings, Ansaru's speciality thanks to AQIM training.

Returning to ideological drivers, in a statement circulated in Kano, Ansaru vowed to restore "the lost dignity of Muslims in black Africa" through the revival of the Sokoto Caliphate.[96] The group's full name itself, *Supporters of the Muslims in Black Africa*, indicates a greater affinity with MUJWA, the *Movement for Unity and Jihad in West Africa*, which claims to draw inspiration from historical figures of Islam in West Africa such as Ousman Dan Fodio (the founder of the Sokoto Caliphate), El Hadj Omar Tall and Amadou Cheikhou "who all fought colonial invaders",[97] and which underpins a broader, i.e. regional, outlook compared to Boko Haram which remains, in spite of some regional experience, a group with a distinctly Nigerian agenda.

Ansaru equally resents "colonial invaders" (and here I do not mean to imply that Boko Haram is not opposed to Western interference), has proved to be more aware of the regional context and has capitalised on it. For example it has launched retaliatory attacks against the military operation in Mali including the kidnapping of a French man in Katsina in December 2012, claimed to have been carried out in retaliation for Paris' presence in Mali and for the French ban on wearing the Islamic veil in public places. The claim came with a threat of future attacks: "We inform the French government that this group will continue launching attacks on the French government and French citizens…as long as it does not change its stance on these two issues."[98] In January 2013 Ansaru fired on a convoy of Nigerian troops leaving Kogi—a state south of Abuja that had hitherto seen no Boko Haram/Ansaru activity—en route to deployment in Mali, killing two officers and wounding eight soldiers, as part of a mission to stop Nigerian troops joining Western powers in their "aim to demolish the Islamic empire of Mali."[99]

Indications of Ansaru's closer ties with AQIM and related groups included the discovery of Ansaru's flyers in Gao in the compound of Mokhtar Belmokhtar, the veteran senior AQIM commander, in early 2013. Khalid al-Barnawi, suspected leader of Ansaru, is believed to have fought under the leadership of Belmokhtar in Algeria in the mid-2000s in Algeria and Mauritania, and he, together with Adam Kambar (the "main link with AQIM and al-Shabaab") and Abu Muhammed (mastermind of the McManus and Lamolinara kidnapping), had been trained by AQIM.[100] In addition, and as Jacob Zenn has noted, from its early days Ansaru had issued videos through Agence Nouakchott d'Information (ANI), the Mauritanian news agency contacted by AQIM to circulate its messages, and had used the same Mauritanian hostage negotiator employed by the al-Qaeda franchise.[101]

Al-Shabaab

Al-Qaeda's affiliate group in Somalia, al-Shabaab [The Youth], emerged out of the now extinct Union of Islamic Courts in 2006 and has been causing mayhem in Somalia and Kenya ever since, including through the infamous three-day siege at the popular Westgate shopping mall in Nairobi, killing sixty-seven people and injuring nearly 200 in 2013, and a series of smaller attacks in Nairobi, Mombasa and other Kenyan tourist destinations. The group formally became part of the al-Qaeda franchise in 2012 when leader Ahmed Abdi Godane, known as Mukhtar Abu Zubair, "pledged obedience" to al-Qaeda's Ayman al-Zawahiri. It has attracted fighters from abroad, including from Europe.[102]

US General Carter Ham and others have over the years alluded to links between Boko Haram and the Somalis although the relationship appears to be less established than in the case of AQIM. Most notably, and often cited in this context, Adam Kambar has been known as the "main link with AQIM and al-Shabaab."[103]

Boko Haram first revealed its alleged connections in the Horn of Africa through a statement circulated in 2011:

> Very soon, we will wage jihad…We want to make it known that our jihadists have arrived in Nigeria from Somalia where they received real training on warfare from our brethren who made that country ungovernable.[104]

While there may be connections at an individual level, institutionalised ones are harder to be confident about. In particular, the mastermind of the bombing of the UN building in Abuja in 2011, Mamman Nur, is thought to have received explosives training in Somalia.[105]

Although not proving any collaboration, following the mass abduction of girls in Chibok, Borno state, al-Shabaab published online statements supporting Boko Haram's actions, going as far as claiming that Shakau's group had "rescued" the girls from government injustice against Muslims.[106]

Tactical implications of foreign influence

Besides AQIM-style kidnappings and statements issued by the groups' spokesmen supporting one another, how has foreign interaction impacted on Boko Haram's modus operandi?

The starkest observation is that Boko Haram is, to date, the only African group alongside AQIM and al-Shabaab that carries out suicide attacks and disseminates martyrdom videos. Until the battle of Maiduguri in 2009 Boko Haram resembled a guerrilla group "striking en masse on police, security and government facilities before dissipating".[107] Following the pause in violent activities between 2009 and 2010 during which members travelled abroad including to Sudan and Pakistan, Boko Haram re-grouped and revealed new tactics including stealing pick-up, "technical", trucks. A Nigerian security official explained to me that they were now using them to mount machine guns—something the group had never done prior to 2010 and this, according to the same official, they had learnt abroad. But this was, regrettably not the only novelty. In fact, effective improvised explosive devices (I was told that it is not easy to master them), vehicle-borne improvised explosive devices, suicide vests and rocket propelled grenades (RPGs) were all part of the new repertoire.[108] The flow of RPGs had apparently increased in the post-Gaddafi era, reaching Nigeria and other countries in the region such as Mali.[109]

Overall the better planning of attacks (at times coordinated) made possible by increased resources indicated some forms of external support. Most significantly, Boko Haram's bomb-making is of a standard that the Nigerian military considers as being far beyond local capabilities. Forensic investigation following the UN attack in Abuja revealed that the high volatility and large quantity of plastic explosive used by the group was not believed to be within the reach of a local outfit unless it had access to external know-how and resources.[110]

Will Boko Haram become the next al-Qaeda franchise?

In the preceding pages I discussed the different relationships established by Boko Haram and Ansaru in neighbouring countries as well as with other jihadists further afield. I believe it has the potential, if unchecked, to expand to other West African nations. To this effect there have already been reports, indicating a possible presence in Senegal where the Federal Government held secret talks with the group in 2012.[111]

If we look at other al-Qaeda branches in Africa, al-Shabaab's formal alignment with al-Qaeda had been discouraged and occurred only after the death of bin Laden in 2012. He had wanted the relationship to remain secret, warning the Somalis that the al-Qaeda "label" could deter support and alienate the local population. It is also possible that al-Shabaab's enforcement of sharia law was deemed too strict and hence counterproductive—as is often the case among the regional groups, including in Mali. AQIM's leader Droukdel had in fact cautioned that

Ansar al-Dine's ruthless implementation of *hudud* punishment and sharia law in northern Mali would undermine public support and prompt international intervention. Both predictions have since proven prescient.

For this reason, the relationship is likely to continue, even though the military operation in Mali has placed AQIM and associated groups in a less favourable position from which to support their junior partners in Nigeria, but Boko Haram is not necessarily going to become an official member of the club. And frankly, it might not make much of a difference to Boko Haram's trajectory.

6

GOVERNMENT RESPONSES

Till now the focus of this book has been Boko Haram, how it has emerged and evolved. It is now time to look at the other parties in the conflict—in particular the Nigerian government and security forces. In an earlier chapter I touched upon official responses to extremist groups in northern Nigeria highlighting that violent repression had usually been the preferred approach at the expense of a more holistic attempt to address some of the grievances put forward by the groups.

The reason an entire chapter is devoted to this topic is because, possibly more than ever before, the government's response to Boko Haram violence has very much shaped the sect's latest development phase. More specifically, growing insecurity in Borno state and elsewhere in the north-eastern parts of Nigeria led to the establishment of Joint Task Force Operation Restore Order (JTF ORO) in the summer of 2011 to provide a multi-service response to the insurgency. Abuses and extra-judicial killings at the hands of the JTF have been widely reported and have undermined the efficacy and credibility of the operation, and, arguably, had the perverse side-effect of increasing support for Boko Haram.

To Nigeria's credit, the approach to Boko Haram has not been an exclusively military one and changes have been evident also at the institutional level. New legislation has been adopted, the position of a National Counter-Terrorism Coordinator had been created and a National Counter-Terrorism Strategy has been devised, including provisions for counter- and de-radicalisation programmes. In addition, in

April 2013 President Jonathan announced the establishment of an Amnesty Committee to evaluate the feasibility of pardoning the militants, which followed on from more informal attempts to engage Boko Haram in dialogue. Some of these new measures look better on paper than in practice and have suffered from a number of shortcomings including the politicisation of certain proposals such as the amnesty, and the lack of adequate resources.

But Nigeria is not alone. Beside collaboration with its immediate neighbours as illustrated in the previous chapter, non-African partners including the United States and Britain have worked quite closely with their Nigerian counterparts by providing military training, advice and equipment as well as through the adoption of measures such as the terrorist proscription of Boko Haram and Ansaru and some of its top leaders. And this of course comes in addition to pre-existing historical and economic ties, especially with London.

The military response

Nigeria possesses the best equipped and best funded military forces in West Africa and can rely on 80,000 active troops (in addition to 82,000 paramilitaries) and a broad spectrum of capabilities. Nevertheless, its armed forces are paying for defence spending mistakes during decades of military rule (until 1999), which witnessed a deterioration of military equipment and procurement aimed at state-to-state conflict as opposed to the current asymmetric threats of insurgency and terrorism. Fortunately recent years have witnessed repair and refit programmes to improve equipment,[1] and counter-terrorism and counter-insurgency training, carried out primarily at the army's Counter-Terrorism and Counter-Insurgency Centre, situated at the Armed Forces Command and Staff College in Jaji, Kaduna, where soldiers are exposed to training in urban patrolling, unarmed combat, and humanitarian law.[2]

Defence spending has also been increased dramatically throughout the years of the Boko Haram insurgency. Most significantly, in May 2014 Minister of Finance, Ngozi Okonjo-Iweala announced that the approved 2014 budget included a 20 per cent allocation for the defence sector—N968.127 billion ($5.949 billion) out of N4.962 trillion ($30.488 billion)—and added:

> No amount of budgetary provision can be enough for the military... The military all over the world that engages in war does not always have enough,

particularly in this new type of war against terror, which requires equipment to assist them. I don't think the Nigerian military would be different from any other in the world in the same circumstance.[3]

The police have been engaged in skirmishes with the sect from the latter's inception. In their support the military was deployed to counter Boko Haram as early as 2003, when, following the Christmas Eve attacks in Yobe state, a joint police and military crackdown was launched. In 2004 the military pursued Boko Haram fighters in to the Mandara Mountains in the Nigeria-Cameroon border area.[4] My account of the 2009 events further evidenced the involvement of the military alongside the police in the days leading up to the killing of Mohamed Yusuf. In fact, as the crisis unfolded, first the Police Mobile Force, including from neighbouring states, and the Police Mobile Training School in Gwoza, and then the military, deployed to support regular police forces in the areas affected by the violence.[5] It was in fact the Army 3rd Armoured Division that led the attack on the sect's headquarters in Maiduguri on 28 July 2009.[6]

> Nevertheless, it was not until the Battle of Maiduguri in July 2009 that the group became seen as a serious threat and it took its re-emergence following the 14–15 month hiatus between July 2009 and the September 2010 Bauchi prison break before the government truly began looking seriously at ways to address the threat more systematically.

Growing insecurity in Borno state and elsewhere in the North East of Nigeria led to the formation of JTF ORO, which began its operations on 15 June 2011. The mandate of the task force was to restore law and order to the north-eastern part of Nigeria and Borno state in particular. The rules of engagement are not publicly available.[7] This army-led task force was composed of the Nigerian Air Force 79th Composite Group in charge of aerial reconnaissance (and later aerial attacks), the Defence Intelligence Agency (DIA) and State Security Service (SSS) responsible for gathering intelligence, the Nigerian Customs Service with responsibility for tracing weapons, IEDs and other illegal goods, the Nigerian Police Force to deal with people on the ground, the Nigeria Immigration Service to monitor people's movements, and the Army 21st Armoured Brigade including counter-terrorism trained units responsible for the entire coordination of ground operations.[8]

Increased military activity in Borno state, and particularly large scale house-to-house searches in Maiduguri where JTF ORO was headquartered, prompted several Boko Haram members to relocate to Damaturo, the capital city of Yobe state. Later that year, the Federal Government approved the establishment of permanent operational bases for JTFs in Yobe alongside Bauchi, Borno, Gombe, Taraba and Adamawa.

From the very beginning JTF ORO had to confront several challenges. Overall, inadequate intelligence, exacerbated by the reluctance of local people to share information with the security forces, limited progress in seizing Boko Haram's weapons and IEDs, and extensive porous borders (800 km in North East Nigeria) have made the security forces' task extremely difficult.[9] With regard to the latter, JTF ORO spokesman Lt. Col Sagir Musa described the almost insurmountable hurdle facing government forces:

Nigeria's borders are massive with hundreds of footpaths crisscrossing to neighbouring countries of Cameroon, Chad and Niger with links to Mali, Libya and Sudan. From conservative estimate by locals, there are well over 250 footpaths from Damaturu/Maiduguri axis that link or lead direct to Cameroon, Chad or Niger. These paths are mostly unknown by security agencies, are unmanned, unprotected and thus serve as leaky routes for arms and ammunitions trafficking in to Nigeria.[10]

A first state of emergency is declared

2011 saw an intensification of attacks but President Goodluck Jonathan remained optimistic, at least in public: "[t]he challenge is only a temporary setback and we shall get over it", he reassured participants of the 17th Nigerian Economic Summit in November.[11] Yet the growing spiral of violent incidents left him no choice but to declare a state of emergency on 31 December. The measure, which was adopted in the aftermath of multiple attacks over Christmas, affected fifteen local areas across four states—Borno, Yobe, Niger, and Plateau—and included the granting of Emergency Powers, whose provisions include "the detention of suspects; the taking of possession or control of any property in the emergency area; the entry and search of any premises; and the payment of compensation and remuneration to people affected by the order".[12] In addition he ordered curfews in a number of other states, including Adamawa, and the shutting of the border with Chad and Niger in the areas affected by recent attacks to prevent militants from escaping from Nigeria's jurisdiction and, at the same time, to stop Boko Haram from receiving external help. In total, 30,000 security personnel were deployed on the ground.[13]

Boko Haram's reaction was immediate: the next day the group's spokesman Abu Qaqa (a *nom de guerre* used by subsequent spokesmen) gave Christians in the north a three day ultimatum to leave northern states and announced that the group was ready to fight government troops in the areas under the State of Emergency.[14]

The state of emergency had a six-month time limit under the Constitution which elapsed at the end of June 2012 and was not renewed by the National Assembly. This decision did not however reflect an improvement of conditions on the ground. In fact, during the emergency period it became clear that Qaqa's threat had not been an empty one. Most notable were the multiple attacks on government buildings in Kano (January), countless jailbreaks and suicide attacks against churches and Christians, a car bomb against *This Day* newspaper building in Kaduna (April), and many other incidents occurring almost on a daily basis.[15] Moreover, the US government issued a warning indicating that Boko Haram was plotting attacks in Abuja, including against hotels frequented by Westerners.[16]

The response to Boko Haram's attacks was widely criticised as being ineffective. This weakened the image of President Goodluck Jonathan who, in spite of ambitious promises, proved unable to contain the violence. In addition, the threats and repeated attacks against Christians fuelled additional criticism from the Christian Association of Nigeria (CAN) whose leader announced "[t]he Christian community is fast losing confidence in government's ability to protect our rights."[17] These sentiments were not transient, and I sensed a similar frustration when interviewing CAN's General Secretary Reverend Dr Musa Asake in 2013. Reverend Asake felt that the president did not listen to the grievances of Christian communities and that no help was available to victims of the violence. He also denounced the lack of firmer condemnation of violence by Muslim clerics.[18] Interestingly, during my visit at the Supreme Council of Islamic Affairs I was reminded that most victims were actually Muslims and here as well, clerics were critical of the government approach but believed Jonathan was strongly influenced by CAN.[19] Although CAN is not representative of all Christians in Nigeria, it is telling that both on the Muslim and Christian sides views of Jonathan's strategy have been particularly negative—and even more so when the issue of amnesty for Boko Haram militants was raised.

But this frustration was also felt on the ground. Following multiple attacks on churches in Zaria in June 2012, Christians killed an unconfirmed number of Muslims in Kaduna state which resulted in the imposition of a 24-hour curfew across the region.[20] Most of this was attributed to a failure of leadership with the president being accused of having ignored for too long the gravity of the Boko Haram crisis, dismissing the violence as a by-product of political sentiment. In fact, north-eastern and north-western Nigeria were the areas from which he had received the fewest votes during the 2012 elections and critics argue that he simply read the Boko Haram violence as a sign of his lack of popularity in those states without acknowledging the extent of the inter-ethnic and inter-sectarian divisions that had come to characterise that part of Nigeria.[21]

Between two emergencies

The lifting of the 2012 emergency provisions did not reflect improvements on the ground; quite the contrary. The fighting continued in spite of several arrests and even the alleged killing of Shekau in October. Boko Haram destroyed more than two dozen mobile phone masts accusing telecommunications providers of assisting the Nigerian intelligence, killed three Chinese nationals and possibly a Ghanaian and two Indians near Maiduguri, and targeted St Rita's church in Kaduna as well as the convoy of the Emir of Kano. It was also in this period that the targeting of health workers became more apparent with the killing of nine female polio vaccinators in Kano and three North Korean doctors in Potiskum.[22]

Worryingly, in this phase Boko Haram's transnational links became clearer than ever. As French-led troops fought to re-take northern Mali from the Islamists, Boko Haram and Ansaru were believed to be supporting Ansar al-Dine and MUJWA's operations although there had been reports of their involvement already in early 2012. Ansaru kidnapped a French engineer in Katsina and seven foreign workers in Bauchi.

As the violence showed signs of diminishing, in November 2012 the JTF placed a bounty of N50 million on Shekau, N25 million on the heads of four other individuals believed to be, together with Shekau, part of the Shura Committee, and N10 million on fourteen top commanders, encouraging anyone with information leading to the capture of the wanted men to come forward without fear their anonymity would be compromised.[23]

March 2013 marked the first presidential visit to Maiduguri—Boko Haram's heartland—since the start of the insurgency. Jonathan had been heavily criticised for his absence and his perceived 'fear' of travelling to Borno state had no doubt done nothing to improve his public image.[24] It was in the aftermath of the visit that the security serviced disclosed the foiling of a plot to bring down the presidential plane in Borno. And this statement was supported by JTF recovering "three anti-aircraft guns, two technical vehicles mounted with anti-aircraft stands and ten rocket propelled grenades"[25] in Maiduguri, alongside a vast assortment of weapons during several operations in the state, including:

3 anti aircraft guns; 10 rocket propelled grenade tubes; 3 general purpose machine guns; 17 AK47 rifles; 3 G3 rifles; 1 pistol (lama); 20 RPG bombs; 12 RPG chargers; 1x 36 hand held grenade; 1 teargas rifle; 33 AK 47 magazines; 11 FN magazines; 3 G3 magazines; 11,068 assorted ammunitions; 2 technical vehicles with mounted anti aircraft stands; 1 box of weapons cleaning kit; 4 swords and two knifes; 5 walking [sic] talkies; 4 VHF hand held sets; 1 multi links router; and assorted uniforms and kits.[26]

Shortly afterwards, another alleged plot was uncovered, this time spreading terror across the entire country as the target was believed to have been Lagos—Nigeria's financial hub. A large cache of weapons was recovered under the suspicion that they would be used to stage an attack on the international airport.[27] But this was not the only scare in the southern city. Screening and deportation of illegal migrants from Chad, Niger and Mali were all conducted as the individuals in question were suspected of having ties with Boko Haram.[28]

Negotiations and amnesty

In this "inter-state of emergency" period, there extensive discussion on the issue of negotiation and a possible amnesty for those fighters willing to renounce violence.

The possibility of starting a dialogue had long been discussed and, naturally, remains a sensitive issue. Negotiations have been tried but failed owing to unreasonable demands, such as Shakau's request that all detained members would be set free—a unacceptable condition. On other occasions, engagement between the government and elements within the groups was given too much media attention, and ended badly. Most infamously, former President Obasanjo became involved in visits to Yusuf's brother-in-law, Babakura Fuggu, whose father had also been killed in 2009, first in 2011,[29] and for the last time in August 2012. The latter visit amounted to a death sentence for Fuggu who was murdered by Boko Haram. The issue around the extrajudicial killing of Yusuf, his father-in-law and many others in 2009 was, and still is (with the trial against the police officers believed responsible for Yusuf's killing reopening in February 2014) lingering. Compensation for the family and, of course, brokering a possible deal with Boko Haram had been on the agenda of the meeting, including a discussion on amnesty, future employment opportunities for Boko Haram members, and Shakau's request for the release of fighters and the withdrawal of the JTF.[30]

This visit, and Obasanjo's high profile involvement more broadly, were highly criticised both by those set against the idea of negotiating with terrorists but also by those fearing that it would jeopardise chances for real dialogue as well as putting Fuggu and his family at risk or, at a minimum, would result in them losing any leverage they may have with Boko Haram. Regrettably, the sceptics were right. The next day Fuggu was shot dead in broad daylight by suspected a Boko Haram member.[31]

At other times elements claiming to represent Boko Haram showed their willingness to talk to the government but were very quickly dismissed by Shekau. In March 2013 the leader released a video statement following claims by a certain Sheikh Abdulaziz Ibn Adam that Shekau had agreed to a ceasefire and hinting at a possible deep fracture within the movement with unruly elements perpetrating violence and ignoring orders coming from the top.[32] This was not the first time that news of what turned out to be a fake ceasefire or dialogue had made headlines. The March 2013 transcript is reproduced below as it offers a good example of Shakau's rhetoric, determination and complete unwillingness to compromise, let alone surrender.

> May the peace and blessings of Allah be upon you all. This is an important message to all people.
>
> There is this wicked rumour making the rounds that we have dialogued with government of Nigeria which led to a ceasefire on our part. We have also heard how some of our operations and attacks are being credited to criminals. As such the security agents have been killing our armed members in the name of criminals. We have seen how our members who were out on holy mission are being attacked and killed with the label of criminals.

We are telling the world that whoever kills any of our members in the name of being criminals, would surely be avenged unless such person repents now.

We are stating it categorically that we are not in any dialogue or ceasefire agreement with anyone. And we have never asked anybody in the name Abdulazeez to represent me, Abubakar Shekau, the leader of this movement.

I swear by Allah that Abdulazeez or whatever he calls himself did not get any authority from me to represent me in any capacity. I do not know him. And if we per adventure encounter Abulazeez and his group, I swear by Allah we are going to mete them with the grave judgment that Allah has prescribed for their likes in the holy book.

I want the world to know that *we have no dialogue with government. I have on several occasions attempted to pass this message across via the Internet and Youtube and we later realised that some agents of government kept removing our messages from the net and preventing its online publication so that our messages will not be heard. They know that If the world hears our position on this fake dialogue, their efforts of deceit would be exposed.*

We are also sending this strong message to the people of Yobe, Borno, Bauchi, Kano, Kaduna, Taraba, Adamawa, and any state that whoever kills any of our members should await a grave retaliation from us. God knows that we don't kill unjustly except those that conspired against us or those that directly fight us, or the government that is waging war upon Allah and His Prophet. *We will continue waging war against them until we succeeded in establish an Islamic state in Nigeria.*

This message is prepared by me and targeted towards clarifying the issue of ceasefire. We have never had any dialogue with anyone. *How would we have had dialogue with the government when our members are being killed and detained in cells, both women and children. Do you call this dialogue? That is not dialogue or truce in Islam.* In Islam there are condition prescribed for us to go into dialogue, and there are also situation in which we cannot go in to dialogue. What we are doing now is what is prescribed for us by Allah and his holy prophet. We are workers in the vine yard of Allah.

We are not out to cause destructions, but correct the ills of the society. And Allah is more powerful than all, and He has the might. Allah will surely assist us to victory. This is my message to you. If you have not heard from me all this while, now my message should have reached you all.[33]

President Jonathan adopted contradicting stands vis-à-vis dialogue, possibly reflecting the sensitivity of the issue and uncertainty around it. In March 2013 he rejected a proposition by the Sultan of Sokoto Alhaji Muhammad Sa'ad Abubakar III for an amnesty programme but a month later he announced the establishment of a committee to evaluate the feasibility of pardoning the militants. This move was a turning point for a president who had long refused to enter into dialogue with "ghosts"—a phrase often used by Jonathan in reference to the fact that in all the videos released by the group, Shekau was the only one not to cover his face—but who finally seemed to acknowledge that the military strategy had produced limited results. His change of mind may have been prompted by growing pressure exerted by the Northern Elders Forum on the president and the fact that his visit to Borno had gone badly in addition to his already poor track record in the North. For these reasons, creating the Committee was designed both to relieve the political pressure and acknowledgement that ignoring the North was no longer feasible.

One of those who had long advocated an amnesty was Governor Kashim Shettima of Borno State who had put the idea forward as early as 2011, before his gubernatorial appointment. Shettima, preferring a three-pronged approach including defence, diplomacy and dialogue, has argued that the former, i.e. the military approach, had as its original goal the defence of Nigerians against external enemies rather than the targeting of fellow countrymen and women. Therefore, as other world leaders have done elsewhere, the Nigerian government should meet and discuss with the enemy even when there exist deep differences of beliefs.[34]

The Presidential Committee on Dialogue and Peaceful Resolution on Security Challenges in Northern Nigeria, aka the Amnesty Committee, working closely with the National Security Adviser, was given the following mission:

To consider the feasibility or otherwise of granting pardon to the Boko Haram adherents,

Collate clamours arising from different interest groups who want the apex government to administer clemency on members of the religious sect; and

To recommend modalities for the granting of the pardon, should such step become the logical one to take under the prevailing circumstance.[35]

In addition, the members of the Committee, led by Alhaji Kabiru Turaki,[36] were tasked with a nationwide tour to discuss the possibility of offering amnesty with a number of stakeholders.

However the announcement was quickly followed by Shekau stating that Boko Haram had done "nothing wrong" and it was the group, if anyone, that should consider offering amnesty to the government for the atrocities committed against Muslims.

While some supported the idea of dialogue, including the Arewa Consultative Forum (ACF, an association of Northern Nigerian leaders),[37] the issue of amnesty remains a highly politicised one (ACF was for instance accused of supporting Boko Haram) and has created much disagreement within and outside government. And having arrived in Nigeria only a few days following the establishment of the Amnesty Committee, I saw for myself how and why officials (and non) disagreed on the subject, although the majority of those I spoke to had many reservations.

Interior Minister Abba Moro seemed optimistic in April 2013, believing that a pardon was key to a long-lasting solution, hence it was vital for the government to be sincere in its approach to dialogue; it also had to separate those willing to negotiate from the more radical elements who wanted to destabilise the country.[38] Others believe that by offering amnesty to some factions or elements it would be easier to extract intelligence from former militants to be used to tackle the more radical core.[39] However given the cell-based structure of the group it is unlikely that individual members have much knowledge beyond their immediate remit of operation.

The once militant Yoruba nationalists of the Oodua Peoples Congress (OPC) also seemed in favour of the initiative citing the Niger Delta militants as an example of peace resulting from amnesty.[40] Others I interviewed however mentioned the Niger Delta as a negative case. There is the risk that amnesty would translate into simply throwing money at the problem. In a country where the minimum wage is around $130 per month, and former Niger Delta militants receive monthly payments of $500, it is easy to see why this is so controversial (and expensive) and fuels the feeling that the country is held hostage by "former" militants who threaten to resume attacks as soon as there is a delay in their payments.[41] More cynically, a security expert I spoke to believed that Boko Haram could afford to carry on with the attacks a little longer before accepting an amnesty—after all they seem to be winning.

Senior military commanders, who naturally were reluctant to express their personal views especially as they differed from the official line, admitted to me that they did not believe this new initiative would work. "Boko Haram cannot be trusted hence amnesty is risky…There is no indication they would stop the violence"[42] worried one. The same officer also deemed it impossible to have a dialogue because the group was ideologically motivated and therefore highly unlikely to compromise. Another officer with direct access to imprisoned Boko Haram militants had a more pragmatic view: "amnesty may not work because of corruption", funds would end up in the wrong hands and projects that have been promised such as the building of schools would simply not happen. In addition to this, Shekau's demand for the removal of the JTF was simply impossible to meet as insecurity persisted.[43]

Another interviewee, while conceding that the criminal elements within the group may accept an amnesty offer, worried that the core of Boko Haram consisted of ideologically driven individuals "waiting for heaven, not amnesty".[44] And bearing this in mind, money set aside for amnesty payments could instead be used to strengthen intelligence capabilities to infiltrate the group's ranks and "flush them out".[45]

The Christian Association of Nigeria (CAN) was not against the amnesty in principle, but strongly believed that before considering amnesty for terrorists and criminals the Federal Government should first compensate victims and put in place provisions for poverty alleviation for the communities that had been affected by the violence. Also, Boko Haram should come forward, show their faces and explain their grievances. Many Christians felt the president had forgotten about them while Northern Elders had come to hold sway over the presidency even though they, unlike Christians, would never vote for him. Moreover, the flawed leadership of President Jonathan was likely to cost him Christian votes at the next elections. In other words, had the Federal Government not failed to prosecute Boko Haram members it would have been easier for CAN to forgive and enter into a dialogue.[46]

Overall, even those in favour of the amnesty seemed to agree that unless Shakau himself was behind the negotiations (to be conducted away from the limelight) and amnesty was part of a larger programme including development, job creation and so on, there was no hope for success.

A second state of emergency is put in place

Prompted by the Baga incident in April 2013, which I discuss later in the context of human rights abuses, President Jonathan had to cut short a trip to southern Africa to return to Abuja and deal with the deteriorating security situation. On 14 May he declared a state of emergency in the states of Borno, Yobe and Adamawa—an area of some 60,000 sq miles (155,000 km sq) of the Sahel bordering Cameroon, Chad and

Niger. During a televised address he indicated that the challenge faced by the country was "not just militancy or criminality, but a rebellion and insurgency by terrorist groups which pose a very serious threat to national unity and territorial integrity" and that "[a]lready, some northern parts of Borno state have been taken over by groups whose allegiance is to different flags and ideologies".[47]

This declaration coincided with the deployment of 2,000 additional security personnel, accompanied by fighter jets and other military equipment, in Borno; later another 1,000 soldiers were sent to Adamawa, bringing the total to approximately 8,000 and marking the largest military deployment since the Nigerian Civil War. In addition, the president introduced a curfew in Adamawa, and granted the military full search, arrest and detention powers in a move that prompted contrasting reactions. While Boko Haram's increased strength warranted a more decisive military intervention, many, including locals, feared that expanded powers would be abused. Moreover, with such a large army deployment, the likelihood of collateral damage was probably the biggest concern for many civilians in the affected states.

While the deterioration of security in the North East required a more decisive form of intervention, one could argue that the suspension of constitutional rights that accompanied the state of emergency may have proved counterproductive in states that were already on edge and that featured a large Kanuri population who already had some sympathy with Boko Haram. In addition, such a heavy display of force may prompt Boko Haram to adopt more unconventional methods when faced by security forces it cannot otherwise defeat.

Furthermore, even within political circles the declaration prompted mixed reactions and the politicisation of the state of emergency with leaders of opposition parties such as General Muhammadu Buhari (rtd.), leader of the Congress for Progressive Change (CPC) and Senator Bola Ahmed Tinubu, leader of the Action Congress of Nigeria (ACN) voicing their disagreement. Ironically the party controlling Yobe and Borno states—the All Nigeria Peoples Party (ANPP)—supported the President's initiative possibly because, unlike previous states of emergency, local authorities were allowed to stay in office.[48]

On 16 May a military offensive was launched in Borno with raids on Boko Haram camps in the Sambisa Game Reserve and increased patrols along national borders, before aerial targeting with jets and attack helicopters was launched. Within a week the army announced the destruction of several Boko Haram camps and the capture of up to 200 militants; women and children held hostage by the sect were also rescued. Boko Haram was "in disarray", the military claimed, and fleeing across the border into Niger and Cameroon. However sect leader Shekau painted a different picture in a video obtained by AFP at the end of May. In the recording, which included images of wrecked military vehicles, he claimed that militants were fighting back against the offensive, as Nigerian soldiers dropped their weapons and "ran like pigs".[49] None of these claims were verifiable, nor were reports that unarmed US spy drones were assisting government operations from a US military base in neighbouring Niger—a collaboration denied by the Nigerian Defence Headquarters.[50] A few months later, the government claimed that 1,000 Boko Haram members had been captured in the first three months of the state of emergency and that JTF ORO's gains had gradually helped dislodge Boko Haram first from Maiduguri and then all the way to the Sambisa Game Reserve and the Gwoza Hills of the North-East.[51]

Speaking to a local journalist who had returned from Maiduguri in June 2013 it appeared that in places such as Marte, in Borno state close to the Chad border, insurgents had left before the arrival of the JTF. Similarly, locals in Yobe state had reported seeing the passing of some 200 trucks carrying alleged Boko Haram members across the border into Niger ahead of the state of emergency deployment. If these accounts are to be believed, one could conclude that a large proportion of the young men rounded up by the security forces during the May operations were probably innocent local youths.[52] Many questions are however likely to remain unanswered as the suspension of mobile phone communication in the areas under emergency—introduced to limit Boko Haram's ability to coordinate attacks—also had an impact on the amount of reporting coming out of, particularly, Borno state. The ban was only lifted in July 2013.[53] More dramatic downsides of the communication blackout became evident as people were unable to raise the alarm in case of emergency. In the summer, schools in Yobe state came under attack. In the deadliest incident twenty-two pupils were burnt alive as their boarding school was set on fire on 6 July. Ibrahim Gaidam, the Yobe Governor, had no doubt that "[t]he lack of [Global System for Mobile Communications] service has prevented patriotic citizens who have hitherto been collaborating with security agents from reporting suspicious movements in their neighbourhoods".[54] Needless to say, in addition to the abovementioned criticism of the communication black-out, many questioned how coordinating and executing such an attack had been possible given, first, the state of emergency, i.e. the large presence of security forces, and second, the knowledge that Boko Haram had attacked many schools before.

Locals in Borno fear JTF more than Boko Haram. Regrettably a hostile barrier was thrown up between the security forces and the population with every civilian being considered a potential fighter and harassment becoming the norm.[55] The situation had become such that many sought refuge abroad as evidenced by an appeal by the Borno state Deputy Governor to the 20,000 civilians who had escaped into Cameroon to return to their homes. This plea had little effect as the fear of being killed by the military prevailed.[56]

The indiscriminate round-ups of innocent men prompted some youths to set up vigilante groups, self-styled as "Civilian JTFs", to identify the real Boko Haram and point them out to the JTF. This appeared to be a self-starting initiative by young men armed with sticks and machetes. It too caused concern: locals would be stopped and searched by young man who, effectively, had no official authority. And civilians were not alone in worrying. Director of Defence Information, Brigadier General Chris Olukolade cautioned:

> We are also concerned about the activities of the Civilian JTF, a lot of us are carefully relating with them. The fact however, still remains that they are very useful to us and I am sure that the government should have a plan for them after their operations…Meanwhile, what happened recently (near Bama, Borno where about 40 were killed in ambush) is unfortunate, which was borne out of exuberance, and also the rivalry among them has not officially come to our notice but we are closely monitoring them…We really do not want to give too much prominence to the Civilian JTF. They were stepping out of boundaries and that is what happened when about 40 of them were killed at Bama.[57]

Fairly rapidly, however, the JTF began monitoring and supporting the vigilantes, who gained quasi-formal roles under military supervision. They were praised by the army which encouraged people to support the civilian JTFs.[58] Indeed, in Borno young men were officially encouraged to set up self-defence groups.[59] Within nine months of their inception the groups gained even greater recognition and became more structured, with their own commanders, sectors and membership cards. In an April 2014 interview Sector 5's commander shed some light on the Civilian JTFs. Vigilantes were still scared of being targeted by the military as suspected Boko Haram and for this reason every member would tie a piece of white nylon cloth on their left hand to differentiate himself from the insurgents. In addition, and unlike Boko Haram, they do not carry guns. Their weapons, normally including sticks, daggers and machetes, but also some tasers and pepper spray, are donated by residents but, usually, are bought by the same vigilantes. Commander Buba also indicated that all units were operational in Maiduguri although, at times, they were engaged in Adamawa and Yobe states.[60]

Boko Haram did not fail to respond to this development. On the contrary the group promptly declared war on the vigilantes in Yobe and Borno launching a manhunt for the youths.[61] Reports of deadly clashes between the group and the Civilian JTFs were soon reported, such as those in Benisheik, Borno (September 2013). The incident highlighted some of the reasons why "officialising" the role of untrained civilians prompts unease. Although intelligence indicated the imminent approach of Boko Haram in Benisheik, the vigilantes were taken by surprise and ambushed in the early hours. Some of the youth later claimed that the military had failed to come to their support, as planned, during the attack. This incident followed an earlier one in which Boko Haram members disguised in military uniforms killed at least twenty-four vigilantes in Monguno, also in Borno.[62] On another occasion a mosque came under attack in Konduga amid speculation that the vigilantes praying there had been the real target.[63] Several other such incidents have since taken place and they are unlikely to end any time soon. A video released by Shekau in spring 2014 left no doubt:

> Your name is not Civilian JTF but Civilian Trouble. My advice to you so-called Civilian-JTF is to flee, take up arms, get conscripted into the army or police, because I am telling you is that I have started a war against you. The war against you has just begun. In this world, there are two kinds of people; there are those who are with us or those who are against us, and the latter group are those I'll kill once I spot them. From now on, my focus of attack is going to be the Civilian-JTF. Let the Civilian-JTF know that this is me, Shekau talking. You will now really understand the person called Shekau. You don't know my madness, right? It is now that you will see the true face of my madness. I swear by Allah's holy name that I will slaughter you. I will not be happy if I don't personally put my knife on your necks and slit your

throats. Yes! I'll slaughter you! I'll slaughter you! And I'll slaughter you again and again.[64]

There have been other occasions in which ineffectiveness—real or perceived—on the part of the Nigerian government has prompted civilians to take matters in their own hands. Relatives of the missing girls kidnapped en masse from a rural school in Chibok, Borno state (April 2014) raised funds to hire around 100 okadas [local motorcycle taxis] to go into the Sambisa forest to look for the girls. Others had themselves vainly attempted to locate their children. The information around the search remains sketchy. According to some accounts, those who had searched the forests were simply unable to find the victims but others claimed that the okada drivers had been warned by Boko Haram to abort the search as failing to do so would result in their deaths and that of the girls'.[65] The slow pace with which the government has responded to the incident—in terms of issuing official statements, launching a rescue operation, and the failure to release pictures and names of the victims—has caused outrage with protests taking place in Nigerian cities and around the world and an online campaign under the banner of #BringBackOurGirls.[66]

The mass kidnapping of the Chibok girls serves a number of purposes for Boko Haram, from undermining the government's credibility (including its timing ahead of the Word Economic Forum in Abuja in May 2014), to financial gain through the sale of the schoolgirls and possible ransoms; from building bargaining power (in light of a possible exchange of arrested Boko Haram members) to promoting morale within the group by providing 'brides' for the fighters; but also, and significantly I would argue, in retaliation for the government's practice of apprehending the wives and children of suspected fighters and using them to exert pressure on the group and show concessions when they are released. In late May 2013, officially as a sign of goodwill and in the spirit of a possible amnesty which was under discussion, JTF ORO released fifty-eight women and children (twenty in Borno and thirty-eight in Yobe state) who were accused of helping Islamist militants. In fairness Borno state governor Kashim Shettima announced that the women would receive job training to ease their reintegration into society and the parents of the pardoned children would be given cash rewards if they could keep their kids in school.[67] However, according to other accounts this was in fact a prisoner exchange: local hostages in return for wives and children of Boko Haram militants.[68] Moreover, it appears that among those held by the security forces there were one of Shakau's wives, Hassana Yakubu who had been captured ten months earlier, Malama Zara, wife of the deceased Mohamed Yusuf, and wives and children of others senior figures within Boko Haram.[69]

In what some may describe as contradictory, or perhaps carrot and stick-like, the massive military offensive under the state of emergency was conducted in parallel with continued discussions on the issue of amnesty. Indeed, shortly after the declaration of a state of emergency it emerged that the Amnesty Committee had held secret meetings in Kaduna with Boko Haram members,[70] and in July the Committee announced that negotiations had led to Boko Haram declaring a cease-fire—only two days after dozens of children were killed in Mamudo, Yobe state, in one of the many infamous attacks against schools. One of the requests put forward by the group was the release of women and children held by the security forces.[71] This came in spite of the proscription of Boko Haram (and Ansaru) as a terrorist organisation in June 2013. The latter indeed was received with mixed feelings. The Northern Elders Forum for one saw the banning as counter-productive and undermining efforts to solve the crisis by indicating that the Federal Government was not genuinely committed to negotiations.[72]

These talks, taking place amid continued violence, left many perplexed. Human Rights Watch, which had released a report (October 2012) deeming Boko Haram's attacks likely to amount to crimes against humanity, immediately cautioned the Amnesty Committee to hold accountable those who had committed such crimes and to exclude them from any amnesty programme as justice was essential for peace.[73] In doing so, the NGO stressed that following a preliminary examination launched in 2010, in 2012 the Office of the Prosecutor of the International Criminal Court (ICC) had concluded that "there was *reasonable basis to believe* that Boko Haram had committed crimes against humanity."[74]

But Human Rights Watched didn't need to worry (relatively speaking of course). In true Shekau-style, a week after the alleged ceasefire agreement, the group's leader made it clear that "[t]he claim that we have entered into a truce with the government of Nigeria is not true. We don't know Kabiru Turaki. We have never spoken with him. He is lying."[75]

Turaki's Committee insisted on the veracity of the agreement and described Shekau's video as the action of a man afraid of what might happen to him if some of his lieutenants were to see him manifesting weakness. It is fair to say that the continuation, and escalation, of violence that followed proves that no real ceasefire was ever reached. Moreover, it shows confusion in the government approach and, as several people I had interviewed cautioned, without Shakau's full backing of an amnesty no such agreement can even be reached.

Moving beyond JTF ORO

In a rather surprising—and I dare say ill-advised—move, in August 2013, JTF ORO was replaced by the newly-established Army 7th Infantry Division, headquartered in Maiduguri and headed by Major General Obida Etnan, in leading the counterinsurgency campaign against Boko Haram.[76] Evidently, this change coincided with the drawing down of a multi-agency effort that, in spite of its faults, had characterised the JTF and its counter-terrorism and counter-insurgency trained components.

In announcing the end of the JTF era, the Director of Defence Information, Brigadier General Chris Olukolade noted that the change was in line with existing planning:

> The phase being concluded on Monday was executed by a Joint Task Force, JTF, composed by troops drawn from the services of the Armed Forces as well as other security agencies who conducted Operation BOYONA. The acronym for the code name, Operation BOYONA, is derived from the names of the three states of Borno, Yobe and Adamawa, covered by the state of emergency declaration. The effort was meant to constitute the first phase of the counter-terrorists operation. The Nigerian Army will now be solely in charge of the operations, but still under the routine guidance of the Defence Headquarters.[77]

At the time of its inception the 7th Division was believed to consist of 8,000 troops: 1,000 redeployed from Mali, with the remaining 7,000 mostly from commands in northern Nigeria: specifically, comprising elements include the 1st Mechanised Brigade (Sokoto, and part of the 1st Division), the 21st Armoured Brigade (Maiduguri) the 23rd Armoured Brigade (Yola) and both parts of the 3rd Armoured Division. However its actual composition may vary and additional (or alternative) troops may be re-deployed from elsewhere.[78]

In an October 2013 interview the Chief of Army Staff (COAS), Lieutenant General Azubuike Ihejirika admitted that the armed forces had gone "into the operation in the North East without joint deployment training" and although he was "impressed with the level of cooperation so far" he did not deny that there had been "limited success with the operation".[79]

One of the reasons for this lack of greater success has been Boko Haram's adaptability and resilience. In response to the military offensive they have adopted new tactics such as the use of children and women as spies to infiltrate targets and wearing military uniforms or disguising themselves as women. Interestingly and often unreported, women have been welcome among the Civilian JTF precisely to tackle the growing use by Boko Haram of women to smuggle weapons, conceal IEDs and run errands. Female Civilian JTFs, usually the wives of male vigilantes, can in fact perform searches of suspected women while men cannot.[80]

Militants also began resorting to mob-like tactics and deploying basic weapons. By now a well known ruse, at times they would arrive at villages, some wearing military uniforms, and claiming to be part of a joint military-vigilantes unit only to lure out Civilian JTFs and kill or capture them. Arrests and army seizures in Sokoto (August), and arrests linked to suicide attack plots in Kano (November), also indicated that while the military operation had been relatively successful in containing the violence in the three states under emergency, Boko Haram was indeed considering secondary fronts.[81]

September saw an increase in troops levels alongside Alphajets and Mi 35 and Mi 34 attack helicopters. The use of air power and aerial targeting in fact played an important role in the destruction of Boko Haram's camps and hideouts, such as the joint 7th Division-79th Composite Group (Maiduguri, Air Force) air and ground assault on 21 October on a camp in Alagarno village, Borno state.[82] Militants also well understood the importance of air operations for the Nigerian military when, on 2 December, 200–300 insurgents on twenty-three Hilux trucks attacked the Air Force 79th Composite Group based at Maiduguri International Airport (alongside other attacks in the area) resulting in the destruction of three decommissioned MIG 21 aircraft, two operational Mi 24/35 variant helicopters and several vehicles, and the imposition of a curfew and temporary air traffic ban in and out of Borno state.[83] Nigerian forces retaliated with an air strike with helicopters and fast jets from the Air Force base in Yola.

It came as no surprise that the state of emergency was extended in November for an additional six months until May 2014.

Operations have highlighted Boko Haram's reliance on the border-lands with Cameroon, Chad and Niger and, as a result, Nigeria has strengthened border controls and entered into policing and intelligence cooperation agreements with its neighbours, including Benin. France and Britain have also offered to increase their support. Cameroon—often accused by Nigeria of not doing enough—had increased border controls in the Far North region and boosted military units there as a result of Boko Haram's presence, more skirmishes on Cameroonian territory and kidnappings such as those of a French priest (November 2013, released), the yet-to-be-claimed kidnapping of two Italian priests and a Canadian nun (April 2014, released) and the kidnap of ten Chinese workers (May 2014, released)—not to mention the earlier abduction of a French family.

In December 2013 the United Nations released figures indicating that since the declaration of a state of emergency in May, over 1,200 civilians, militants and security personnel had died as a result of the insurgency in addition to an unknown number of people who have been wounded. The report also stated that "of the 11 million Nigerians living in the state of emergency states, up to six million have been affected by the insecurity, four million of whom live in Borno state." The UN also expressed concern over reporting of abduction and forced conversion of Christian women then forced into marriage and the recruitment of child soldiers, some as young as twelve.[84] In the first three months of 2014 alone over 1,500 people lost their lives.[85]

Amid speculation that President Jonathan was losing patience with the military leadership's inability to curtail the violence in the North East, in January 2014 he replaced Admiral Ola Sa'ad Ibrahim as Chief of Defence Staff with Air Marshal Alex Badeh. He also sacked and replaced with immediate effect the Chiefs of Naval, Air and Army Staff.[86]

Soon after his appointment Chief of Army Staff, Lt. Gen. Kenneth Minimah relocated to the North East to more closely monitor the military offensive, now led by Maj. Gen. A. Mohammed, in the aftermath of attacks on schools which had produced much public outcry. The move was sanctioned by the Senate:

> The Senate Committee on Defence and Army condemned the atrocity being unleashed by Boko Haram elements on innocent citizens and in particular the massacre of students of the Federal Government College, Buni Yadi in Yobe State. The committee has by this, issued a directive that the Chief of Army Staff take the following actions (a), Re-strategise on possible new ways

of curbing these excesses, (b) mobilise all available military resources and face the insurgents, relocate his office to Maiduguri for urgent actions to curtail the repeated attacks by the insurgents on innocent Nigerians.[87]

All in all, by spring 2014 the security forces had made some gains, destroying Boko Haram's hideouts, killing and arresting many fighters (including senior commanders)[88] and being able to broadly contain the violence within the three states under state of emergency through coordinated offensives in Sambisa Forest, the Lake Chad area, Gwoza Hills and Mandara Mountains.

However the early months of 2014 left little room for optimism owing to high fatality levels—1,500 between January and March alone according to Amnesty International bringing the total deaths since the start of the insurgency to well over 5,000 since 2010,[89] as well as bolder attacks such as the one at the Giwa barracks and prison in March[90] and the two IED attacks in the outskirts of Abuja in April 2014 (one week apart) as the capital was preparing to host the World Economic Forum.[91] The mass kidnapping of over 200 school girls in Chibok, Borno state in April prompted countries such as the UK, the USA, Canada, France, China and Israel to offer support in the form of military advisers, hostage situation experts, intelligence sharing, surveillance aircraft and so on. France even hosted an international summit on Boko Haram in May to discuss a joint plan of action.[92] The Chibok incident, and the Federal Government's delays in responding to it, have prompted enormous criticism of President Jonathan and were a great embarrassment for the Nigerian authorities, who had been claiming that their military campaign against the militants was succeeding. The apparent inability to prevent such an attack and deal with the aftermath have made foreign involvement inevitable.

Boko Haram attacks have not been the only security preoccupation for Northern and North-Central Nigeria. Communal violence and ethno-religious tensions that have long been a feature of the country's Middle Belt[93] escalated in early 2014 with suspected Fulani herdsmen allegedly responsible for deadly clashes in Kaduna and Benue states and even further north in Katsina causing the death of over 100 people in each attack and prompting the deployment of 600 police officers in Benue in March. Less deadly clashes were also reported in Plateau state. These events, which also required the deployment of special forces and the temporary relocation of the Army 82nd Division to Benue, came as a setback after the peace agreement reached by the Fulani and Berom communities in Plateau in May 2013 and the ceasefire agreement signed by the Fulani and Alago in July.[94]

With all this fighting taking place, the idea of amnesty for Boko Haram was at this point far from the top of anyone's agenda. Nevertheless in November 2013, fourteen months after its inauguration, the Presidential Committee on Dialogue and the Peaceful Resolution of the Security Challenges in the North submitted its report to President Jonathan. Besides highlighting the human impact of the insurgency and recommending the creation of a victims' support fund, the report pointed at tensions among security forces and the lack of up-to-date equipment. In addition, it suggested the establishment of a new committee, including some of the current members, to continue the dialogue.[95] Interestingly, Minister of Special Duties and Head of the Committee Kabiru Tanimu Turaki admitted that although the team had interviewed Boko Haram members in prison, they had been unable to contact the leadership at large,[96] which is a cause of concern, given that any dialogue that excludes Shekau is highly unlikely to bring an end to the violence.

Allegations of human rights abuses

Accusations of human rights abuses have marred the government's response from the onset of the fight against Boko Haram: such practices have certainly had a negative impact on the perception of the government's approach, have prompted retaliation by the group and have alienated the public.

Discussion of extra-judicial killings featured earlier in this book in the account of Mohamed Yusuf's death. Regrettably, it seems that for too long the security forces have been following the order to "crush" Boko Haram at the expense of the right to fair trial and the rule of law. Discussing the 2009 events, Abdulkarrem Mohammed highlights how such killings, besides being unlawful, deprived the counter-insurgency effort of valuable information on the sect, its motives and sponsors, that could have been gathered through interrogation. A former Commissioner of Police has also shared his concerns that the quick disposal of suspects might have served to cover up collusion between high profile individuals and Boko Haram.[97]

The use of the military can be problematic as, by nature, soldiers are not trained to deal directly with the civilian population and, increasingly, human rights abuses have been reported following army deployments in the north, while several Boko Haram attacks have been carried out in response to the actions of government forces. A widely discussed Amnesty International report[98] released in 2012 documents various cases of summary executions, extra-judicial killings, house burnings and forced evictions, not to mention the lack of adequate investigations and witness protection programmes; while an earlier document by the same NGO had described how, following Boko Haram attacks, the JTF would carry out house-to house searches and round up men, who would frequently be shot on the spot, and beat women.[99] Contacts in Nigeria have sent me pictures showing summary executions in which groups of men are lined up in what seems to be the middle of nowhere, then the same individuals are lying on the ground, and a few pictures later have bullet wounds in their heads. Although such images are normally unverified, given the number of stories that have surfaced over the years regarding summary executions and the footage that is easily accessible online, it is hard to dispute their authenticity.

There is no shortage of examples that could be cited. In spring 2013, to mention an infamous incident, the town of Baga, Borno, became the stage of a fierce exchange lasting several hours between Boko Haram and the military, resulting in at least 187 deaths, dozens of injuries and the destruction of over 2,000 houses between 16 and 17 April. The Baga incident was later put under close scrutiny following allegations of excessive use of force on the part of the military. Satellite images corroborated this account and identified 2,275 destroyed buildings with another hundred or so severely damaged, during a military raid to hunt down Boko Haram.[100] An interim report by the Nigerian National Human Rights Commission released in June 2013 highlighted concerns about compliance with international norms concerning human rights as well as proportionality of the use of force. Worryingly, the Commission identified the existing tendency to tolerate "certain numbers of killing" provided they were not too high.[101]

To be fair to the security forces, it has to be pointed out that, in the context of the Baga incident, JTF ORO was supported by the presence of the Multinational Joint Task Force (M-JTF) consisting of approximately 700 Nigerian troops, 700 Chadians, 500 Cameroonians and 500

Nigeriens cooperating with the Air Force 79th Composite Group based in Maiduguri. M-JTF had originally been conceived in 1998 as Operation Flush to target Chadian rebels. Unlike JTF ORO, members of the M-JTF are not trained in counter-terrorism or counter-insurgency: they are infantry with no urban warfare training and lack many of the key components at the disposal of JTF ORO such as reconnaissance and intelligence.[102]

Another interesting example is that of Kano. When I interviewed residents in this northern city memories of the attacks of 20 January 2012 were still fresh in their minds. It was the day that radically altered the urban landscape (many checkpoints were set up in its aftermath) and people's lives when a series of coordinated explosions resulted in the death of over 200 people including one of the highest profile killings by Boko Haram, an assistant commissioner of police. Residents told me that for days after the explosions more bodies were found even on roads quite far from the scene of the blasts giving rise to suspicion that the JTF was responsible for some of those deaths. Moreover when Boko Haram distributed leaflets to take responsibility for some but not all of the deaths, a propotion of local residents tended to believe them because the sect had never shied away from claiming responsibility for attacks it had carried out.[103] And although there was a recognition that a military presence was necessary, locals were afraid of the security forces who were known for "brutalising" people, "killing easily" and "extorting money at roadblocks".[104] Whereas they condemned Boko Haram's violence, some interviewees also admitted that they understood why the group was so critical of the government.[105]

A human rights activist in Kano suggested in a discussion with me, that the actions of the JTF were likely to facilitate Boko Haram recruitment. People have developed grudges against the institutions prompted by the looting, harassment and raping carried out by the JTF during some of their raids, or the fact that at check-points they would demand bribes more often than screen vehicles. They are also known for destroying people's houses on the suspicion that one of those living there was a member of Boko Haram—and of course no compensation is ever paid for any of those wrongdoings.[106]

To compound these grudges, the judicial system suffers from an incredible backlog with pre-trial detention lasting up to three years in some cases—as the Minister of Interior admitted to me in Abuja.[107]

Some people I spoke to believed that the problem with the huge number of court cases waiting to be heard almost indefinitely may encourage police officers to take justice into their own hands and kill arrested individuals on the spot, especially when it comes to suspected Boko Haram members. This links back to the 2009 killings which some explained as triggered by the sense of humiliation and frustration felt by the police, not only because the sect had killed a number of its officers, but also because the police were aware that Mohamed Yusuf had previously been arrested and taken to court only to be released by the judiciary, and therefore, in the eyes of some, an immediate execution was the only way to serve justice.[108]

Minister Moro even admitted that some people end up awaiting trial for periods longer than the actual sentence they will be given. In other words, if a person is sentenced to serve two years in prison but they have already spent three years in pre-trial custody, they will be released on the day of the sentence having effectively wasted a year of their life and receiving, in the Minister's words, no compensation.[109] Instances of this sort, which apparently are the norm, contribute to undermining the already fragile relationship between the authorities and the public and weaken trust in the judicial system, not to mention that anyone who has been the victim of this level of injustice would probably feel extremely disgruntled. As a way of alleviating this problem, the minister has been considering designing alternative forms of punishment such as suspended sentences, non-custodial measures and the possibility of handing over convicts to local leaders.[110] The latter reminded me of a diplomatic cable from the American Embassy in Abuja in 2008 made public by Wikileaks discussing the common practice of releasing terrorist suspects into the hands of imams or northern traditional leaders for re-education. Some of those imams in Kano and Kaduna, however, "contended that the so-called de-radicalisation efforts of the State Security Service were not only ill-conceived, but also ineffective, counter-productive, and unimpressive".[111]

Beside the broader discussion, it is important to consider the human/individual level to understand the extent of the damage families are suffering. When I visited a local a NGO providing legal support to victims of the judicial system, I was told the case of a woman, S.U., from Bauchi who had been arrested and held in custody for six months with her three children—a ten month old baby she was still breastfeeding, a three year old and a five year old. In prison she had no medication or food provision. One wonders what crime she had committed. It turned out that her husband was a suspected Boko Haram leader, still at large, and the authorities hoped he would turn himself in so that his wife and children would be set free. He did not do so, and after having spent six months in a prison in Abuja the wife and children were freed. She won damages of N15mil (£60,000) in early 2012, which had still not been paid to her as I learnt her story over a year later.[112]

Another telling case was one involving A.T., a man arrested on September 2010 in Borno because he too was believed to be a member of Boko Haram. A magistrate's court ordered his release on bail but the police never obliged. Instead the man was transferred to a prison facility in Abuja. Bail was then granted in March 2011 but, again, he was simply transferred, this time back to Borno state. Apparently this is a common tactic used by the police to break the prisoner and extract information from him. Throughout his ordeal he was never allowed to see his family and his relatives had no idea of his fate. When the Legal Defence and Assistance Project (LEDAP) got involved, it took A.T.'s case to the Federal High Court in Abuja and, subsequently, to the ECOWAS Court.[113]

Sadly, cases of this sort are not uncommon and most of them are not brought to justice. People are disillusioned with the police and the judicial system and often families, after not hearing of or from their relatives for some while, assume they have been killed in custody and see no point in trying to protest or complain. Due process is severely undermined by the fact that people are immediately presumed guilty upon arrest and in the case of certain crimes such as kidnapping or terrorism, officers appear eager to remove the problem by executing the suspects. The judicial system is also hindered by corruption. Early arrests revealed that some Boko Haram militants were the children of the affluent upper class. In subsequent investigations, tardiness, absence of transparency and lack of convictions suggested a willingness to protect some of those detained.

In October 2013, Amnesty International reported that over 950 people had died in military custody in the first six months of 2013 alone.[114] This statistic was published in the wake of rumours indicating a shocking number of bodies being taken from Maiduguri prison— about ten to fifteen every day. These were the result of killings but also of sub-human conditions with little water and food provided to inmates who were kept within the Giwa military barracks, home to the 21st Armoured Brigade, in over-crowded cells.[115] Amnesty International has corroborated the information and collected details regarding an underground "dungeon" used for punishment.[116] In June 2013 a source from Maiduguri discussed with me some anecdotal evidence of "dozens" of bodies brought daily to the two morgues in Maiduguri carrying clear signs of torture, their identity unknown and autopsy forbidden. The same source estimated that 7,000 men had "disappeared" in Maiduguri alone during the previous three years.[117] Equally sub-human conditions are said to exist in the grimly named "Abattoir", a former meat-processing unit in Abuja used as a detention facility for Boko Haram suspects by the Special Anti-Robbery Squad (SARS).[118]

Given the horrific stories emanating from Giwa, it was hardly a surprise when hundreds of Boko Haram fighters launched an attack on the barracks in March 2014. Besides the attempt to free their fellow group members, Giwa is an evocative place in the context of the fight between Nigeria and Boko Haram. Around 600 people were killed by the army in an attempt to thwart the raid and prison escape. The government said that the vast majority of those killed were either Boko Haram members or criminals, while Amnesty International has claimed that civilians had died in the incident and most of the victims were unarmed inmates who should have been re-arrested rather than shot.[119]

A softer approach

In April 2013 I interviewed Dr Fatima Akilu from the office of the National Security Adviser (NSA). The Terrorism Prevention Act of 2011 (section 1A) granted the NSA office responsibility for coordinating activities related to counter terrorism and provided it with the mandate to:

> ensure the formulation and implementation of a comprehensive counterterrorism strategy, build capacity for the effective discharge of the functions of relevant security, intelligence, law enforcement and military services under the act and do such other acts or things that are necessary for the effective performance of the function of the relevant security and enforcement agencies under the act.[120]

This resulted in the creation of the position of counterterrorism coordinator in 2011 first held by former Director General of the Nigeria Intelligence Agency and army General Ambassador Zakari Ibrahim. At that point the National Focal Point on Terrorism, in existence since

2007 and consisting of elements from Customs, Immigration, the Ministry of Foreign Affairs and the State Security Service (SSS), appeared to have scaled down its activities and, to date, little is known about whether it still functions or not.[121]

Ambassador Ibrahim's career as counterterrorism coordinator was short-lived. In the aftermath of the Boko Haram attack on the UN building in Abuja in August 2011, President Jonathan removed him from office and in September appointed the former JTF Commander in the Niger Delta, Major General Sarkin Bello.[122] In his capacity as head of the Counter Terrorism Centre he has designed a counter terrorism strategy—NACTEST—that at the time of writing has yet to be released.

Dr Akilu heads the NSA's branch dealing with de-radicalisation and also a branch that seeks to lay the foundation for a softer approach to extremism—the Directorate of Behavioural Analysis and Strategic Communication. Akilu admitted that pre-Boko Haram, militants had been dealt with exclusively as a military matter and, perhaps owing to the larger scale of the current insurgency, a more sophisticated approach was needed—including de-radicalisation and counter-radicalisation programmes as well as strategic communications.[123]

Nigeria's programme is inspired by the experience of other countries—particularly Australia, Singapore, Indonesia, the UK, the US, Bangladesh and Turkey—and officials were often eager to describe it to me as the Nigerian equivalent of the British Prevent—one of the four 'Ps' in the UK counter-terrorism strategy "Contest" alongside Prepare, Pursue and Protect.[124]

Dr Akilu has ambitious plans to counter the radicalisation of young Muslims through community-inclusion programmes across the North, to work with local government and NGOs, and to map schools and religious teaching institutions to identify extreme preachers. A classification of imams has already been carried out at the state level in Katsina and Niger and the Federal Government is now proposing to extend the survey to other states, producing a register of "good" imams that would be part of a network of credible and moderate preachers and teachers. Longer term plans include a messaging platform to build long-term resilience to radicalisation in the broader sense beyond the Boko Haram threat, to teach individuals not to be afraid to question teachings that may fuel intolerance and violence, and to build a stronger sense of national identity and self-esteem. In addition, it is vital to promote inter-faith dialogue, which, albeit difficult, should at a minimum encourage religious leaders to speak with one single voice against extremism.[125]

De-radicalising Boko Haram militants poses several challenges but, like counter-radicalisation, there is no shortage of proposals coming from the National Security Adviser's office, including provisions for after-care following release from prison and involving cognitive behavioural methods to facilitate reintegration into society through sport, the arts, poetry, vocational training (in partnership with prospective employers) and even family therapy for some. As of 2014, only two convicted terrorists had been put through the de-radicalisation programme, suggesting that they had yet to be fully implemented. Besides, it is difficult to recruit people to run such programmes for fear of retaliation by Boko Haram, not to mention the shortage of those qualified to do the job who are properly trained to deal with prisoners.[126]

The lack of convictions of Boko Haram members, although they reached ten by August 2013 and forty by February 2014, is linked to several factors.[127] First, it cannot be denied that judges are afraid. In this sense the new approach involves selection, training and protection for judges ruling over terror cases. Similar arrangements are to be put in place for prosecutors and defence attorneys. Second, one could argue that the low number of convictions is a by-product of weak terror legislation. It was only in June 2011 that the president passed into law the Terrorism Prevention Act of 2011 and although this represented a significant step forward, the Act was ambiguous with regard to which agency should lead terror investigations.[128] Furthermore, as admitted by Interior Minister Abba Moro, an enormous judicial backlog and resulting extended pre-trial detention are severely affecting the expediency of the judicial system.[129] Trial delays were indeed identified by the US government as one of the key weaknesses of Nigerian counter-terrorism legislation.[130] Attempts were made at strengthening the legislation through an amendment of the Terrorism Prevention Act in June 2013. At that time, nearly a month after the state of emergency was declared in the North East, both Ansaru and Boko Haram were placed under the Act and proscribed as terrorist organisations. A minimum twenty year sentence was introduced for anyone directly or indirectly helping them.[131]

In spring 2014, National Security Adviser Mohammed Sambo Dasuki formally rolled out Nigeria's soft approach to countering terrorism during a press conference in Abuja on 14 March, only days after the Giwa barracks incident in Maiduguri.[132] Dasuki outlined the four-pronged "Prevent" strategy resulting from work conducted by Akilu's Behavioural Analysis and Strategic Communication units over an eighteenth-month period. The pillars of this approach are: (1) prison-based de-radicalisation run by the Ministry of the Interior; (2) counter-radicalisation through community engagement, the building of societal resilience the to counter extremist views, and education (this second pillar will benefit from support from the UN for training and capacity-building aimed at NGOs operating in the country—it also consists of a Countering Violent Extremism Programme involving federal, state and local government as well as NGOs, civil societies and religious leaders); (3) training in strategic communication for law enforcement and the military, public diplomacy courses for civil servants, and media training for reporters and public relations practitioners reporting on conflict; and (4) economic revitalisation, designed in partnership with the NSA's Economic Intelligence Unit, to alleviate poverty, revitalise the economy in the states most vulnerable to extremism—hence attempting to eliminate some of the root causes of terrorism. This last aspect has been championed by President Jonathan who in December 2013 had tasked the NSA and North-eastern leaders with designing a joint revitalisation plan.[133]

This softer approach did indeed evolve in 2013 and 2014 and, although projects are yet to be implemented and evaluated through a planned monitoring framework, these efforts show a move in the right direction. Resources are still limited but at least Akilu's Directorate is no longer two-people strong. As of 2014 there are teams specialising in de-radicalisation and counter-radicalisation, as well as cooperation with the Defence Academy and the civil service to deal with, respectively, strategic communication and public diplomacy. The latter, albeit less talked about, is of particular value to avoid unfortunate instances of "communication mistakes". For instance, following multiple bomb attacks on beer parlours in Kano in July 2013, the military issued a statement blaming the public for having failed to be vigilant and spot suspicious packages being placed in the area which turned out to contain explosives.[134] Given the already fragile, not to say tense atmosphere in some areas, and fraught relationship between the authorities and the public, statements of this sort do nothing but further victimise civilians, who not only fear Boko Haram first, and the military second, but are now being blamed even when they are the victims of violence.

There have been advances in the training of prosecutors, in witness protection and in crime scene management, and there are plans to have two dedicated prisons to exclusively house convicted terrorists and those awaiting trial on terror charges. According to a reliable source, one facility will be in Abuja while the location of the second one has not been disclosed.[135] Given the issues related to the high number of out-of-school children and the *almajirai* that I discussed extensively earlier in the book, the fact that many of the counter-radicalisation efforts are centred on education is no doubt encouraging. Indeed a new education platform unveiled in May 2014 and a "creative" curriculum is to be introduced as early as primary school level to encourage arts, sport and music and to build moral responsibility and a sense of belonging. These extra-curricular activities also have the aim of countering the unintended segregation that is often manifested in schools. In fact, many children attend schools wherein the demographic is quite homogenous in terms of ethnicity and faith. By encouraging activities such as sports in stadiums, pupils from different schools can be brought together and experience diversity. Strategically, there are plans to link education to national objectives, i.e. as the country tries to diversify its economy away from one that is almost entirely reliant on the oil industry, education can be targeted to provide the skills required for the sectors that will be prioritised in the future such as agriculture and technology.[136]

These promising plans are hindered by several challenges, including the lack of schools and the often poor conditions and standards of the existing ones, the absence of a more robust policy framework for education, and the controversial, albeit widespread, stigmatisation of the *almajirici* system. As for the latter, not enough schools have been built and the authorities are arguably not targeting the youth groups most at risk of radicalisation and recruitment into the ranks of Boko Haram. In April 2013 a plan to establish over a hundred such schools at the cost of 5 billion naira was unveiled. By the summer, Minister of State for Education Ezenwo Nyesom Wike announced that 124 of the 148 *Tsangaya* (Qur'anic schools) built by the Federal Government would open in September.[137] [138] The *Tsangaya* are likely to have no impact on youth groups that have no affiliation to the Qur'anic school system such as the *Yan-ci-rani* (migrants fleeing harsh conditions bro in rural areas)

of the US administration.
m extremism and terror-
ed as a country that was
nce keen on cooperating
TSCTP[152]—even though
nowledge the extent of the
as to be noted that even
gh levels, there was a ten-
al connections in speeches
se of the use of the word
ntion and, with it, aid.
have trained the Nigerian
the latter's 72nd Counter-
ed as the first ever entirely
try training by 3rd Special
53 Regrettably, the US later
the latter was not believed,
54 As a result of allegations
DRO, limitations have been
assistance under TSCTP.[155]
014 of the Nigerian Army's
tackle terrorism and insur-
nce from AFRICOM, the
d the Office of Security
n also agreed to the transfer
C.[157] It is telling that the
ny Staff during the "Counter-
Learned Exchange" between
er indicates the continuing
e US stood by Nigeria in the
tions of 2014 and the State
e Nigerian government, con-
though no details were made
s followed a resolution intro-
overnment to assist a rescue
l the setting up of a special
Abuja, comprising military,
situations, to help locate the

and the *Yan Tauri* (street urchins) who, because of their socio-economic situation, are susceptible to negative influences.

COIN vs CT: What strategy?

Given that this volume refers throughout to the Boko Haram "insurgency", one might be puzzled by the preceding discussion on counter-"terrorism". There is anti-terror legislation in place in Nigeria, a counterterrorism coordinator in office, and President Jonathan himself had often described Boko Haram as terrorists even before formally designating the group in June 2013.

Beside the mere issues of definition and labelling, should we consider Boko Haram as a counter-insurgency (COIN) or a counterterrorism (CT) problem?

Counter-insurgency expert David Kilcullen describes insurgency as:

> a struggle for control over a contested political space, between a state (or group of states or occupying powers), and one or more popularly based, non-state challengers. Insurgencies are popular uprisings that grow from, and are conducted through pre-existing social networks (village, tribe, family, neighbourhood, political or religious party) and exist in a complex social, informational and physical environment.[139]

Although others might describe insurgency slightly differently, this is a broadly accepted way of depicting the phenomenon.[140] When it comes to terrorism, things are more complicated, as no widely accepted definition exists; indeed, the debate is ongoing.[141] The British government's convincing definition of terrorism is as follows:

> [t]he use or threat of action designed to influence the government or an international governmental organisation or to intimidate the public, or a section of the public; made for the purposes of advancing a political, religious, racial or ideological cause; and it involves or causes: serious violence against a person; serious damage to a property; a threat to a person's life; a serious risk to the health and safety of the public; or serious interference with or disruption to an electronic system.[142]

Boko Haram's activities can be characterised as an insurgency campaign involving a terrorist component, as represented by suicide attacks against high-profile targets such as the UN building and the Police HQ in Abuja in 2011. Terrorist tactics are used to raise the group's standing and to further Boko Haram's ultimate goal to Islamise Nigeria, which is

at the heart of their insurgency. Boko Haram represe
the convergence of terrorist, insurgent, and criminal
turn requires a full-spectrum counter-insurgency ap
counter-terrorism and regular law enforcement eleme
out when the Nigerian Army's Counter-Terrorist an
gency Centre, based at the Armed Forces Command
in Jaji, Kaduna, began training an additional 3,000
and counter-insurgency specialists on subjects ran
patrol to unarmed combat and humanitarian law.

These efforts fall under the category of Military C
Than War (MOOTW) within Nigerian military doc
counter-insurgency and counter-terrorism operations
ples. More specifically, MOOTW initiatives have prom
turing of military forces to ensure Nigeria possesses th
address a full spectrum of challenges requiring the rapid
troops locally, nationally or internationally. An example c
the establishment of a Quick Deployment Force within t
2010. In the context of the campaign against Boko Haram
the deployment of a Light Utility Helicopter to the In
Operations (ISO) in Borno and Bauchi states and of N
helicopters to Maiduguri.[143]

Western response

Given the scale of the Nigerian economy, its strategic role
nent, and the large presence of foreign nationals in the coun
as no surprise that a number of non-African states are w
unfolding Northern insurgency with concern—especially t
the United States and the United Kingdom.

The United States (US)

Nigeria-US relations strengthened in 1999 when the first civ
dent took office in Abuja. Nigeria is now the US' number o
partner in Sub-Saharan Africa[144] and through the US-Nigeria
Commission, inaugurated in 2010, the two countries engag
aimed at fostering progress in four areas: good governance, tran
and integrity; Energy and investment; Food security and ag

threats of African partners differed from that
A case in point was Senegal, which did not de
ism as priorities. Conversely Nigeria was cit
particularly vulnerable to such threats and h
with the US and others under the aegis of the
the Nigerian authorities had been slow to ack
Boko Haram insurgency. Nevertheless, it h
before the violence had reached its current h
dency to overblow Boko Haram's internation
aimed at a foreign audience knowing that u
"terrorism" is sure to attract international att

As alluded to earlier, US Special Forces
Army for some time, the best example bein
terrorist Battalion, which in 2010 was deplo
Special Forces Battalion following in-coun
Forces Group, Fort Bragg, North Carolina.
decided to suspend training for the 72nd as
by the Americans, to be achieving its goals.
of human rights abuses perpetrated by JTF
imposed on the continued US training and
[156] Nevertheless, the establishment in early
Special Operations Command (NASOC) t
gency was made possible through assista
Special Operations Command Africa a
Operations at the US Embassy. Washingto
of some equipment destined for NASO
announcement was made by the Chief of Arr
Terrorism and Counter-Insurgency Lessons
the US and Nigeria in Abuja, which furth
cooperation between the two countries. Th
aftermath of the Chibok schoolgirl abdu
Department, further to discussions with th
firmed its willingness to support Nigeria, a
available on the nature of such support. Th
duced by American senators to urge the
operation.[158] In May, the US announce
coordination cell within the Embassy in
law enforcement and experts in hostage
missing girls.[159]

One of the tools available to foreign countries to tackle groups such as Boko Haram and to signal that the threat posed by them and their individual members may have repercussions at home is the proscription process. In the case of the US this translated into the designation as Foreign Terrorist Organisations under Section 219 of the Immigration and Nationality Act or, in the case of individuals, as Specially Designated Global Terrorists under section 1(b) of Executive Order 13224.[160]

The US government has been quite active in this respect and as of mid 2012 it has targeted many individuals and groups active across the Sahel and West Africa including, and affiliated with, MUJWA, Ansar al-Dine, AQIM and the al-Mulathameen Battalion, the latter including the Those Who Sign in Blood Battalion and al-Murabitoun.[161]

On 21 June 2012 the US Department of State designated Boko Haram leader Abubakar Shekau alongside two other members: Khalid al-Barnawi, believed to be Ansaru's leader, and Abubakar Adam Kambar,[162] considered by the Nigerian forces to be Boko Haram's "main link with AQIM and al-Shabaab".[163] Curiously, in June 2013 Nigerian senior officers claimed that Kambar had been killed by the Nigerian Army in March 2012, three months before the official US designation.[164] In an unprecedented move, in June 2013 the Department of State offered a total reward of $23 million for information leading to the capture of five designated terrorists active in West and North Africa, including a $7million bounty on Shekau alone, signalling the US' greater concern for the region and threats emanating from it.[165] Shekau is now a "third-tier" wanted terrorist in the US Rewards for Justice Programme, behind the likes of Mullah Omar, the spiritual leader of the Taleban ($10 million reward) and al-Qaeda leader Ayman al-Zawahiri ($25 million reward) who tops the list.[166]

Some elements within the US government have been very vocal in advocating the proscription of entire groups operating in the region, especially Boko Haram, as opposed to the simple targeting of key individuals.

When after months of discussion, in June 2012 the US Department of State designated Boko Haram's leader Abubakr Shekau, the administration opted not to designate the group as a Foreign Terrorist Organisation (FTO), in a decision later defended by Assistant Secretary of State for African Affairs Ambassador Johnnie Carson before the House of Representatives in July. Carson argued that the designation of senior members was sufficient and that going down the FTO route would grant the group greater status and notoriety than it deserved. This stance has been widely criticised, especially in Republican quarters and in Nigeria where it is seen as an indicator of the Boko Haram threat not being taken seriously in spite of a surge in attacks and reports of collaboration between the Nigerian sect and major Islamist groups.[167]

In this respect, one of the first Western senior officials to raise the alarm vis-à-vis African extremist groups was US General Carter Ham (then AFRICOM's Commander) who in summer 2011 indicated that Boko Haram had made contacts with AQIM and al-Shabaab. At the time it was unclear what links existed among the groups, but Ham reiterated his concerns in February 2012 when he warned the US Congress that Boko Haram, AQIM and al-Shabaab were looking at ways to synchronise their efforts, something which, in his view, would pose a "real challenge" to the United States.[168]

Furthermore, a document published by the Committee on Homeland Security's Subcommittee on Counterterrorism and Intelligence entitled "Boko Haram—Emerging Threat to the US Homeland" (2011) clearly indicated that a portion of the American administration held an alarmist view that Boko Haram would, like al-Qaeda in the Arabian Peninsula (AQAP) and the Tehrik-i-Taliban Pakistan (TTP), defy the intelligence community and transform, going from posing a localised threat to becoming an international terror group capable of staging attacks against the United States.[169]

Unquestionably there have been some Boko Haram statements explicitly mentioning Washington. In 2010, for instance, Shakau identified America as a new target when releasing a message to "Infidels, hypocrites and apostates: do not think jihad is over. Rather jihad has just begun, America, die with your fury",[170] and in January 2012 he pointed his finger at Barack Obama accusing the President of "waging war on Islam."[171] Hence it has become a legitimate question whether the group's intention to attack the US could rapidly move from the aspirational to the concrete.

Similar concerns were voiced in a second report for the House of Representatives in 2013, this time titled "Boko Haram. Growing Threat to the US Homeland", where the Committee staff determined that Boko Haram remained "a lethal and growing threat to the people of Nigeria, the international community, Americans in the region, and potentially the United States Homeland"[172] and again recommended the proscription of the group deeming the designation of key members not sufficient to stop individuals in the US from supporting Boko Haram. The document also emphasised the transnational angle making it clear that capacity-building was needed in Nigeria's neighbours.[173]

Boko Haram and Ansaru were finally designated as FTO on 14 November 2013—a step very much welcomed in Abuja.[174] The proscription amounts to:

> a prohibition against knowingly providing, or attempting or conspiring to provide, material support or resources to, or engaging in transactions with, Boko Haram and Ansaru, and the freezing of all property and interests in property of the organizations that are in the United States, or come within the United States or the control of US persons[175]

It remains reasonable to discount Boko Haram's capability, or even true intention, to stage an attack in the US although there is a substantial Nigerian-American community of over one million people living there and no shortage of direct flights connecting the two countries.[176] Perhaps a true concern is the possibility of attacks against US interests in the region. The first that comes to mind is oil from the Niger Delta. Yet, over the past decade Nigerian oil exports to the US have decreased and accounted for only around 4 per cent of US imports in 2013.[177] Moreover Boko Haram has not been able to penetrate the Niger Delta where the oil is extracted in spite of a warning by Shekau in February 2014 of potential attacks in the region and the targeting of the family home, in Borno state, of the Commander of the Joint Task Force in the Niger Delta.[178] As I have argued elsewhere, establishing a foothold in the South would prove particularly difficult due to the limited support Boko Haram enjoys there and to the presence of a number of groups, the most notorious being the Movement for the Emancipation of the Niger Delta (MEND) and the Niger Delta People's Volunteer Force (NDPVF), which had accepted a lucrative amnesty deal with the central government in 2009 in return for halting attacks on oil installations.[179] Both have spelled out that they will resist any attempt by Boko Haram to disrupt their homeland.[180]

But there are other concerns for the American citizens who are involved in a number of development projects in the North including in the health and education sectors. In particular, the targeting of polio immunisation workers in Kano[181] and elsewhere, and the killing of many teachers and students has forced USAID and other agencies and NGOs to review their practices. For instance, since December 2012 USAID has de-branded its operations in the North for fear of being targeted and diplomats are allowed little freedom of movement outside the capital.[182]

The United Kingdom (UK)

The United Kingdom has close historic ties to Nigeria born of their shared colonial past and today Nigeria remains the UK's second-most important business partner in Sub-Saharan Africa. In military terms, the UK has had a strong influence on Nigeria not least by mentoring senior officers training at the Armed Forces Command and Staff College, Jaji, through the provision of funding for training and military facilities such as the Peacekeeping Wing at Jaji, the delivery of actual training, and the hosting of Nigerian officers at the Advanced Command and Staff Course at the Defence Academy.[183] In addition, over time Nigeria has hosted officers as part of the British Defence Advisory Team (BDAT) to support the professionalisation of the Nigerian Armed Forces to perform both peacekeeping and domestic roles.[184]

A key focus of such cooperation has been insecurity in the Niger Delta where attacks against oil installations, oil bunkering and kidnappings have become a serious threat in both security and economic terms. In March 2013 the two countries signed a five-year Memorandum of Understanding (MOU) strengthening bilateral cooperation against maritime insecurity and terrorism which had at its core the fight against oil theft in the Niger Delta.[185] On signing the document, the British minister Andrew Robathan, MP, emphasised the fact that Boko Haram was perceived as a threat to British interests in the region.[186] The conflation of anti-piracy and anti-oil bunkering on one hand and terrorism on the other is somehow questionable and was indeed criticised.[187] Nonetheless the signing of the memorandum took place less than two months after the British government's announcement of a 240-strong deployment of non-combat troops to Mali, Nigeria and Sierra Leone to build "upstream capacity" through advising and training local militaries. It is not entirely surprising therefore that given the Malian crisis and the proliferation of extremist groups across West Africa and the Sahel, terrorism was high on the agenda and received a special mention in the MOU.[188] Above and beyond that, ongoing links between the Chiefs of Defence Staff of the two countries centred on deepening counter-terrorism cooperation primarily in the form of specialised training assistance that London would provide Abuja.[189]

With the deteriorating security situation in the North, counter-terrorism has indeed become a bigger priority in bilateral relations. In 2011 a heads of government meeting between President Jonathan and Prime Minister Cameron resulted in the creation of a new counterterrorism co-operation framework as part of which Britain would provide advisers, train Nigerian counter-terrorism specialists and help set up a response mechanism for terrorism incidents modelled around the British Cabinet Office Briefing Room (COBR).[190] Possibly the most significant instance of military cooperation occurred in 2012. Then, British Special Forces participated in the failed operation to free Chris McManus and Franco Lamolinara from their Ansaru kidnappers.[191] This led to London proscribing Ansaru as a terrorist organisation later that year under the Terrorism Act 2000.[192]

Military exchanges have occasionally been marred by controversy. A 2013 EU-funded report by the Platform organisation questions the high level of British military aid to Nigeria—nearly £12 million between 2001 and 2010—as being primarily motivated by the protection of British energy interests in the Niger Delta, and without sufficient scrutiny of how newly acquired military equipment and skills would be used by Nigerian security forces, given their reputation for committing human rights abuses.[193] Concerns over human rights abuses that have been holding back the Americans and led to a slow down of their training of Nigerian forces have similarly affected the British. Related problems, for instance, had hampered relations in the past when, in 1993, the decision by the Nigerian government not to move to democratic civilian rule resulted in a ban from British military training facilities of Nigerian officers and the withdrawal of UK military advisers as well as of funding for the National War College in Lagos.[194] More recently, the Head of the FCO's Counter-Terrorism Department, Simon Shercliff, highlighted on-going concerns over Nigerian practices and the dilemma posed by cooperating with countries that at times fail to meet human rights standards:

We cannot afford to be, for example, handing over intelligence on Nigerian terrorists for the Nigerians then to go and find the people and hang them up by their toenails…So we assist the Nigerians to go round the place and find the terrorists, because that is very much in our national interest, and at the same time—from the top level of political exhortation to the practical capacity building level—we continually exhort them to do their work while maintaining international standards of human rights. You can't do one without the other.[195]

The above statement was collected as part of an inquiry by Parliament's Foreign Affairs Committee into Britain's response to extremism and political instability in North and West Africa, which was published in March 2014. Members of the Committee looked into the factors that contributed to the crisis in Mali, whether they were at risk of arising elsewhere in the wider region, and the UK's policy on dealing with them, including its work with international partners to combat extremism and instability.[196] Although it was the In Amenas attack in Algeria in January 2013 and the Malian crisis that galvanised the initial impetus for the inquiry—after all David Cameron himself had spoken (in overly alarmist terms) of an "existential" threat emanating from the region[197]— the interconnectedness of groups operating there, including Boko Haram and Ansaru's presence in Mali, and the declared state of emergency in North Eastern Nigeria led to the broadening of the inquiry's scope to include the Nigerian insurgency. In addition, this was followed by the Woolwich attack (May 2013) in which two British-born Nigerian men killed Private Lee Rigby in south London in what was treated as a terrorist incident. Both were raised as Christians but later converted to Islam, and one of the perpetrators had previously been arrested in Kenya for allegedly trying to travel to Somalia to train with al-Shabaab. In Britain, Michael Adebolajo was also allegedly linked to an outlawed Islamist organisation, al-Muhjiroun.[198]

When I was called to give evidence at the inquiry, I was asked for my views on the threat facing Britain and, more specifically, the risk of a direct Nigerian extremist attack on UK soil. I did not at the time, and still do not now, see a connection between extremist activities in Britain and what is happening in Northern Nigeria; indeed I would categorise the Woolwich attackers as "home-grown terrorists". In my conversations with counter-terrorism practitioners they confirmed my sense that Nigeria is not really seen by Islamist extremists in the West as a "theatre of jihad".

Nor are Mohammed Yusuf or Abubakar Shakau well known outside the region and therefore they are unlikely to be a source of inspiration for extremists beyond Nigeria and its immediate neighbourhood.[199]

Ironically, the day I posted a short piece[200] questioning the threat to Britain posed by Nigerian extremism, the government announced that Boko Haram would join Ansaru on the list of proscribed terrorist organisations.[201] By doing so, the police were granted powers to pursue any individual operating on behalf of Boko Haram or supporting the group in the United Kingdom.[202] This took place in July 2013, one month after Nigeria had gone down the same route. Rather than signifying a perceived direct threat to the UK, the proscription was a way of backing Nigeria's effort in the context of international cooperation, and private conversations with the Foreign Office seemed to confirm this interpretation.[203]

Taking a step back, it was November 2012 when Shekau made his first direct reference to the UK in one of his videos, the first in which he spoke in Arabic instead of Hausa:

> Nigeria and other crusaders, meaning America and Britain, should witness, and the Jews of Israel who are killing the Muslims in Palestine should witness…that we are with our mujahideen brothers in the cause of Allah everywhere.[204]

Again, as in the case of the United States, the localised ambitions, i.e. to Islamise Nigeria, and relatively limited capabilities make it unlikely that Boko Haram would attack Britain. Instead, British nationals living in Nigeria—who number approximately 40,000—and commercial interests may face a more immediate risk.[205] There have been media reports suggesting that the Security Service (MI5) had begun to keep an eye on the Nigerian diaspora in late 2011 and early 2012, ahead of that year's Olympic Games to be hosted in London.[206] This was possibly motivated by concerns that Nigerian nationals with radicalised views might try to enter the UK and that therefore the Service should not discount such a possibility. One should however keep in mind that, although Nigerians represent the largest African diaspora in Britain (figures vary from 190,000, provided by the FCO, to 1.5 million according to the Central Association of Nigerians in the United Kingdom, although discrepancies may depend on whether calculations include UK citizens of Nigerian origin),[207] Muslims represent only around 9 per cent of them and the vast majority of the Nigerian community consists of well-educated professionals, confessionally Christian of one sort or another, from southern Nigerian states. Curiously, Nigerian visitors (non-residents) are among the foreign nationals who spend the most while in the United Kingdom. In 2014 they replaced Russians as the third highest spenders in that league table.[208] This of course does not imply that wealthy individuals may not espouse extremist ideologies or commit violenct acts, nevertheless the evidence indicates that the bulk of the Boko Haram membership consists of unemployed young men. For this reason, initiatives funded by the Department for International Development (DFID), such as the Nigeria Stability and Reconciliation Programme (NSRP)—implemented by the British Council in eight states, including five affected by Boko Haram—are very important as, among other strands of work, they address key economic factors driving violent conflict and work to reduce grievances related to the lack of job opportunities for the youth and uneven distribution of resources.[209]

Canada

Perhaps surprisingly, the latest Western country to take measures against Boko Haram has been Canada, proscribing the group under the Canadian Criminal Code in December 2013.[210] Canada is involved in regional capacity-building in the Sahel, particularly in the context of the Global Counter-Terrorism Forum, and already in 2012 had pledged to support Abuja's efforts to counter the northern insurgency as well as to increase business cooperation.[211] Regrettably, a Canadian national was kidnapped in April 2014 in Cameroon. The nun had been a missionary in the country since 1979 and it is likely that she was targeted for being a Westerner and, possibly, a Christian, rather than because of her nationality.[212]

7

CONCLUSIONS

So, what is Boko Haram? The people I encountered in Nigeria, from religious leaders (Muslims and Christians) to generals, from government ministers to taxi drivers, from foreign diplomats to academics, from human rights activists to security specialists, all had an opinion, often at variance from one another. I was told that the group was "completely political",[1] but then someone else argued that Boko Haram was a mainly ideological (read religious) entity with sleeper cells everywhere "to instigate religious warfare".[2] Another opinion offered was someone who saw Boko Haram as "a clear example of Samuel Huntington's *Clash of Civilizations*" built on deep-seated suspicion of anything Western.[3] The same interviewee, an Admiral, characterised militants as "criminals who appeal to collective sensitivities".[4]

I prefer to describe it as a violent Islamist movement waging an insurgency campaign that includes terrorist tactics such as suicide attacks. Given the escalation of violence, the diversification of attacks into suicide operations and kidnappings, the use of more sophisticated weapons, including those favoured by the army and armoured fighting vehicles (stolen from the military) and a significant criminal element, I would place Boko Haram in the category of a hybrid security challenge.

Recent years have seen an increase in the number of conflicts that less and less resemble traditional warfare and instead increasingly manifest themselves as hybrid forms of insecurity overwhelmingly affecting developing countries. All regions of the developing world present case studies indicating a convergence of conflict, insurgency, terrorism and criminal elements. This often results in high numbers of casualties and displaced persons, the slowdown or suspension of economic activities, and even the loss of state control over parts of the territory. All these consequences have been experienced in northern Nigeria.

Settling upon a definition, and I do not expect to have the last word on this, is rather important, not so much because of any real need to label a group, sect or movement, but rather in order to design an appropriate approach that includes *effective* countermeasures tackling both violence and the underlying narrative. In order to respond to hybrid security challenges state responses have to be more imaginative and to combine different strategic approaches and tactics which may, or may not, prove successful. In this respect, the deployment of JTF-ORO, featuring military *and* civilian components, was a shrewd move although one may argue that using the military in a civilian context, where the enemy hides among the local population, may result in a number of unfortunate consequences, not least because soldiers are normally trained to inflict maximum damage on their opponents (as per conventional conflict situations), whereas in internal security operations restraint should be exercised to avoid alienating one's fellow citizens.[5]

Addressing such challenges is likely to highlight pre-existing structural weaknesses that undermine the effectiveness of the security and defence apparatus of the countries in question, and determines whether foreign intervention is ultimately necessary to bring back stability, as in the case of French intervention in northern Mali in January 2013 and, to an extent, the several offers of support for Nigeria following the Chibok abductions in April 2014.

Receiving foreign help, be it in the form of capacity-building, advisory roles or boots on the ground is no simple panacea, an easy fix to end all problems. Indeed it is likely to crystallise tensions between seeking foreign support and keeping one's partners at an arm's length for fear of facing domestic criticism. These interactions can be challenging to deal with when partners have different priorities, such as the protecting of human rights, or when a party becomes reluctant to share intelligence or work too closely with a foreign partner for fear that corruption or collusion between government forces and militants or criminals may be exposed.

Throughout the preceding chapters we have observed the cyclicality with which extreme religiously motivated movements have emerged over time in Nigeria, particularly in the post-colonial period, and how the government has dealt with them—usually through ignoring demands, crushing the groups in question and forcing the remaining members to go underground only to re-emerge a few years later under a different name but with often similar objectives. Frustratingly, it has been possible to observe how—in spite of the many historical precedents I described above—the Nigerian security forces found themselves unprepared in the face of Boko Haram's campaign of violence. There was nothing particularly innovative about Boko Haram—the only real novelty is that in the twenty-first century groups of this sort benefit from advances in communication and information technology their predecessors could never have imagined. This has made it possible for Shakau's followers—and other otherwise localised groups with national rather than international agendas—to expand their repertoire of tactics and draw financial support, training and weapons from more sophisticated, better established and internationalised violent extremists. Moreover, for too long the Nigerian government refused to admit that a problem that had started in the form of a secluded, isolated sect had turned into a force for social mobilisation—at times to be exploited for political gain—and then degenerated into an uncontrollable monster with links to al-Qaeda. And when that admission came it was, sadly, too late.

I did not embark on this project with the aim of pointing my finger at the Nigerian government and its security forces. Mistakes have been made—whether the initial denial of the problem's magnitude, the extra-judicial killings, or the (in my view premature) removal of the JTF as the leading force in the anti-Boko Haram effort, to mention some of the most significant issues. Nevertheless, I fully acknowledge the complexity of the theatre in which the operation is being conducted—a friend of mine recently reminded me that Borno state alone was 2.5 times the size of Helmand province in Afghanistan, in which the British military had deployed an entire division. Geographical factors aside, Boko Haram or not, Nigeria presents a challenging environment. It is indeed an African super-power economically, militarily and diplomatically but is also a country facing a range of challenges, from corruption[6] to the effects of climate change,[7] which require political attention, effort and resources.

The Way Ahead?

Regrettably living conditions have continued to decline among those people inhabiting the areas where the state of emergency was declared in May 2013, particularly as concerns food scarcity and a wider economic slowdown. Curfews and restrictions on movement have seen food prices tripling, and the costs of transport and communications have also gone up. The temporary closure of borders has naturally affected trade on both sides, Nigerian and foreign.[8] In November 2013 the State Ministry of Agriculture indicated that 20,000 farmers had been displaced in Borno and farmers in the Northeast had lost three billion naira in food crop revenues as a direct result of the Boko Haram crisis.[9] Even though agriculture has been so badly affected by the insurgency, it could still offer the way out of poverty for people in Borno and neighbouring states if more is done to support this sector. A Borno government official was adamant when I spoke to him that "the North can feed the South" and that if agriculture were properly developed it would create many jobs and that up to 300,000 hectares could be exploited in Borno alone. It would also rejuvenate the North East. It could even address the imbalance whereby "all the resources go to the South".[10] A more aggressive focus may even translate into an export-led economy and in this respect the Finance Minister Ngozi Okonjo-Iweala announced in January 2014 the forthcoming introduction of a 5 billion naira intervention programme, the Federal Initiative for the North East (FINE), aimed at rehabilitating the Northeast and providing assistance to farmers.[11] This initiative is no doubt worth monitoring and it is to be hoped it involves ameliorating electricity supply, one of Nigeria's greatest infrastructural weaknesses. The issue of repeated power shortages may sound trivial to a non-Nigerian audience, but when one visits the country one realises the level of disruption they cause in spite of the use of generators. And this becomes even more serious a consideration as unreliable electricity supply is an impediment to economic development. A 2006 report commissioned by Public Services International (PSI) on water and electricity concluded that "[t] here is general agreement that the system currently suffers from inefficiency and corruption" and emphasises the mistakes made through the privatisation process.[12] Therefore, ensuring a steady supply of electricity is paramount to kick-start the economy in areas that are unable to cash in on "petrol dollars" and that are suffering from severe poverty, such as the states of the North Eastern Nigeria where the Boko Haram insurgency is primarily concentrated.[13]

Education is the other area where more work needs to be done. At the World Economic Forum in Abuja (April 2014), the UN Special Envoy for Global Education Gordon Brown announced Safe Schools, an initiative made possible by the Nigerian business community to ensure the right to education for the millions of children in Nigeria who currently have no access to it or who can no longer attend classes for fear of being killed or abducted by Boko Haram. It would be interesting to see the results of the pilot scheme and, following the initial support offered by business, who will fund (and to what extent) the initiative so that it can be rolled out across the North. The vicious attacks on schools that Boko Haram has carried out have already prevented millions of kids from going to school, learning, taking their exams and building a path out of poverty. Over time this is going to translate in to many fewer graduates from northern states as only the children of the elite, those who can afford education elsewhere, will be able to attend school. This is going to further hinder the development of the region and create an additional imbalance between North and South as senior positions in Nigeria's public life will likely be held by those with higher levels of education in a way that is worryingly reminiscent of the post-colonial era.

This divide is also manifested in the way many outside the affected states think of Boko Haram as "a problem of the North". This is true of my friends in Lagos but also of many politicians. The latter is perhaps one of the reasons why it took so long before the Federal Government acknowledged the seriousness of the problem. If nothing else, the international protests and online campaign following the mass abduction of over 200 girls in Chibok have put Boko Haram on the international community's map and alerted the public to their existence (although the Western media continue to cover attacks very selectively). More importantly for Nigeria, the widespread outrage about the kidnapping but also over the highly criticised government response to it brought home to President Jonathan the fact that he is perceived internationally as ineffectual, which, one hopes, should prompt some reflection on his part.

If President Jonathn does stand for re-election in 2015, how will the millions of Northerners who already oppose his current term react?[14] One should anticipate some violence during the campaign, as is often the case, while Boko Haram—not exactly a fan of democracy—has previously targeted polling stations. One cannot help but recall how some founder members of Boko Haram were hired by politicians to act as their personal thugs and to intimidate electoral rivals, only to evolve into something much more sinister. Have Nigeria's politicians learnt their lesson, and will they resist this old practice?

The other aspect that it is impossible to ignore is how the Boko Haram problem has become politicised, with parties accusing one another and even claiming that rivals support the group or are members of it. A recently published cartoon neatly encapsulates this tension. An FBI officer asks the President for a list of all Boko Haram militants. The President replies: "That's easy! I'll let you have the list of APC members!" Such grandstanding apart, there is a real danger that the Boko Haram threat will become just another political football ahead of the elections while, in fact, not being really addressed the way it should.

Beyond addressing the obvious and serious shortcoming of the Nigerian military, namely human rights abuses it is fundamental that trust is built/re-built between the security services as a whole and the civilian population. This should go hand in hand with additional training and ensuring that a greater defence budget actually results in better pay for the soldiers and better equipment so that they can do their job without getting killed. What does the future hold for a country whose people fear those who are meant to protect them almost as much as they do Boko Haram? This feeling is paralelled by a broader sense of pervasive injustice that makes people abandon hope when their relatives are arrested, knowing that in all likelihood they will never see their husbands, brothers or sons again, regardless of whether or not they are actually guilty of something, Boko Haram-related or otherwise. Changing the culture of impunity, redressing wrongs and providing compensation for those who deserve it are essential steps in establishing a social contract between the government and its people, which is something that appears to be broken in many parts of the country and makes citizens reluctant to report incidents, suspected terrorist activities or other issues to the authorities.

While I would like to end this book on a positive note, unless structural and societal issues are addressed, no state of emergency, military deployment or even foreign intervention will grant lasting stability to

Nigeria. Even if the military is successful in crushing the current manifestation of Boko Haram, a new version will most likely present itself, sooner or later, feeding on unresolved grievances and inequality.

EPILOGUE

A few months have passed. Records indicate that over 6,300 civilian lives were lost over the course of 2014 in addition to the lives of more than 1,200 security forces and militants.[1] Violence has indeed escalated: attacks were up 40 per cent on 2013 and the announcement of an alleged ceasefire in October once again proved unfounded.[2] The supposed agreement went as far as involving the release of the Chibok girls—who, sadly, remain missing as I write these final thoughts in February 2015.

The states of Borno and Adamawa in particular have been heavily targeted: abductions and suicide bombings (many featuring women as the perpetrators) have continued unabated, the city of Kano has been the stage of bloody attacks including one allegedly aimed at the new Emir, former Governor of the Central Bank Lamido Sanusi.[3] Controversially, he would later call on Nigerians to arm themselves against Boko Haram and, as a result, Abubakar Shekau has issued a direct threat accusing the Emir of being a "fake Muslim".[4] Today, 13 February, the headlines read "Nigeria's Boko Haram militants attack Chad for first time".[5] Niger was subjected to the same fate a week ago.[6]

Boko Haram's advance has been relentless. A swathe of territory that according to some estimates might be as large as Belgium is believed to have fallen under Shekau's control in what he calls his 'caliphate'. The latter term is itself rather controversial. As more accurate translations of the Arabic language message become available, it is likely that Shekau had been announcing the establishment of a state in Gwoza rather than a caliphate.[7] Regardless, either label is misleading: there is no evidence indicating that any form of administration or governance is being implemented in this 'Islamic state'.

In a move that appeared to amount to the encirclement of Maiduguri, the group proved determined to gain control over Borno's capital city which had been Boko Haram's key stronghold before the military effort pushed fighters to rural areas. Besides, Maiduguri has a double symbolic value: first as the set of the infamous 2009 Battle of Maiduguri which resulted in the killing of Mohammed Yusuf. Second, Maiduguri seats on the remnants of the Kanem-Bornu Empire which, arguably, Shakau aims to recreate, as suggested by his choice of targets in neighbouring countries which fall within what was once the Empire.[8]

These already grim accounts have, if possible, an even darker tone. Increasingly, the vulnerability of the now over 1.5 million conflict-displaced persons has been exploited by unscrupulous individuals. Reports are emerging of girls taken from refugee camps and sold as slaves. Sexual and physical abuse is common. The same camps also present an opportunity for child traffickers to prey on the many orphans left behind by the insurgency.[9]

The crescendo of violence beyond Nigerian borders is what has catalysed international attention to possibly an unprecedented extent. Attacks in Cameroon, repeated abductions, including of the wife of Deputy Prime Minister Amadou Ali (released in October)[10] and the mass kidnapping of children in January sparked a wave of international outrage and—I dare to say, finally—a sense of urgency. This is not to suggest that the Chibok incident and the resulting #BringBackOurGirls campaign had not resonated around the world. Yet, at the risk of being excessively harsh, hashtags do little to save young girls from captivity, let alone end an insurgency. Furthermore, offers of help had been predominantly confined to intelligence and surveillance (and I explained in chapter six how difficult that form of cooperation and exchange can be) and proposed initiatives including the formation of a regional multinational force failed to materialise. This force, in particular, had been agreed upon back in July at the time when Nigeria, Niger, Chad and Cameroon had pledged to jointly deploy 2,800 troops at a summit hosted by Britain.

What is now clear is that the borderlands that had for years been used by Boko Haram as safe havens have become fighting grounds. Cameroon is now playing a more decisive military role as a result of increased Boko Haram's activity in its territory. President Paul Biya has himself been threatened and there is no doubt that greater Cameroonian involvement against Boko Haram has prompted retaliatory actions by the militants following an escalatory pattern well-known by Shekau's group. The eventful month of January witnessed, for the first time, the deployment of foreign troops in Cameroon in support of local forces: the Chadian parliament had in fact voted, 150 to 0, in favour of sending troops to help its neighbour.[11] This development has the potential—short of turning the tide on the counterinsurgency campaign—for making a significant contribution, given the reputation of Chadian soldiers as effective desert fighters who played a key role in Mali at the time of France's Operation Serval. Two weeks in, Chadian forces had already claimed the lives of over 200 militants.[12]

The arrival of 2,000 Chadians complements Cameroon's decision to add an aerial component to this strategy. In fact, following Boko Haram's seizure of Assighasia military camp in December President Biya decided the time had come to begin air strikes.[13] This approach had already proved rather effective when adopted by Nigerian forces.

Regional efforts finally appear to be consolidating as the African Union (AU) endorsed the plan for a 7,500 strong force at the AU Summit in late January. The proposal for this anti-Boko Haram standby force—which will comprise elements from Nigeria, Chad, Cameroon, Niger and Benin—awaits endorsement by the UN Security Council before troops can be deployed as part of this yet to be created force.[14] Possibly the first question that comes to mind is how the AU, already stretched in Mali, Central African Republic and Somalia, can sustain a further engagement. Deputy Chairman of the AU Commission Erastus Mwencha seems to be hoping for mobilisation of funds from across the continent and through UN channels.[15]

In all of this however, I wonder how much appetite there truly is in Abuja for foreign intervention (read: interference). Nigeria is a proud sovereign country. And certainly within the continent it is an economic, diplomatic and military giant. For all the talk about Boko Haram not being exclusively a Nigerian problem, accepting foreign troops would not be easy to swallow. In spite of escalating violence and amid international calls for action, National Security Adviser Sambo Dasuki rejected the need for AU or UN troops stating that regional partners were best placed to deal with the problem and that with nearly 50 per cent of

Nigerian troops deployed against Boko Haram the problem was being taken more than seriously.[16]

Among all the externals actors now looking at the Boko Haram crisis—German Chancellor Angela Merkel even proposed the European Union should fund an anti-Boko Haram force[17]—France has distinguished itself with an unprecedented level of involvement in Nigeria. France has long played an important role in Francophone Africa. Latterly, this was exemplified by the 2013 intervention in Mali and subsequent reorganisation of French troops across the Sahel. These include bases in Chad, Niger and Burkina Faso home to, respectively, Rafale and Mirage jets, Reaper and Harfang drones, and Special Forces. Chadian capital N'Djamena also hosts the headquarters of the 3,200 strong Barkhane, France's latest counter-terrorism operation across the region.[18]

Leveraging its influence in former colonies, Paris had first convened a Summit (May 2014) to discuss a regional approach to fighting Boko Haram and is now sending Niger-based military advisers to the border with Nigeria and conducting reconnaissance flights along the Niger-Chad border.[19] There is likely to be some reluctance on the part of the French government to deploy combat troops against Boko Haram (troops remain committed in Mali and Central African Republic). Nevertheless, France's own interests in the countries that have come under attack such as Chad and Niger, the kidnapping of French nationals at the hand of the group, and the justified concern with Boko Haram's destabilising impact across the region—not just in Nigeria—are prompting France to take a more prominent stance. It is also possible that Chad's decision to intervene in Cameroon and the latter's acceptance of foreign help might have been 'encouraged' by France. Similar speculations can also be made vis-à-vis Niger's decision to pledge troops for a multinational force against Boko Haram.[20] Sadly this has provoked retaliatory attacks on Nigerien soil.

Against this rapidly evolving security backdrop, the long-debated general elections scheduled to take place between 14 and 28 February 2015 were delayed by six weeks. A number of people had called for a postponement on security grounds and owing to the alleged inability of the Independent National Electoral Commission (INEC) to deliver Permanent Voters' Cards to millions of Nigerians in the north east of the country. National Security Adviser Dasuki had been particularly vocal.[21] It appears that the decision by INEC to move the elections to 28 March (national) and 11 April (state) was driven by the fact that the military were concentrating their efforts on fighting the insurgency and therefore were unable to guarantee the security of polling stations. Interestingly however, Inspector General of Police Suleiman Abba declared his force ready to provide security around the elections—something that is, in fact, a police rather than a military function. A further reason or, some say, excuse, was given.[22] On 5 February INEC's Chairman Attahiru Jega was informed that the military were about to launch a major six-week offensive against Boko Haram.[23] Naturally, some scepticism is in order: the likelihood that this latest offensive would, in the span of just six weeks, normalise an insurgency that has been worsening for the past two years seems remote. And what if it does not succeed? The power of INEC is already under question as the Commission appears to have been manipulated by the military. Moreover, public confidence in the democratic process is under threat and it is not unthinkable that people would take the streets.

President Jonathan's Peoples Democratic Party (PDP) party and some small parties have welcomed the delay. Many, including opposition All Progressives Congress (APC) and presidential candidate retired General Muhammadu Buhari were frustrated. Messages of disappointment were sent from abroad, including from the United States.[24] President Jonathan and former military ruler Buhari are about to contest what are likely to be the closest elections ever run in the country—the first that may eventually break the PDP's track record of winning every single election since democratic rule was adopted in 1999. Sceptics see the postponement as a political manoeuvre to give the PDP more time to improve ratings and discredit Buhari—whose birth certificate and academic qualifications have already been put under the microscope as part of an on-going disqualification lawsuit.[25]

Regardless of all the machinations that may be going on behind the scenes, it is not going to be easy for voters, let alone fully satisfactory, if we consider that the choice is between a former dictator and a failed president, as the *Economist* puts it in an article unsubtly titled "The least awful".[26] Jonathan's leadership failure is likely to push those Christians who would have normally voted for him to cast their preference in favour of northerner Buhari who, in spite of masterminding a military coup and other unsavoury claims to fame, has a reputation for being an anti-corruption hard-liner. Yet again, many Christians may see him as a religious zealot and decide to stick with Jonathan.[27] Meanwhile, Boko Haram is urging people to boycott the elections.[28]

There is no doubt that what I call in chapter five 'the internationalisation of Boko Haram' has now reached a whole new level: the battlefield has firmly expanded beyond Nigerian borders and foreign involvement in the anti-Boko Haram campaign is consolidating. Personally, I struggle to make predictions: naturally, part of me is hopeful that greater foreign commitment combined with air power will lead to the defeat of Boko Haram. On the other hand, I cannot help but think of Boko Haram's resilience and adaptability which have allowed the group to survive, evolve and flourish over the years. All that is left is to observe how the latest multinational offensive progresses and whether gains can be consolidated; and hope that when the general elections eventually take place Nigerians will be given hope for a future that is less bleak and more in line with Nigeria's status as the largest economy in the continent.

APPENDIX

SELECTED CHRONOLOGY OF KEY EVENTS

15th Century	Hausa kings convert to Islam.
1804	Usman Dan Fodio & Fulani "warrior-scholars".
1800s	Fulani families replace Hausa kings. Expansion of the empire east and south. Insurgencies against Islamic rule.
1902–3	Colonial period: British Indirect Rule inaugurated.
1960	Independence: power shifts south.
1963–6	First Republic under President Nnamdi Azikiwe.
1966–79	First military junta under Major General Aguiyi-Ironsi, General Yakubu Gowon, Brigadier Murtala Mohammed, General Olusẹgun Obasanjo.
1967–70	Nigerian Civil War (Biafran War).
1973	Discovery of the Niger Delta Nembe Creek Oil field. Oil boom.
1978	Izala reformist anti-Sufi movement (Jos), funding from Saudi Arabia.
1979	Shehu Shagari elected president.
1980	Maitatsine movement (Kano).
1983–98	Second military junta under Major General

	Muhammadu Buhari, General Ibrahim Babangida, Ernest Shonekan (brief return to democracy in 1993), General Sani Abacha, General Abdulsalami Abubakar.
1990s	Islamic Movement of Nigeria (IMN), Shiite.
Late 1990s	Movement for the Islamic Revival (MIR),[1] Sunni (Kano).
1999	End of military rule, election of Olusegun Obasanjo as the new President of Nigeria.
1999–2001	Sharia law adopted in twelve northern states.[2]
2002	Nigerian Taleban.
2003	Mohamed Yusuf's students set up the Al Sunna Wal Jamma [Followers of the Prophet's Teaching] community in Yobe state, after relocating to Kanama following conflicts with locals.
Dec 2003	Police stations and government buildings in Kanama and other northern cities come under attack prompting the intervention of the military. Surviving group members return to Maiduguri. Yusuf travels to Saudi Arabia.
Sept 2004	Following attacks against police stations in Gwoza and Bama, Borno state, Boko Haram militants retreat to the Mandara Mountains, near the Cameroon border.
2005–7	Boko Haram's recruitment and fundraising phase. Yusuf is arrested several times.
April 2007	Ja'afar Mahmud Adam is murdered in Kano.
2007	Umaru Yar'Adua elected President.
June 2009	Yusuf threatens the government with reprisals following the killing of some of his followers in Borno.
July 2009	Battle of Maiduguri. Uprisings in Borno, Bauchi, Yobe, Gombe, Kano, and Katsina. More than 800 suspected Boko Haram militants are killed.
30 July 2009	Extrajudicial killing of Mohamed Yusuf.
5 May 2010	Muslim President Umaru Yar'Adua dies.

	Christian Vice-President Goodluck Jonathan is sworn in the next day.
June 2010	Abubakar Shekau releases video announcing he is the new leader of the sect.
Sept 2010	Bauchi prison escape. At least 100 of the 700 prisoners escaping during the attack are believed to belong to Boko Haram.
24 Dec 2010	Attacks against churches in Maiduguri and Jos spark a spate of sectarian violence.
8 April 2011	Goodluck Jonathan is declared Nigeria's president. Post-electoral violence ensues in the north.
12 May 2011	British and Italian workers Chris McManus and Franco Lamolinara are kidnapped in Kebbi state. The attack is later claimed by "al Qaeda in the land beyond the Sahel".
15 June 2011	Establishment of Joint Task Force Operation Restore Order (JTF-ORO)
16 June 2011	The first suicide attack in the history of Nigeria targets the police HQ in Abuja.
July 2011	Five police officers are charged with the murder of Mohamed Yusuf.
Aug 2011	First Boko Haram attack reported in Adamawa state with banks and police stations being targeted.
26 Aug 2011	25 people are killed and more than 100 are wounded during a suicide attack against the United Nations building in Abuja.
Sept 2011	Yusuf's brother-in-law Babakura Fugu is shot dead after acting as intermediary in negotiations between former President Olusegun Obasanjo and the sect.
Nov 2011	Over 150 people are killed following a series of attacks in Yobe.
22 Dec 2011	Multiple bombings and firearms attacks across Borno and Yobe states.
25 Dec 2011	Suicide attacks at Saint Theresa Catholic Church in Medulla, Niger State, in Damaturo and Jos.

31 Dec 2011	A state of emergency is declared in parts of Borno, Niger, Plateau, and Yobe states. Northern borders are temporarily closed.
Jan 2012	The sect issues a three-day ultimatum urging Christians to abandon the North.
Jan 2012	President Jonathan voices concerns that Boko Haram has infiltrated branches of the government.
20 Jan 2012	Multiple attacks in Kano leave 250 dead. Between 50 and 100 members escape from prison in Kano.
Jan 2012	German engineer Edgar Fritz Raupach is kidnapped in Kano by Ansaru and later killed (in May).
March 2012	Failed UK-Nigeria rescue operation in Sokoto results in the death of hostages Chris McMannus and Franco Lamolinara alongside several of what were later believed to be Ansaru members.
8 April 2012	Easter Sunday suicide bomb attack in Kaduna.
8 April 2012	Boko Haram is believed to have executed its spokesman Abu Qaqa II.
26 April 2012	Bombing of *This Day* building in Abuja and of a building in Kaduna hosting several media outlets.
21 June 2012	The US Department of State designates Abubakar Shekau, Adam Kambara and Kalid al-Barnawi "Specially Designated Global Terrorists".
Sept 2012	Boko Haram begins to destroy mobile phone towers in northern Nigeria.
Sept 2012	The JTF announces the killing of Boko Haram commander Abubakar Yola and the arrest of 156 militants in Adamawa.
6 Oct 2012	Three Chinese workers are killed in Maiduguri.
7 Oct 2012	The JTF announces the killing of Abubakar Shekau.

28 Oct 2012	An attack against St. Rita's church in Kaduna prompts Christian reprisal against Muslims.
Nov 2012	The United Kingdom proscribes Ansaru.
Nov 2012	Amnesty International releases report documenting human rights violations carried out by Nigerian security forces.
20 Dec 2012	Francis Collomp, a French engineer working in Katsina, is kidnapped by Ansaru.
Jan 2013	France launches *Operation Serval* in Mali. Boko Haram and Ansaru are believed to be present in the country and operate alongside AQIM, MUJWA and Ansar al-Dine.
Jan 2013	Ansaru launches an attack in Kogi state against Nigerian troops heading to Mali.
Feb 2013	Polio vaccination workers in Kano and three North Korean doctors in Potiskum are killed by suspected Boko Haram.
16 Feb 2013	Ansaru kidnaps seven foreigners working for Lebanese construction company Setraco in Bauchi. They are executed on 10 March 2013.
Feb 2013	A French family is kidnapped in northern Cameroon. Boko Haram later claims responsibility. All seven family members are released in April 2013.
7 March 2013	President Jonathan's first visit to Maiduguri. Security forces foil a plot to shoot down the presidential plane.
18 March 2013	Bombing in Sabon Gari, Kano kills over 70 people.
April 2013	President Jonathan sets up the Presidential Committee on Dialogue and Restoration of Peace in the North-East to explore the feasibility of offering amnesty to Boko Haram elements. Minister of Special Duties Tanimu Turaki is appointed chairman of the committee.
11 April 2013	Shekau rejects any possible amnesty.

16–17 April 2013	More than 185 people die as a result of clashes between Boko Haram and the JTF in Baga, Borno state. Over 2,200 homes are destroyed and the security forces are heavily criticised for excessive and disproportionate use of force.
14 May 2013	President Jonathan declares a state of emergency in Borno, Yobe and Adamawa and deploys the largest military contingent since the Civil War.
May/June 2013	Emergence of Civilian JTF.
June 2013	Nigeria proscribes Boko Haram and Ansaru.
July 2013	The United Kingdom proscribes Boko Haram.
6 July 2013	At least 25 schoolchildren are killed in Boko Haram-linked attacks against a school in Mamudo, Yobe state.
Aug 2013	The newly established Army 7th division replaces JTF ORO in the counterinsurgency campaign against Boko Haram.
Aug 2013	The Defence HQ announces that over 1,000 militants had been captured in the previous three months.
Aug 2013	The Army claims Shekau died following clashes with the JTF in the Sambisa forest.
Sept 2013	Shekau issues a video.
28 Sept 2013	40 students are killed in a Boko Haram attack against College of Agriculture in Gujba, Yobe.
13 Nov 2013	Boko Haram kidnap French priest Fr. Georges Vandenbeusch in northern Cameroon. He is released in December.
Nov 2013	State of emergency renewed for additional six months.
13 Nov 2013	The US Department of State designates Boko Haram and Ansaru "Foreign Terrorist Organizations".
Dec 2013	Militants attack Maiduguri airport and military air-base destroying two helicopters.

Dec 2013	Canada designates Boko Haram a terrorist organisation.
Jan 2014	President Jonathan replaces Chief of Defence Staff and the Army, Navy and Air Force Chiefs of Staff.
Feb 2014	Boko Haram suicide bombers stage a major attack in the northern city of Bama.
14 Mar 2014	More than 600 inmates are extra judicially killed following a Boko Haram attack on Giwa barracks and prison in Borno state.
4 April 2014	Two Italian priests and Canadian nun are kidnapped by Boko Haram in northern Cameroon. They are freed on 1 June.
April 2014	Following the rebasing of GDP, Nigeria replaces South Africa as Sub Saharan Africa's biggest economy.
14 April 2014	Boko Haram abducts nearly 300 schoolgirls in Chibok, Borno. Protests and an international online campaign follow. The US, the UK, France, China, Israel and Canada offer support.
14 April 2014	88 people die when two bombs are detonated by Boko Haram in Abuja.
April 2014	Mass killings continue in Borno state.
2 May 2014	A car bomb is detonated only 200 metres from the site of the 14 April attack in Abuja.
7–9 May 2014	Abuja hosts the World Economic Forum on Africa.
May 2014	Shekau issues a video claiming that Christian girls abducted in Chibok have been forced to convert to Islam and threatening to sell some of them. He requests a prisoner exchange which is rejected by the government.
May 2014	The state of emergency in Yobe, Borno and Adamawa is renewed.
May 2014	Paris hosts the Regional Summit on Security in Nigeria to devise a strategy against Boko Haram.

1–3 June 2014	Over 200 people are killed in the Gwoza area.
8 June 2014	Nigeria's first female suicide attack is carried out in Gombe state.
8 June 2014	Former governor of the Central Bank and government critic Lamido Sanusi is named Emir of Kano, the second highest Islamic authority in Nigeria.
12 June 2014	Nigeria, Chad, Benin, Niger and Cameroon, with the support of the US, the UK and France, agree on a regional intelligence unit to fight Boko Haram with multinational patrols along the border.
June 2014	Around 60 women and children are abducted in villages across Borno.
25 June 2014	A bomb attack against a popular shopping centre in Wuse, Abuja, kills at least 21 people. In Lagos, militants attack a fuel depot.
June 2014	Follow up summit in London.
29 June	Dozens are killed in villages near Chibok, Borno state.
21 July 2014	Boko Haram takes control over Damboa, Borno state.
23 July 2014	At least 82 people die in bomb explosions in Kaduna.
27 July 2014	Boko Haram kidnaps the wife of the Cameroonian deputy prime minister and kill three.
30 July 2014	Two Boko Haram members are arrested with a 10 year old girl wearing a suicide belt in Katsina.
24 Aug 2014	Shekau declares the establishment of an Islamic caliphate in Gwoza, Borno state.

NOTES

1. INTRODUCTION

1. 'Nigeria's Boko Haram crisis: 'Many dead' in Damboa', *BBC News*, 18 July 2014 http://www.bbc.co.uk/news/world-africa-28374679
2. 'Nigeria (Ethno-religious violence). Human Security', *Armed Conflict Database*, accessed 7 May 2014 https://acd.iiss.org/
3. 'Graph 3. Cumulative weekly violent deaths in Nigeria by perpetrator', *Nigeria Security Tracker*, accessed 24 August 2014 http://www.cfr.org/nigeria/nigeria-security-tracker/p29483 [Note on data: the Nigeria Security Tracker begun recoding fatalities on President Jonathan's inauguration on 29 May 2011].
4. 'Nigeria (Ethno-religious violence)—Human Security, July 2014', *The Armed Conflict Database*, August 2014 https://acd.iiss.org/en/conflicts/nigeria-ethno-religious-violence-4494
5. Michael Olugbode, 'Nigeria: NEMA—400,000 Internally Displaced Persons in North-East', *This Day*, 14 August 2014 http://allafrica.com/stories/201408 141400.html
6. Matt Egan, 'Boko Haram threatens Nigeria's economic future', *CNN Money*, 12 May 2014 http://money.cnn.com/2014/05/12/investing/nigeria-kidnapping-investing/
7. It should be noted that the Nigerian oil industry is affected by serious problems ranging from severe environmental degredation, to militancy and corruption. Chief among many, although 2 million barrels of crude are produced every day, the local oil infrastructure is unable to refine crude as the four existing refineries operate at around 23% of their capacity. The vast majority of crude produced in Nigeria is therefore exported and the government has to import fuel, thereby paying importers to keep the prices low. On 1 January 2012 President Goodluck Jonathan announced the removal

of fuel subsidies (this new measure, already vainly attempted by previous administrations, resulted in fuel prices rising from 65 naira (US$0.40) per litre to 140 naira ($0.89) at petrol stations, and from 100 ($0.64) to 200 naira ($1.28) on the black market) lamenting the high costs of this practice—in 2011 1.3 trillion naira (around $8bn) were spent, as opposed to the budgeted 248bn naira. The announcement prompted week-long strikes across the country as citizens grew frustrated with Jonathan's inability to address the problems causing the high spending—namely corruption and mismanagement—and instead proposing to eliminate the subsidies, hence undermining the lives of average Nigerians. (*Strategic Survey 2012. The Annual Review of World's Affairs*, Oxon: Routledge, 2012, pp. 279–80).

8. The development, which had been under discussion for some time, was made possible through the rebasing of the country's gross domestic product (GDP)—outstanding since 1990—which now includes economic sectors such as information technology, airlines, telecommunications, music, online sales and film production. With a GDP of $509.9bn for 2013, Nigeria has therefore replaced South Africa ($370.3bn) as the number one economy in the continent although, per capita, South Africans are three times richer than Nigerians and wealth distribution in the West African nation remains highly uneven (Keyur Patel, 'Nigeria: No. 1 in Africa by 2014?', Beyondbrics, *Financial Times*, 8 February 2012 http://blogs.ft.com/beyond-brics/2012/02/08/nigeria-no-1-in-africa-by-2014/).

9. 'Africa's new Number One', *The Economist*, 12 April 2014 http://www.economist.com/news/leaders/21600685-nigerias-suddenly-supersized-economy-indeed-wonder-so-are-its-still-huge

10. As a way of comparison: South Africa (59), Niger (59), Ghana (60), Afghanistan (60), United Kingdom (81). (World Health Organisation, *Life Expectancy at birth. Both Sexes 2012*, accessed August 2014 http://gamapserver.who.int/gho/interactive_charts/mbd/life_expectancy/atlas.html).

11. 'Nigerians living in poverty rise to nearly 61%,' *BBC News*, 13 February 2012 http://www.bbc.co.uk/news/world-africa-17015873

12. This is a reflection of the fact that the development of the petroleum industry starting in the 1950s has been carried out at the expense of all other economic sectors, has generated fewer jobs than expected, and caused a steep decline in agricultural exports beginning in the 1960s. In early 2013 the Nigerian Association of Chambers of Commerce, Industry, Mines and Agriculture (NACCIMA) accused the oil sector of "killing the economy" and noted that "the advent of the oil sector (petrol dollars) assuming a prominent place in contributing to the GDP had created a distortion in the manufacturing and agricultural sectors of the economy". (Zakariyya Adaramola, 'Nigeria: Naccima Says Oil Sector Is Killing Economy', *Daily Trust*, 13 February 2013 http://allafrica.com/stories/201302130929.html).

13. George Oguntade, 'The Social Contract: Which way Nigeria?', *The Nation*, 29 October 2013 http://thenationonlineng.net/new/social-contract-way-nigeria/

14. Gary Haugen and Victor Boutros, *The Locust Effect: Why the End of Poverty Requires the End of Violence*, Oxford University Press: New York, 2014.

15. Ibid., p. 181.

16. 'Nigeria: Gruesome footage implicates military in war crimes', *Amnesty International*, 5 August 2014 http://www.amnesty.org/en/news/nigeria-gruesome-footage-implicates-military-war-crimes-2014–08–05; 'Boko Haram and Nigerian military both accused of war crimes as conflict escalates', *The Independent*, 5 August 2014 http://www.independent.co.uk/news/world/africa/boko-haram-and-nigerian-military-both-accused-of-war-crimes-as-conflict-escalates-9649909.html

17. Ola' Audu, Sani Tukur and Nnenna Ibeh, 'Boko Haram: Mutiny as Nigerian soldiers shoot at commanding officer's vehicle', *Premium Times*, 14 May 2014 https://www.premiumtimesng.com/news/160762-boko-haram-mutiny-nigerian-soldiers-shoot-commanding-officers-vehicle.html

18. 'Boko Haram crisis: Nigerian soldiers 'mutiny over weapons'', *BBC News*, 19 August 2014 http://www.bbc.co.uk/news/world-africa-28855292

19. Oladunjoye Patrick and Omemu Felix, 'Effect of Boko Haram on school attendance in northern Nigeria', *British Journal of Education* 1(2) December 2013 http://www.eajournals.org/wp-content/uploads/Effect-of-Boko-Haram-on-School-Attendance-in-Northern-Nigeria.pdf

20. Farouk Chothia, 'Boko Haram crisis: Nigeria's female bombers strike', *BBC News*, 6 August 2014 http://www.bbc.co.uk/news/world-africa-28657085

21. With over 165 million inhabitants Nigeria is the most populous country in the whole continent and accounts for around 50 per cent of West Africa's population. It is also an extremely diverse country, with over 250 ethnic groups, around 250 languages and a population that is divided more or less equally between Muslims, primarily concentrated in the North, and Christians, mainly in the South.

22. 'Sub-Saharan Africa', *The Military Balance* 114(1), Routledge: Abingdon, 2014, pp. 451–3.

23. The term 'Islamist' (both as noun and adjective) is used throughout the book to indicate groups, movements or individuals espousing Islamism, also described as political Islam or Islamic activism, and not necessarily equating to violence or militancy. Rather, it indicates a diverse range of movements as varied as the Taliban, Hizb ut-Tahrir and al-Qaeda placing Islam at the centre of their political ideology (Trevor Stanley, 'Definition: Islamism, Islamist, Islamiste, Islamicist', *Perspectives on World History and Current Events*, July 2005). The latter is in fact driven by legal rules drawn

from the Qur'an and Sunna (Islam's sacred texts). The rise of political Islam in the latter part of the twentieth century coincided with the desire among many Islamists for a return to Sharia, the revealed law (Ziba Mir-Hosseini, 'Classical *fiqh*, contemporary ethics and gender justice', in Kari Vogt, Lena Larsen and Christian Moe (eds), *New Directions in Islamic Thought*, London/ New York: I.B. Tauris, 2009, pp. 78–9). In the post 9/11 period the Western world has looked at political Islam with greater concern and although the emergence of the concept is linked to Shia Islam and the 1979 Iranian Revolution, it is Sunni Islamism, and its many, often conflicting, forms that preoccupies Western governments more. Nevertheless, too often the mistake has been made to deem all forms of Islamism as radical and threatening to the West. On the contrary, political and missionary types exist in addition to jihadists committed to violence ('Understanding Islamism', *Middle East/North Africa Report* N°37, International Crisis Group, 2 March 2005 http://www.crisisgroup.org/~/media/Files/Middle%20East%20North%20Africa/North%20Africa/Understanding%20Islamism.pdf)

2. ISLAM IN NIGERIA: HISTORICAL BACKGROUND

1. Isak Svensson, 'Fighting with Faith: Religion and Conflict Resolution in Civil Wars', *The Journal of Conflict Resolution* 51 (6) (Dec., 2007), pp. 930–49.

2. 'Nigeria's Boko Haram rejects Jonathan's amnesty idea', *BBC News*, 11 April 2013 http://www.bbc.co.uk/news/world-africa-22105476

3. Femi Ibrahim, 'Boko Haram's "Just War" Critique and Opinion', *Terrorism, Research and Analysis Consortium*, Beacham Publishing, 2013 http://www.trackingterrorism.org/article/boko-harams-just-war-critique-and-opinion

4. Toyin Falola, *Violence in Nigeria: The Crisis of Religious Politics and Secular Ideologies*, Rochester, NY: University of Rochester Press, 2009.

5. Ibid.

6. Nathaniel Dominic Danjibo, 'Islamic Fundamentalism and Sectarian Violence: The "Maitatsine" and "Boko Haram" Crises in Northern Nigeria'. Peace and Conflict Studies Programme, Institute of African Studies, University of Ibadan, 2009, p. 3

7. Nicolas van de Walle, 'A History of Nigeria; Faith and Politics in Nigeria: Nigeria as a Pivotal State in the Muslim World', *Foreign Affairs*, Nov/Dec 2008http://www.foreignaffairs.com/articles/64593/nicolas-van-de-walle/a-history-of-nigeria-faith-and-politics-in-nigeria-nigeria-as-a-

8. Walter Van Beek, *Purity and statecraft: The Fulani jihad and its empire*, Mouton: Berlin, 1988 https://openaccess.leidenuniv.nl/bitstream/handle/1887/9002/ASC_1241507_152.pdf

9. Johannes Harnischfeger, *Democratization and Islamic Law: The Sharia Conflict in Nigeria*, Frankfurt/New York: Campus, 2008, p. 42.

10. Open letter from Boko Haram, August 2011 reproduced in Sahara Reporters, 'Boko Haram: Why We Struck In Kano', *Sahara Reporters* 22 January 2012 http://saharareporters.com/news-page/boko-haram-why-we-struck-kano (block capitals in the original).

11. The origins of the Wahhabi movement can be traced back to the Islamic ideology that was formed in the Arabian peninsula in the eighteenth and nineteenth centuries centred on the teachings of Muhammad ibn Abd-al Wahhab. Wahabism rejects traditional rulers and scholars, emphasises monotheism and aims at purifying Islam. Whereas it rejects traditional forms of worship and deems other Muslims to be outside of Islam, it encourages believers to form their own interpretation of sacred texts regardless of their theological knowledge or level of understanding. In addition, one of the most contentious and concerning aspects of Wahhabism is the belief, among the most extreme elements, that reforming Islam can be pursued through violent means, which is coupled with the tendency to selectively use verses of the Qur'an to justify radical ideology (and departing from Islam's tradition of tolerance) ('Islamic Radicalism: Its Wahhabi Roots and Current Representation', The Islamic Supreme Council of America, accessed on 28 August 2014 http://www.islamicsupremecouncil.org/understanding-islam/anti-extremism/7-islamic-radicalism-its-wahhabi-roots-and-current-representation.html). Today, Wahhabism is normally used to describe Salafi Sunnism in Saudi Arabia.

12. Walter Van Beek, *Purity and statecraft: The Fulani jihad and its empire*, Berlin: Mouton, 1988 https://openaccess.leidenuniv.nl/bitstream/handle/1887/9002/ASC_1241507_152.pdf pp. 155–6.

13. Jonathan Hill, 'Sufism in northern Nigeria: Force for counter-radicalization?', 2010, p. 15 http://www.strategicstudiesinstitute.army.mil/pdffiles/pub989.pdf

14. Van Beek, *Purity and statecraft*, pp. 157–8.

15. F. H. El-Masri, 'The life of Shehu Usuman dan Fodio before the jihad', *Journal of the Historical Society of Nigeria* 2, No. 4 (December 1963), p. 442.

16. Van Beek, *Purity and statecraft*, pp. 157–8.

17. Assa Okoth, *A History of Africa: African societies and the establishment of colonial rule, 1800–1915*, Nairobi/Kampala/Dar el Salam: East African Educational Publishers, 2006, p. 2–3.

18. Ibid.

19. Harnischfeger, *Democratization and Islamic Law*, pp. 43–4.

20. Frank A. Salamone, *The Hausa of Nigeria*, Lanham, Maryland: Univeristy Press of America, 2010, p. 111.

21. Martin Z. Njeuma, *Fulani Hegemony in Yola (Old Adamawa) 1809–1902*, Bamenda: Langaa, RPCIG, 2012, p. 54.

22. Charlotte A. Quinn and Frederick Quinn, *Pride, Faith, and Fear: Islam in Sub-Saharan Africa*, Oxford/New York: Oxford University Press, 2003, p. 21.

23. Harnischfeger, *Democratization and Islamic Law*, pp. 45–46.

24. 'Ethnic groups', *The World Factbook* 2013–14. Washington, DC: Central Intelligence Agency, 2013 https://www.cia.gov/library/publications/the-world-factbook/fields/2075.html

25. Harnischfeger, *Democratization and Islamic Law*, p. 49.

26. Sardauna of Sokoto, 1949, quoted in Martin Meredith, *The State of Africa*, London: Free Press, 2005, p. 75.

27. In 1822 the Egyptian ruler Muhammad Ali, a provincial governor of the Ottoman Empire, invaded the Sudan. In taking control over Sudan, men were forced into conscription with the Egyptian army, Egypt imposed heavy taxes on the Sudanese, took full control over local trade and placed many locals in slavery. The latter practice soon became an integral feature of the local economy. In 1863, the arrival of the new Egyptian governor Ismail coincided with the beginning of an anti-slavery campaign, later intensified by General Charles Gordon, who was appointed governor of Sudan a decade later. By then, London, eager to protect its interests in the Suez Canal and to see his loans to the Egyptian government re-paid, had decided to broaden its presence in the region. Sudanese Arab leaders, however, equated British involvement with a Christian attempt to undermine the dominant role occupied by Muslim Arabs. This resentment soon translated into a call to wage holy war: in 1881, the Sudanese Islamic cleric Muhammad Ahmad proclaimed himself the Mahdi and formed an army to fight against Egypt and Britain. Joint British-Egyptian forces suffered extensive casualties, including the beheading of General Gordon, the commander of the British-Egyptian forces, alongside almost the entire Anglo-Egyptian garrison protecting Khartoum. Amid great public outcry back home, the British evacuated Sudan only to return in 1896. By then, the Mahdist movement had been weakened by infighting following the death of Ahmad in 1885. The new commander of the Anglo-Egyptian army Horatio Kitchener was determined to take advantage of this opportunity. The final battle was fought in September 1889 resulting in the death of 11,000 Mahdists. Over 16,000 of them were wounded. The killing of Khalifa, Ahmad's successor, the next year marked the official end of the Mahdist state [Andrew Kurt, 'Mahdist Revolt' in Immanuel Ness (ed.), *The International Encyclopedia of Revolution and Protest*, Blackwell Publishing, 2009 http://www.revolutionprotestencyclopedia.com/public/tocnode?id=g9781405184649_yr2012_chunk_97 81405184649956].

28. H. R. Palmer, *Attitude of the Muslim Provinces of Nigeria*, 2 March 1917 http://www.waado.org/colonial_rule/british_nigeria/muslim_wwi.pdf
29. Harnischfeger, *Democratization and Islamic Law*, p. 55.
30. Martin Meredith, *The State of Africa*, London: Free Press, 2005, p. 77.
31. 'Biafra's ghost haunts Nigeria as Igbos demand N2.4 trillion reparation over civil war ordeal', *News Express* 15 July 2014 http://www.newsexpressngr. com/news/detail.php?news=6631
32. 'Half of a Yellow Sun film approved by Nigeria censors', *BBC News* 8 July 2014 http://www.bbc.co.uk/news/world-africa-28212955
33. Biyi Bandele, 'Why can't Nigerians watch the country's biggest movie?', *CNN* 21 May 2014 http://edition.cnn.com/2014/05/21/opinion/why-cant-nigerians-half-yellow-sun/
34. Chinua Achebe, *There Was a Country: A Personal History of Biafra* (London: Allen Lane, 2012).
35. Eghosa E. Osaghae and Rotimi T. Suberu, 'A History of Identities, Violence, and Stability in Nigeria', *CRISE Working Paper* 6, January 2005, p. 7 http:// r4d.dfid.gov.uk/PDF/Outputs/inequality/wp6.pdf
36. Levi Akalazu Nwachuku and G. N. Uzoigwe (eds), *Troubled Journey: Nigeria Since the Civil War*, University Press of America: Lanham, MD 2004, pp. 32–3.
37. Ibid., p. 33.
38. Ibid., p. 36.
39. Mark Curtis, 'Nigeria's war over Biafra, 1967–70', February 2007 http:// markcurtis.wordpress.com/2007/02/13/nigeriabiafra-1967–70/ extracted from Curtis, *Unpeople: Britain;'s Secret Human Rights Abuses*, London: Vintage, 2004.
40. Phili Efiong, *Nigeria and Biafra: My Story*, Africa Tree Press: NY, 2007, p. 3.
41. Hilary M. Njoku, *A Tragedy Without Heroes: the Nigeria-Biafra War*, Fourth Dimension: Nigeria, 1987, p. 174.
42. 'Remembering the nightmare of Biafra: E.H. Johnson was at the centre of saving lives in Biafra 35 years ago', *The Free Library* 2004 http://www. the-freelibrary.com/ Remembering+the+nightmare+of+ Biafra%3a+E.H.+ Johnson+was+at+the+centre...-a0122700689
43. Sakah Mahmud, 'Nigerian Islamist Activism and Religious Conflict' in Stig Jarle Hansen, Atle Mesoy and Tuncay Kardas (eds), *Borders of Islam. Exploring Samuel Huntington's Faultlines, from Al-Andalus to Virtual Ummah*, London: Hurst, 2009, p. 116.
44. Daniel E. Agbiboa, 'The Ongoing Campaign of Terror in Nigeria: Boko Haram versus the State', *Stability: International Journal of Security and Development* 2(3):52, 2013 http://www.stabilityjournal.org/article/view/ sta.cl/145#n1

45. Monica Mark, 'Boko Haram vows to fight until Nigeria establishes sharia law', *The Guardian*, 27 January 2012 http://www.theguardian.com/world/2012/jan/27/boko-haram-nigeria-sharia-law

46. Ibid.

47. Agbiboa, 'The Ongoing Campaign of Terror in Nigeria'.

48. *Religion and Conflict*, Immigration and Refugee Board of Canada, 1 March 1993 http://www.refworld.org/docid/3ae6a80510.html

49. See Martin Meredith, *The State of Africa*, London: Free Press, 2005, p. 586.

50. Philip Ostien, *Sharia Implementation in Northern Nigeria*, Ibadan: Spectrum Books, 2007 p. viii http://www.sharia-in-africa.net/pages/publications/sharia-implementation-in-northern-nigeria.php

51. BBC News, 'Sharia court frees Nigerian woman', *BBC News*, 25 March 2002 http://news.bbc.co.uk/1/hi/world/africa/1891395.stm

52. BBC News, 'Analysts: Nigeria's sharia split', *BBC News*, 7 January 2003 http://news.bbc.co.uk/1/hi/world/africa/2632939.stm

53. J.N. Paden, *Muslim Civic Cultures and Conflict Resolution: The Challenge of Democratic Federalism in Nigeria*, Washington DC: The Brookings Institute, 2005.

54. J.N. Paden, *Islam and Democratic Federalism in Nigeria*, Washington D.C: Africa program, Center for Strategic and International Studies, 2002 http://bit.ly/16YznPg

55. Paden highlights seven Muslim identities in northern Nigeria: "Emirate authorities and traditional non-sectarian mainstream Muslim groups; Sufi brotherhoods, especially the Qadiriyya and Tijaniyya; Anti-innovation legalists, especially the *Izala*; Intellectual reformers; Anti-establishment syncretists, especially remnants of the Maitatsine movement; Antiestablishment "Muslim Brothers" (*Ikhwan*), sometimes referred to as 'Shi'ites;' unemployed urban youth and Qur'anic student movements, formed around local schools and teachers" [Paden, *Islam and Democratic Federalism in Nigeria*, pp. 2–5].

56. Toyin Falola, *Violence in Nigeria: The Crisis of Religious Politics and Secular Ideologies*, Rochester, NY: University of Rochester Press, 2009, p. 69.

57. Ibid.

58. Hill, 'Sufism in northern Nigeria', p. 20.

59. Hanna Hoechner, 'Traditional Qur'anic students in Nigeria: Fair game for unfair accusations?', *Democracy in Africa*, 16 December 2012 http://democracyinafrica.org/traditional-quranic-students-in-nigeria-fair-game-for-unfair-accusations/

60. G.K. Brown, 'Paper commissioned for the EFA Global Monitoring Report 2011. The hidden crisis: Armed conflict and education', *Education for All Global Monitoring Report*, United Nations Educational Scientific and Cultural Organisation (UNESCO), 2010, p. 18.

61. C. Jarmon, *Nigeria: Reorganization and Development since the Mid-twentieth Century* (Monographs & Theoretical Studies in Sociology & Anthropology in Honour of Nels Anderson), Leiden: Brill, 1988, p. 109.
62. Interview with anonymous source#8, 2013.
63. Paden, *Islam and Democratic Federalism in Nigeria*, p. 2.
64. Ibid.
65. Loimeier, *Islamic Reform and Political Change in Northern Nigeria*.
66. Harnischfeger, *Democratization and Islamic Law*. pp. 74–5.
67. Loimeier, *Islamic Reform and Political Change in Northern Nigeria*, p. 17.
68. Harnischfeger, *Democratization and Islamic Law*. p. 75.
69. Ibid., p. 34.
70. I do not imply that north and south are two homogenous blocks. Indeed, differences within the north and the south should not be overlooked.

3. THE GENESIS OF RADICAL GROUPS

1. *Almajiri* (pl: *almajirai*): this word, from Arabic, refers to someone who leaves home in search of Islamic instruction.
2. Wole Soyinka, 'The Butchers of Nigeria', *Newsweek Magazine* 16 January 2012, pp. 1–5. http://thebea.st/17tJIl5
3. In spite of the fact that Salafism is often characterised as being itself an ideology (e.g. 'Who are the 'Salafis'?' AS-Sunnah Foundation of America, accessed on 29 August 2014 http://sunnah.org/publication/salafi/salafi_unveiled/who.htm), the term refers to a particular methodology used to evaluate textual sources which aspires to emulate beliefs and practices of the first three Islamic generations, i.e. those closest to the Prophet's era and hence believed to represent the purest Islam (Yasir Qadhi, 'On Salafi Islam', *Muslim Matters*, 22 April 2014 http://muslimmatters.org/2014/04/22/on-salafi-islam-dr-yasir-qadhi/). Salafism does not represent any specific community and indeed there are several, and somewhat different, groups that espouse Salafi methodology [ibid.]. Its origins can be traced back to the time of the Abbasid caliphate (750–1519) and the Ahl al-Hadith, a movement focused on the study of the *hadith* [teachings and traditions of the Prophet] to rid Islam of non-Muslim influences. In doing so, Salafists reject the four traditional schools of thought (*madhhab*) of Sunni Islam (Maliki, Hanbali, Shafi'i and Hanafi) and encourages direct interpretation of the *hadith* and the Qur'an using both a scripturalist and literalist approach (Roel Meijer (ed.), *Global Salafism: Islam's New Religious Movement* (New York: Columbia University Press, 2009), p. 4). Among the contentious issues over which adherents of Salafism disagree are militancy in the context of jihad, the extent to which it is allowed to criticise an Islamic ruler; the degree to which one should dis-

sociate from religious innovations (including interaction with non-Salaf-
ists), and whether it is acceptable to follow one of the jurisprudential schools
(Qadhi, 'On Salafi Islam').

4. Moghadam, 2011 in Alex P. Schmid (ed.), *The Routledge Handbook of
Terrorism Research*, Abingdon: Routledge, 2011, p. 25.

5. Roman Loimeier, *Islamic Reform and Political Change in Northern Nigeria*,
Evanston/Chicago: Northwestern University Press, 1997.

6. Adesoji, 'Between Maitatsine and Boko Haram'.

7. Jacob Zenn, 'A Brief Look at Ansaru's Khalid al-Barnawi—AQIM's Bridge
into Northern Nigeria. Personalities Behind the Insurgency', *Militant
Leadership Monitor* Volume 4, Issue 3, 2013 p. 4.

8. Adesoji, 'Between Maitatsine and Boko Haram'.

9. Dan Isaacs, 'Nigeria's firebrand Muslim leaders', *BBC News*, 1 October 2001
http://news.bbc.co.uk/1/hi/world/africa/1573491.stm

10. Hill, Sufism in Northern Nigeria, p. 24.

11. Ibid.

12. Ibid.

13. Interview with anonymoussource #1, 2013.

14. Zenn, 'A Brief Look at Ansaru's Khalid al-Barnawi', p. 4.

15. Loimeier, *Islamic Reform and Political Change in Northern Nigeria*, pp. 248–9

16. Ibid, p. 84.

17. Ibid, pp. 248–249.

18. Adesoji, 'Between Maitatsine and Boko Haram'.

19. Abdulkareem Mohammed; Mohammed Haruna. *The Paradox of Boko
Haram Nigeria*, p. 42.

20. Ibid.

21. *Ulama*: Islamic elite and intelligentsia. Mohammed notes their role in northern Nigerian society as being significant. They take such names, notes
Mohammed, as "*Sheikh*", "*Ustaz*" and "*Malam*". The singular tense is "*alim*"
and an *alim* would often take several students under his wing, teaching
them "Islam in all its ramifications" (Mohammed, *The Paradox of Boko
Haram Nigeria*, pp. 15–16).

22. Mohammed, *The Paradox of Boko Haram Nigeria*.

23. Loimeier, *Islamic Reform and Political Change in Northern Nigeria*, p. 73.

24. Mohammed, *The Paradox of Boko Haram Nigeria*, p. 43.

25. Ibid. p. 44.

26. Ibid, p. 41.

27. Loimeier, *Islamic Reform and Political Change in Northern Nigeria*.

28. Ibid, p. 14.

29. Ibid.

30. As pointed out earlier, outside the ambits of the established Islamic order,

and with a sufficient following, it appears such ideologues can indeed flourish—as was arguably the case for both Marwa Maitatsine (Isichei, 'The Maitatsine Risings in Nigeria 1980–85') and Mohammed Yusuf (Mohammed, *The Paradox of Boko Haram Nigeria*). Nonetheless, the position adopted within this study is that the concept of transformation, especially that of gradual transformation, is more applicable to the Boko Haram over the years of the network's existence, than it was to the Maitatsine.

31. Mohammed, *The Paradox of Boko Haram Nigeria*, p. 40.
32. Adesoji, 'Between Maitatsine and Boko Haram', p. 105.
33. Zenn, 'A Brief Look at Ansaru's Khalid al-Barnawi'.
34. J.N. Paden, *Muslim Civic Cultures and Conflict Resolution: The Challenge of Democratic Federalism in Nigeria*. Washington DC: The Brookings Institute 2005, pp. 58, 60.
35. Loimeier, *Islamic Reform and Political Change in Northern Nigeria*.pp. 14–15.
36. Ibid.
37. Mervyn Hiskett, 'The "Community of Grace" and its opponents, the "rejecters": A debate about theology and mysticism in Muslim West Africa with special reference to its Hausa expression', *African Language Studies* 17, 1980, pp. 99–140.
38. Loimeier, *Islamic Reform and Political Change in Northern Nigeria*.
39. Isichei, 'The Maitatsine Risings in Nigeria 1980–85'; and Toyin Falola, *Violence in Nigeria: The Crisis of Religious Politics and Secular Ideologies*, Rochester, NY: University of Rochester Press, 2009.
40. Adam Higazi, 'The origins and transformation of the Boko Haram insurgency in northern Nigeria'; published in French translation as 'Les origines et la transformation de l'insurrection de Boko Haram dans le nord du Nigeria', *Politique Africaine*, 130, 2013, pp. 137–64.
41. Higazi, 'The origins and transformation of the Boko Haram insurgency in northern Nigeria'.
42. Andrew McGregor, "Central African Militant Movements: The Northern Nigeria, Niger, Chad, and Cameroon Nexus". *Instability in Nigeria: The Domestic factors*. Select conference proceedings from "Threats to Nigeria's Security: Boko Haram and beyond". Jamestown Foundation, 2012, p. 31.
43. Higazi, 'The origins and transformation of the Boko Haram insurgency in northern Nigeria', p. 9.
44. Mohammed, *The Paradox of Boko Haram Nigeria*.
45. Andrew Walker, 'What is Boko Haram?' *Special Report 308*. Washington D.C: United States Institute of Peace (USIP), 2012, p. 7.
46. Xan Rice, 'The Changing Face of Boko Haram', *Financial Times*, 22 May 2012 http://on.ft.com/17qcRzq
47. Ibid.

48. Ibid.

49. Murray Last, 'Nigeria's Boko Haram: The Anatomy of a Crisis', E-International Relations Website, 30 January 2012 http://bit.ly/Awmh5J

50. Patrick Meehan and Jackye Speier, 'Boko Haram: Emerging Threat to the US Homeland'. Report to US House of Representatives Committee on Homeland Security; Subcommittee on Counterterrorism and Intelligence, 30 November 2011, p. 23.

51. Ibid, pp. 2, 8, 17, 20.

52. Ibid, p. 28.

53. Freedom Onuoha, 'The Islamist challenge: Nigeria's Boko Haram crisis explained', *African Security Review*, 19: 2, 2010, p. 55.

54. Andrew Lebovich and Paul M. Lubeck, *Salafist Insurgencies in West Africa: The Enigma of Boko Haram*, Washington DC: John Hopkins—SAIS African Studies Program, 2011 Youtube video of the conference available at http://bit.ly/1e0lZxR

55. Loimeier, *Islamic Reform and Political Change in Northern Nigeria*, p. 248.

56. Ibid., pp. 248–9.

57. Ibid.

58. IMN is also known as the Muslim Brothers (Harnischfeger, *Democratization and Islamic Law*, pp. 202–203).

59. Who founded his own Islamist network, Ahl al-Sunnah wal-Jamâ'ah, Jâ'amutu Tajidmul Islami (Movement for the Islamic Revival (MIR).

60. Hill, Sufism in northern Nigeria, p. 24.

61. Ibid.

62. Ibid., p. 23.

63. *Biography of Sheikh Zakzaky*, Official Website of the Islamic Movement of Nigeria, 18 September 2011 http://www.islamicmovement.org/index.php?option=com_content&view=article&id=108&Itemid=142

64. Hill, Sufism in northern Nigeria, pp. 20–24.

65. The Izala are an area of particular focus here, as this chapter is more focused on fundamentalist groups with a history of and tendency towards clashing with state security agencies, but also because, with the formation of the Izala, the gauntlet had now been thrown down, so to speak. Indeed, and especially with its success in the years and decades that followed, it now became clear to other fundamentalist ideologues that the existing Islamic establishment could be successfully challenged; and if so, then why not the state? In this context, the Yan Izala fit this book's explanatory model: first because of its repeated clashes with authorities and other movements (Loimeier) but also due the "template" for anti-establishment and fundamentalist revivalism that it laid out, as well as due to its categorization as "a Nigerian manifestation of the radical Islamist movements of the Islamic

world" (Ibid, p. 18). It is noteworthy however that Izala is by no means the only fundamentalist network established "from scratch".

66. Loimeier, *Islamic Reform and Political Change in Northern Nigeria*, pp. 16, 209.

67. Ibid, p. 17.

68. Ibid. It would appear as though the authorities had a vested interest in maintaining the order brought about by the Sufi Brotherhoods and the *turuq*; which could explain the clashes of the Izala with the authorities. For instance Loimeier (p. 214) contends that Isma'ila, who was with the Nigerian Army prior to the formation of the Yan Izala, "was dismissed from the army on 7th April 1978"; two months after the Izala movement was officially established. Idris was arrested the same month by security forces, and would also be arrested in the years that followed.

69. Loimeier, *Islamic Reform and Political Change in Northern Nigeria*, p. 210.

70. The suffix recommended by Gumi had a powerful connotation, and may well have helped shaped the Izala's militant opposition to the Sufis in the decades to come. It showed that the Izala were not only, as a movement, anti-innovation legalists (*Jamâ'at Izâlat al-Bid'a*), but that in addition they were anti-establishment (*wa Iqâmat as-Sunna*) and in particular opposed to the concept of Sufism and what it had come to represent at the time. Indeed, the underlying ideology behind the name, taken together, was what informed the "declaration of war" alluded to by Loimeier (p. 209).

71. Loimeier, *Islamic Reform and Political Change in Northern Nigeria*, pp. 207–330.

72. Ibid, p. 222.

73. "Innovation" here is a reference to cultural innovation from traditional Islamic teaching and practice (Paden, p. 62)

74. Paden, *Islam and Democratic Federalism in Nigeria*, pp. 60–1.

75. JNI: *Jamâ'at Nasr al-Islâm* [Movement for the Support of Islam]. A new Islamic organization created by Ahmadu Bello. Gumi, as a vassal of Ahmadu Bello was closely affiliated with the JNI. Indeed, Loimeier argues that Gumi was the brain behind the idea to create the JNI, in his role as adviser to the Prime Minister and states that "Ahmadu Bello…had been convinced of the necessity of such an organization by Gumi and saw the creation of the JNI as a strategy to win the 'ulama' [faithful] for his religious policy" (p. 135). However it appears that Gumi's influence and support within the JNI waned in the years after Ahmadu Bello was killed in the 1966 coup (p. 208).

76. Loimeier, *Islamic Reform and Political Change in Northern Nigeria*, p. 208.

77. Ibid, p. 16.

78. Ibid, p. 108.

79. Ibid, pp. 208–9.

80. Ibid, p. 208.
81. Ibid, p. 214.
82. Ibid, p. 216.
83. David McCormack, 'An African Vortex: Islamism in Sub-Saharan Africa', *Occasional Paper Series No. 4*, Washington, DC: Center for Security Policy, 2005, p. 10.
84. Loimeier, *Islamic Reform and Political Change in Northern Nigeria*, p. 17.
85. Debbie West, *Combating Terrorism in the Horn of Africa and Yemen*. Program on Intrastate Conflict and Conflict Resolution, Belfer Center for Science and International Affairs, John F. Kennedy School of Government, Harvard University. Cambridge, Massachusetts, 2005, p. 18.
86. Isichei, 'The Maitatsine Risings in Nigeria 1980–85'; and Falola, 'Violence in Nigeria'.
87. McCormack, 'An African Vortex', p. 4.
88. West, *Combating Terrorism in the Horn of Africa and Yemen*, p. 2.
89. Ibid.
90. Isichei, 'The Maitatsine Risings in Nigeria 1980–85', p. 194.
91. Falola, 'Violence in Nigeria', p. 142.
92. Falola, 'Violence in Nigeria', pp. 141–2.
93. Ibid.
94. Danjibo, 'Islamic Fundamentalism and Sectarian Violence: The "Maitatsine" and "Boko Haram" Crises in Northern Nigeria'. Peace and Conflict Studies Programme, Institute of African Studies, University of Ibadan, 2009, p. 6.
95. Ibid.
96. Socio-economic and political environment of the times, arguably also played a role in this religious and social entrapment of many 'Yan Tatsine.
97. Falola, 'Violence in Nigeria', p. 143.
98. Isichei, 'The Maitatsine Risings in Nigeria 1980–85', p. 194; and Falola, 'Violence in Nigeria', pp. 142–55.
99. Falola, 'Violence in Nigeria', p. 143.
100. Isichei, 'The Maitatsine Risings in Nigeria 1980–85', p. 195.
101. Falola, 'Violence in Nigeria', p. 143.
102. Ibid, p. 141.
103. Ibid, pp. 143–4.
104. Compare for instance this viewpoint to that of the late Ustaz Mohammed Yusuf, the Boko Haram leader. Specifically, in a video debate between Ustaz Yusuf of the Jamā'at ahl al-sunnah li'l-da'wah wa'l-jihād" (Boko Haram) and Ustaz Idris Abdulaziz of the Jamā'at 'izālat al-bid'a wa iqāmat al-sunna (Izala), Ustaz Yusuf was quoted as saying "Western education, as taught in the kinds of schools we have in Nigeria, is haram" (Mohammed, 2010 p. 67). In Yusuf's view, karatun boko was a form of knowledge "that

clashes with Islam" and that could—but not necessarily would—"even lead to shirk [disbelief]" (Ibid).

105. Harnischfeger, *Democratization and Islamic Law*.
106. Ibid.
107. Danjibo, 'Islamic Fundamentalism and Sectarian Violence'.
108. Harnischfeger, *Democratization and Islamic Law*, p. 78.
109. Ibid., p. 75.
110. Ibid.
111. Harnischfeger, *Democratization and Islamic Law*, p. 74; and Isichei, 'The Maitatsine Risings in Nigeria 1980–85', p. 194.
112. Higazi, 'The origins and transformation of the Boko Haram insurgency in northern Nigeria'. See for instance the following media reporting: Aminu Abubakar, 'Death toll from Nigeria clashes climbs to 70', *AFP*, 30 December 2009 http://www.google.com/hostednews/afp/article/ALeqM5iOts2sc MCQ_TmONnGuQaRoMCQYMw; and Ruth Gledhill, 'Nigeria: extremists unleash new "terror"', 29 December 2009 http://www.anglican-mainstream.net/2009/12/29/nigeria-extremists-unleash-new-terror/
113. Mark, 'Boko Haram vows to fight until Nigeria establishes sharia law'.
114. Sakah Mahmud, 'Nigeria-Islamist Activism and Religious Conflict', in Stig Jarle Hansen, Atle Messoy, and Tuncay Kardas (eds), *The Borders of Islam: Exploring Samuel Huntingdon's Faultlines, from Al-Andalus to Virtual Ummah*, London: Hurst Publishers, 2009, pp. 120–1.
115. Ibid.
116. Azubuike Ihejirika quoted in Envisions, 'Boko Haram not Army's only problem, says Ihejirika', *Envision Nigeria* website 12 September 2012 http://www.envisionnigeria.com/index.php?option=com_content&view=article&id=%201858&Itemid=146

4. WHAT IS BOKO HARAM?

1. See for instance Cameron Duodu, 'Mohammed Yusuf's final days', *The Guardian*, 6 August 2009 http://www.theguardian.com/commentisfree/belief/2009/aug/06/mohammed-yusuf-boko-haram-nigeria or 'Boko Haram Fast Facts', *CNN*, 30 June 2014 http://edition.cnn.com/2014/06/09/world/boko-haram-fast-facts/
2. Another name used to describe the group was Muhajirun. Isa, for instance, describes new militant Islamists that emerged in the past ten to fifteen years who grounded their ideology more firmly in the region's deteriorating socio-economic conditions, especially in the northern areas. Among this new wave was *Muhajirun*, whose upper and middle-class leaders from northeast Nigeria recruited unemployed youths to its cell-based network. The introduction of

sharia law in the north was not enough for its members, who wanted the adoption of Islamic rule across the country. Statements issued by the group also indicated an attempt to align the Nigerian struggle to jihad in Palestine, Afghanistan and Iraq. Boko Haram, Isa argues, developed out of Muhajirun (Muhammed Kabir Isa, 'Militant Islamist Groups in Northern Nigeria' in Wafula Okumu and Augustine Ikelegbe (eds), *Militias, Rebels and Islamist Militants*, Pretoria: Institute for Security Studies, 2010, pp. 329–31)

3. Freedom C. Onuoha, *Boko Haram: Nigeria's Extremist Islamic Sect*, Al Jazeera Centre for Studies, 29 February 2012.

4. Andrew Walker, *What is Boko Haram?*, USIP May 2012 http://www.usip.org/files/resources/SR308.pdf

5. Roel Meijer (ed.), *Global Salafism: Islam's New Religious Movement* (New York: Columbia University Press, 2009), p. 4.

6. Mohamed Yusuf, 2009 quoted in Joe Boyle, 'Nigeria's 'Taliban' enigma', *BBC News* 31 July 2009 http://news.bbc.co.uk/1/hi/8172270.stm

7. Ibid.

8. Isa Umar Gusau, 'Boko Haram: How it all began', *Sunday Trust*, 2 August 2009 http://sundaytrust.com.ng/index.php/the-arts/35-people-in-the-news/people-in-the-news/5869-boko-haram-how-it-all-began

9. Roman Loimeier, 'Boko Haram: The Development of a Militant Religious Movement in Nigeria', *Africa Spectrum* 47, 2–3, 2012, pp. 148–9.

10. Walker, What is Boko Haram?.

11. Loimeier, 'Boko Haram: The Development of a Militant Religious Movement in Nigeria'.

12. David Cook, *Boko Haram: A prognosis*, James A. Baker III Institute for Public Policy, Rice University, 16 December 2011, p. 10.

13. As indicated by Hausa linguist Paul Newman, commentators have often claimed the Hausa word "*boko*" to have been adopted by the English language and to etymologically derive from "book". However a more in-depth study disproves the claim and connects the term to *karatun boko* (Western education, as introduced earlier in this volume). Citing analysis the by Hausa scholar Liman Muhhamed, Newman explains that *boko* belongs to the category of "western concepts expressed in Hausa by semantic extension of pre-existent Hausa words" and originally referred to an object or idea that is fraudulent or deceitful—a definition that includes anything that is non-Islamic. Western education introduced during colonial times by the British was frown upon in contrast to highly regarded Islamic education. To this extent the elites would send only their servants to schools set up by the British government while choosing traditional Qur'anic schools for their own children. Western education was considered to be an external imposition and void of any substance and allowing children to attend those

schools would have amounted to turning them into *yan boko* [would-be Westerners]. By extension Western education became synonymous with fraud or sham (Paul Newman, *The etymology of Hausa boko*, Mega Chad Research Network 2013 http://www.megatchad.net/publications/Newman-2013-Etymology-of-Hausa-boko.pdf).

14. Mallam Sanni Umaru (2009) quoted in Kamal Tayo Oropo, Samson Ezea, Onyedika Agbedo and Njadvara Musa, Boko 'Haram Threatens To Attack Lagos, Claims Link To al-Queda', *Nairaland*, 15 August 2009 http://www.nairaland.com/310123/boko-haram-new-leader-teach#4354820

15. Abubakar Shekau (2012) quoted in SaharaReporters.com, 'Nigeria: More Than 170 Perished In Kano Bomb Blasts', 22 January 2012 http://sahara-reporters.com/news-page/nigeria-more-170-perished-kano-bomb-blasts The full message read: "In the name of Allah, Peace and Mercy! We are the group called 'forbidden' that is Boko Haram but we love to call ourselves *Jama'atu Ahlissunnah Liddaawati wal Jihad*. This message is to all inhabitants of Kano State especially the security agencies, those arresting our brothers and telling the media they are arresting thieves or armed robbers. These are our brothers they are arresting. We don't have the right to attack those who don't attack us but our war is with the government fighting Muslims, its security agencies and Christians (under C.A.N.), those killing Muslims and even eating their flesh and all those helping security agents even if they are Muslims. Anybody who becomes an accomplice to arresting our brothers should wait for our visit." The message ended with the words, "Message from Leader Jama'atu Ahlissunnah Liddaawati wal Jihad. Imam Abu Muhammad Abubakar Bin Muhammad (Shekau)."

16. Cook, *Boko Haram: A prognosis*, p. 10.

17. Gusau, 'Boko Haram: How it all began'.

18. Ihuoma Chiedozie, 'Suspected al Qaeda member denies confessional statement', *Punch*, 14 February 2013 http://www.punchng.com/news/suspected-al-qaeda-member-denies-confessional-statement/ and Jide Ajani, 'Nigeria: Trial of Mohammed Ashafa—the Making of Another Mohammed Yusuf, Boko Haram Leader', *Vanguard*, 11 March 2012 http://allafrica.com/stories/201203120553.html?viewall=1

19. Vanguard, 'Danger alert: Al-Qaeda boss in West Africa lives in Kano', *Vanguard*, 8 April 2012 http://tunde.ipaidabribenaija.com/news/item/2087-danger-alert-al-qaeda-boss-in-west-africa-lives-in-kano

20. BBC, 'Nigerian 'trained in Afghanistan', *BBC News*, 2 September 2009 http://news.bbc.co.uk/1/hi/world/africa/8233980.stm

21. Loimeier, 'Boko Haram: The Development of a Militant Religious Movement in Nigeria', p. 149.

22. Integrated Regional Information Networks (IRIN), *What will follow Boko*

Haram?, 24 November 2011, available at: http://www.refworld.org/docid/4ed388292.html (accessed 2 June 2013).

23. Barnaby Phillips, 'Nigeria's Borno state adopts Sharia', *BBC News*, 19 August 2000 http://news.bbc.co.uk/1/hi/world/africa/887355.stm
24. Gusau, 'Boko Haram: How it all began'.
25. See Mohammed, *The Paradox of Boko Haram Nigeria*, pp. 69–70; and Gusau, 'Boko Haram: How it all began'.
26. Mohammed, *The Paradox of Boko Haram Nigeria*, p. 69.
27. Mohammed Yusuf, 14 June 2009, quoted in Mohammed, *The Paradox of Boko Haram Nigeria*, p. 71.
28. See Mohammed, *The Paradox of Boko Haram Nigeria*; Gusau, 'Boko Haram: How it all began'; Nna-Emeka Okereke, 'Financing the Boko Haram: Some Informed Projections' in African Centre for the Study and Research on Terrorism (ACSRT), *African Journal for the Prevention and Combating of Terrorism*, Vol 2, No 1, Dec 2011, pp. 150–2.
29. 'Boko Haram Members Poison Water In Bauchi And Many More', *Nairaland Forum*, 31 July 2009 http://www.nairaland.com/303487/boko-haram-members-poison-water
30. Mohammed, *The Paradox of Boko Haram Nigeria*, pp. 73–80.
31. Olesegun Adeniyi, 27 July 2009 quoted in Mohammed, *The Paradox of Boko Haram Nigeria*, p. 81.
32. Mohammed, *The Paradox of Boko Haram Nigeria*, pp. 81–3.
33. Okereke, 'Financing the Boko Haram: Some Informed Projections', p. 152.
34. BBC News, 'Islamist death 'good for Nigeria'', *BBC News*, 31 July 2009 http://news.bbc.co.uk/1/hi/world/africa/8177681.stm
35. BBC News, 'Nigeria row over militant killing', *BBC News*, 31 July 2009 http://news.bbc.co.uk/1/hi/world/africa/8178820.stm
36. George Gorman, 'Nigerian Taliban leader killed in custody', *The Long War Journal*, 31 July 2009 http://www.longwarjournal.org/archives/2009/07/nigerian_taliban_lea.php
37. Interview with anonymous source #1, Nigeria 2013.
38. Gorman, 'Nigerian Taliban leader killed in custody'.
39. Interview with anonymous source #4, Nigeria 2013.
40. Al Jazeera, 'Video shows Nigeria 'executions'', *Al Jazeera* 9 February 2010 http://www.aljazeera.com/news/africa/2010/02/2010298114949112.html
41. Interview with anonymous source #4, Nigeria 2013.
42. Nasiru L. Abubakar, 'The last interview of our supreme leader Ustaz Mohammed Yusuf; during interrogation by infidel security operatives of the Nigerian state' *Daily Trust Newspapers* 30 July 2009, reproduced in Yusuf Islamic Brothers blog, 20 June 2011 http://yusufislamicbrothers.blogspot.co.uk/2011/06/last-interview-of-our-supreme-leader.html (formatting and spelling as in the original).

43. Spokesman of the Nigerian National Police (2009) quoted in Sharon Bean, 'The Founding of Boko Haram and Its Spread to 32 Nigerian States', *Terrorism Monitor*, Jamestown Foundation, 24 March 2010.

44. 'Boko Haram's divided house', *The Nigerian Voice* 24 July 2011 http://www. thenigerianvoice.com/news/56729/1/boko-harams-divided-house.html

45. Jacob Zenn, 'Can Nigeria exploit the split in the Boko Haram Movement?', *Terrorism Monitor Volume* 9(36) 22 September 2011 http://www.jamestown.org/single/?tx_ttnews%5Btt_news%5D=38442#.U4XKv3JdXAs

46. Jacob Zenn, 'Boko Haram's International Connections', *CTC Sentinel* 14 January 2013 http://www.ctc.usma.edu/posts/boko-harams-international-connections

47. Interview with anonymous source #4, Nigeria 2013; Interview with anonymous source #5, UK 2013; Freedom C. Onuoha, *Boko Haram: Nigeria's Extremist Islamic Sect*, Al Jazeera Centre for Studies, 29 February 2012 http://bit.ly/1dGU7AK; Jide Ajani, 'Boko Haram: A small group becomes a deadly scourge', *Legal Oil*, 26 June 2011 http://www.legaloil.com/NewsItem.asp?DocumentIDX=1309338116&Category=news

48. Interview with anonymous source #1, Nigeria 2013; and Xan Rice, 'Changing face of Nigeria's Boko Haram', *Financial Times*, 22 May 2012 http://www.ft.com/cms/s/0/9d2ab750–9ac1–11e1–9c98–00144feabdc0. html

49. Interview with anonymous source #1, Nigeria 2013.

50. Rice, 'Changing face of Nigeria's Boko Haram'.

51. Walker, What is Boko Haram?, p. 8.

52. Interview with anonymous source #1, Nigeria 2013.

53. Abdullahi Tasiu Abubakar, 'Profile of Nigeria's Boko Haram leader Abubakar Shekau', *BBC News*, 4 June 2013 http://www.bbc.co.uk/news/world-africa-18020349

54. Ibid.

55. Abubakar Shekau, 2012 quoted in AFP, 'Shekau leading Boko Haram from the shadows', *Vanguard*, 28 January 2012 http://www.vanguardngr.com/2012/01/shekau-leading-boko-haram-from-the-shadows/

56. Sagir Musa, 2013 quoted in Ndahi Marama, Uduma Kalu, Dayo Adesulu, 'I am alive, says Abubakar Shekau in new video', *Vanguard* 26 September 2013 http://www.vanguardngr.com/2013/09/i-am-alive-says-abubakar-shekau-in-new-video/

57. BBC News, 'Abubakar Shekau of Nigeria's Boko Haram "may be dead"'; *BBC News*, 19 August 2013 http://www.bbc.co.uk/news/world-africa-23761048

58. Maina Maina, 'Boko Haram: JTF insists Momodu Bama was killed in Bama encounter', *Daily Post*, 14 August 2013 http://dailypost.com.ng/2013/08/14/boko-haram-jtf-insists-momodu-bama-was-killed-in-bama-encounter/

59. Abubakar Shekau, 2013 quoted in Hamza Idris, 'Breaking news: Shekau appears in new video, says "I am alive"', *Daily Trust*, 25 September 2013 http://dailytrust.info/index.php/news/6244-breaking-news-shekau-appears-in-new-video-says-i-am-alive

60. Alex Thurston, 'Boko Haram and Nigeria's elections', *Sahel Blog*, 25 April 2011   http://sahelblog.wordpress.com/2011/04/25/boko-haram-and-nigerias-elections/

61. Walker, 'What is Boko Haram?', p. 5.

62. See for instance the attacks on a police station in February 2012 (Yusuf Mohammed & Ben Adaji, 'Boko Haram Strikes In Kogi, Kills 4; Police Station, Bank Burnt-PM News, Lagos', *Sahara Reporters*, 3 February 2012 http://saharareporters.com/news-page/boko-haram-strikes-kogi-kills-4-po-lice-station-bank-burnt-pm-news-lagos) and on a prison later that month freeing inmates (Atabor Julius, 'Nigeria: Boko Haram Frees Kogi Prison Inmates', *All Africa*, 15 February 2012 http://allafrica.com/stories/2012 02160852.html). An alleged Boko Haram cell was dismantled in late 2013 (Zachary Elkaim, 'Nigerian authorities dismantle Boko Haram cell in Kogi state', *The Long War Journal*, 22 November 2013 http://www.longwarjour-nal.org/threat-matrix/archives/2013/11/boko_haram_cell_busted.php#ixzz2rjIbgH8M).

63. Jacob Zenn, *Northern Nigeria's Boko Haram: The Prize in al-Qaeda's Africa Strategy*, The Jamestown Foundation, November 2012, p. 22.

64. See for instance: Reuters, 'Nigeria arrests 42 Boko Haram suspects in Lagos, Ogun', *Reuters*, 30 June 2013 http://www.reuters.com/article/2013/07/30/us-nigeria-bokoharam-idUSBRE96T0M620130730

65. 'Security forces foil Boko Haram attack on Lagos Int'l Airport', *National Daily*, 25 March 2013 http://www.nationaldailyng.com/current-edition/security-forces-foil-boko-haram-attack-on-lagos-intl-airport

66. Sani Muh'd Sani, 'Nigeria: Attack On Bauchi Prison—Boko Haram Frees 721 Inmates', *All Africa*, 8 September 2011 http://allafrica.com/sto-ries/201009090034.html

67. Matthew Onah, 'Boko Haram Raids Yola Prison, Frees 14', *This Day*, 23 April 2011 http://www.thisdaylive.com/articles/boko-haram-raids-yola-prison-frees-14/90140/

68. Reuters, 'Nigeria's Boko Haram free 40 in prison break: police', *Reuters*, 24 June 2012 http://www.reuters.com/article/2012/06/24/us-nigeria-bokoharam-idUSBRE85N0DP20120624

69. Reuters, 'Boko Haram attack leaves over 50 dead and sees 100 inmates freed from jail in Nigeria', *The Telegraph*, 8 May 2013 http://www.telegraph.co.uk/news/worldnews/africaandindianocean/nigeria/10043005/Boko-Haram-attack-leaves-over-50-dead-and-sees-100-inmates-freed-from-jail-in-Nigeria.html

70. USICF, 'Nigeria: Boko Haram: Religiously-Motivated Attacks', *Nigeria Factsheet*, August 2013 http://www.uscirf.gov/images/Final%20Nigeria%20 Factsheet%20%20August%2019,2013.pdf p. 1

71. BBC News, 'Christmas bombings kill many near Jos, Nigeria, *BBC News*, 25 December 2010 http://www.bbc.co.uk/news/world-africa-12077944

72. Monica Mark, 'After Nigeria's Church Bombings: The Advent of Christian-Muslim Conflict?', *TIME*, 27 December 2011 http://content.time.com/ time/world/article/0,8599,2103163,00.html

73. CNN Staff, '12 killed in attacks on two churches in Nigeria', *CNN*, 26 December 2012 http://edition.cnn.com/2012/12/25/world/africa/ nigeria-christmas-attack/

74. Paschal Ihuoma, 'Kabiru Sokoto bags life imprisonment for terrorism', *Punch*, 20 December 2013 http://www.punchng.com/news/boko-haram-kingpin-kabiru-sokoto-jailed-for-life/

75. ICG, 'Curbing Violence in Nigeria (I): The Jos Crisis', pp. 9–10.

76. Adam Higazi, *Rural Insecurity on the Jos Plateau, Nigeria: livelihoods, land, and religious reform among the Berom, Fulani and Hausa*, Nigeria Research Network (NRN), Oxford Department of International Development, Queen Elizabeth House, University of Oxford, January 2013, p. 16.

77. Ibid., pp. 17–18.

78. Walker, What is Boko Haram?, p. 1.

79. Sahara Reporters, 'Rift in Boko Haram, 'Ansaru' Splinter Group Emerges, Calls BH 'Inhuman' To Muslims', *Sahara Reporters*, 31 January 2012 http:// saharareporters.com/news-page/ rift-boko-haram-%E2%80%98ansaru%E2%80%99-splinter-group-emerges-calls-bh-%E2%80%98inhuman%E2%80%99-muslims?page=4

80. The video is no longer available. Quotes have been taken from LWJ Staff, 'New Islamist group emerges in Nigeria, vows to defend all Muslims in Africa', *Long War Journal*, 4 June 2012 http://www.longwarjournal.org/ threat-matrix/archives/2012/06/new_islamist_group_emerges_in.php

81. Interview with anonymous source #1, Nigeria 2013.

82. AFP, 'Nigeria claims 'global terrorist' Kambar killed', *AFP*, 6 June 2013 http://www.google.com/hostednews/afp/article/ALeqM5jk-K-7JtJP3j6v2 N2zBZAK1QGyMw?docId=CNG.64560c1b7e078b6ee2f2e6180f254326. 61

83. Interview with anonymoussource #1, Nigeria 2013.

84. Matthew Holehouse, 'British hostage murder: timeline of how the kidnap of Chris McManus and Franco Lamolinara by al-Qaeda unfolded', *The Telegraph*, 8 March 2012 http://www.telegraph.co.uk/news/worldnews/afri-caandindianocean/nigeria/9132476/British-hostage-murder-timeline-of-how-the-kidnap-of-Chris-McManus-and-Franco-Lamolinara-by-al-Qaeda-unfolded.html

85. Ibid.

86. Mohammed Abbas, 'Government bans Nigerian Islamist group accused of murder', *Reuters*, 22 November 2012 http://uk.reuters.com/article/2012/11/22/uk-britain-nigeria-islamists-idUKBRE8AL0VQ201 21122

87. Interview with anonymoussource #1, Nigeria 2013; 'Taking the hostage road', *Africa Confidential* 54 (6) March 2013.

88. Interview with anonymous source #4, Nigeria 2013.

89. Yusuf Alli, 'How bombers are chosen, by Boko Haram suspect', *The Nation*, 9 February 2012 http://www.thenationonlineng.net/2011/index.php/news/36248-how-bombers-are-chosen-by-boko-haram-suspect.html

90. Interview with Dr Freedom Onuoha, National Defence College, Abuja 2013.

91. Andrew McGregor, Captured Boko Haram spokesman undergoes "intense interrogation"', *Aberfoyle international Security*, 10 February 2012 http://www.aberfoylesecurity.com/?p=483

92. Interview with anonymoussource #1, Nigeria 2013.

93. Muhammad Bello, 'SARS Attack: New Islamic Sect Claims Responsibility', *ThisDay*, 27 November 2012 http://www.thisdaylive.com/articles/sars-attack-new-islamic-sect-claims-responsibility/131867/

94. Interview with anonymoussource #4, Nigeria 2013.

95. Cited by Emilie Oftedal, 'Boko Haram—an overview', *FFI-rapport*, 2013/01680, Norwegian Defence Research Establishment (FFI), 31 May 2013, p. 29.

96. Interview with anonymoussource #1, Nigeria 2013.

97. ICG, 'Curbing Violence in Nigeria (II): The Boko Haram Insurgency', *Africa Report*, 216, 3 April 2014, p. 22 http://www.crisisgroup.org/~/media/Files/africa/west-africa/nigeria/216-curbing-violence-in-nigeria-ii-the-boko-haram-insurgency.pdf

98. Heather Murdock, 'Ansaru Militants Claim Attack on Nigerian Soldiers', *Voice of America*, 21 January 2013 http://www.voanews.com/content/ansaru-militants-claim-attac-on-nigerian-soldiers/1587952.html

99. NSRP, 'Conflict briefing No. 14, 1 May–15 June 2013', *Nigeria Security and Reconciliation Programme*, June 2013, p. 2 http://www.nsrp-nigeria.org/wp-content/uploads/2013/07/Conflict-Briefing-No-14-1-May-15-June-2013.pdf

100. Ibid.

101. Ibid.

102. Mohammed, *The Paradox of Boko Haram*, pp. 84–6.

103. Freedom C. Onuoha, '(Un)Willing to Die: Boko Haram and Suicide Terrorism in Nigeria', *al Jazeera Center for Studies* 30 December 2012

http://studies.aljazeera.net/en/reports/2012/12/2012122491416595337.htm

104. Victor Ulasi 'Suicide attack, two other blasts rock Nigerian city', *Agence France-Presse*, February 9 2012 via http://www.jihadwatch.org/2012/02/nigeria-suicide-bomber-in-army-uniform-targets-barracks/

105. David Cook, 'Boko Haram: Reversals and Retrenchment', *CTC Sentinel*, 29 April 2013 http://www.ctc.usma.edu/posts/boko-haram-reversals-and-retrenchment

106. Sahara Reporters, 'Boko Haram Claims Responsibility For Tuesday's Maiduguri Attacks', *Sahara Reporters*, 14 January 2014 http://saharareporters.com/news-page/boko-haram-claims-responsibility-tuesdays-maiduguri-attacks

107. Hussaini Abdu, Nigeria Country Director, ActionAid. Interview with the author, Abuja, 17 April 2013.

108. Clement Idoko, 'Mid-Term Review: One out of three Nigerian children still out of school', *Nigerian Tribune*, 13 June 2013 http://tribune.com.ng/news2013/en/component/k2/item/14177-mid-term-review-one-out-of-three-nigerian-children-still-out-of-school.html

109. See my first draft for Voices (link to stat)

110. Charles Kumolu, 'Almajari Education: Modern gang up against ancient tradition?', *Vanguard*, 26 April 2012 http://www.vanguardngr.com/2012/04/almajiri-education-modern-gang-up-against-ancient-tradition/

111. Virginia Comolli, 'The lost boys of Kano', *IISS Voices*, 24 April 2013 http://www.iiss.org/en/iiss%20voices/blogsections/iiss-voices-2013–1e35/april-2013–982b/lost-boys-of-kano-3fe2

112. Daily Post, 'We Were Paid N5,000 to Burn Schools—Child Boko Haram Recruits Confess', *Daily Post*, 2 June 2013 http://newsrescue.com/we-were-paid-n5000-to-burn-schools-child-boko-haram-recruits-confess/#ixzz2WNTUxaOX

113. Rakiya A. Muhammad, 'How we're managing Almajiri Model School, by Sokoto SUBEC boss', *Sunday Trust*, 10 February 2013 http://www.sundaytrust.com.ng/index.php/component/content/article/60-education/education/7714-how-were-managing-almajiri-model-school-by-sokoto-subec-boss

114. Hussaini Abdu, Nigeria Country Director, ActionAid. Interview with the author, Abuja, 17 April 2013.

115. The practice and process of being an *almajiri*.

116. E. Isichei, 'The Maitatsine Risings in Nigeria 1980–85: A Revolt of the Disinherited', *Journal of Religion in Africa*, Vol. 3 Oct., 1987, p. 202.

117. Nathaniel Dominic Danjibo, 'Islamic Fundamentalism and Sectarian Violence: The "Maitatsine" and "Boko Haram" Crises in Northern

Nigeria', Peace and Conflict Studies Programme, Institute of African Studies, University of Ibadan, 2009 p. 6.

118. Ibid.

119. Ibid.

120. More on this has been documented by Hannah Hoechner, *Search for knowledge and recognition. Traditional Qur'anic Students in Kano, Nigeria*, French Institute For Research in Africa, 2013 http://www.ifra-nigeria.org/IMG/pdf/searching-for-knowledge-recognition-hannah-hoechner.pdf

121. Mervyn Hiskett, 'The Maitatsine Riots in Kano: An Assessment', *Journal of Religion in Africa* 17(3) 1987, pp. 209–223.

122. Ibid, pp. 212–213.

123. Abdulkareem Mohammed; Mohammed Haruna. *The Paradox of Boko Haram Nigeria*, Moving Image Limited, Nigeria, 2010, p. 16.

124. Ibid.

125. Hiskett, The Maitatsine Riots in Kano: An Assessment', p. 213.

126. Ibid.

127. Hannah Hoechner, *Search for knowledge and recognition. Traditional Qur'anic student in Kano, Nigeria*, Nigeria: French Institute For Research inAfrica,2013http://www.ifra-nigeria.org/IMG/pdf/searching-for-knowledge-recognition-hannah-hoechner.pdf

128. Hiskett, The Maitatsine Riots in Kano: An Assessment', pp. 212–13.

129. Hoechner, *Search for knowledge and recognition.*

130. Wole Soyinka, 'The Butchers of Nigeria', *Newsweek Magazine* 16 January 2012, pp. 1–5. http://thebea.st/17tJll5

131. Ibid.

132. Hoechner, *Search for knowledge and recognition*

133. Hannah Hoechner, 'Traditional Qur'anic students in Nigeria: fair game for unfair accusations?', *Debating Development* blog, 5 February 2013 http://blog.qeh.ox.ac.uk/?p=82

134. Ibid.

135. Ibid.

136. A.O. Adesoji, 'Between Maitatsine and Boko Haram: Islamic Fundamentalism and the Response of the Nigerian State', *Africa Today* Volume 57, Number 4, summer 2011, p. 113.

137. Hoechner, *Search for knowledge and recognition.*

138. Ibid.

139. Interview with Senior Nigerian Security Officer, Nigeria 2013.

140. Bill Clinton, 2013 quoted in Ini Ekott. 'Bill Clinton counters Jonathan, insists poverty behind Boko Haram, Ansaru insurgency', *Premium Times* 27 February 2013 http://premiumtimesng.com/news/122116-bill-clinton-counters-jonathan-insists-poverty-behind-boko-haram-ansaru-insurgency.html

141. Goodluck Jonathan, 2013. Ibid.
142. Chris Lawrence, 'Gates says Taliban have momentum in Afghanistan', *CNN*, 6 May 2009 http://edition.cnn.com/2009/POLITICS/05/06/mideast.gates/
143. Okereke, 'Financing the Boko Haram: Some Informed Projections', pp. 166–71.
144. Freedom C. Onuoha, 'Countering the Financing of Boko Haram Extremism in Nigeria', *African Journal for the Prevention and Combating of Terrorism* Vol 2, No 1, Dec 2011, p. 113.
145. *FAFT Report. Terrorist Financing in West Africa*, FATT/GIABA October 2013, p. 20 http://www.fatf-gafi.org/media/fatf/documents/reports/TF-in-West-Africa.pdf
146. Ibid., p. 18.
147. Interview with anonymous source #3, Nigeria 2013.
148. Wole Soyinka, 'The Butchers Of Nigeria', *Newsweek Magazine*, 16 January 2012 http://www.thedailybeast.com/newsweek/2012/01/15/wole-soyinka-on-nigeria-s-anti-christian-terror-sect-boko-haram.html
149. Marc-Antoine Pérouse de Montclos, 'Nigeria: comment en finir avec la nébuleuse Boko Haram', *Slate Afrique*, 25 February 2013 http://www.slateafrique.com/101999/nigeria-comment-lutter-contre-boko-haram-interview-perouse
150. Interview with US government officials in Nigeria, April 2013.
151. See for instance Kyari Mohammed, 'The message and methods of Boko Haram', p. 31 and Johannes Harnischfeger, 'Boko Haram and its Muslim Critics: observations from Yobe state', p. 46 in Marc-Antoine Pérouse de Montclos (ed.), *Boko Haram: Islamism, politics, security and the state in Nigeria*, West African Politics and Society Series, Vol. 2, 2014 file://iiss-uk-file03/home$/comolliv/Downloads/Boko_Haram_WAPOSO_2.pdf
152. Onuoha, 'Countering the Financing of Boko Haram Extremism in Nigeria', pp. 113–14.
153. Sahara Reporters, 'Boko Haram: Detained senator admits knowing BH spokesperson', *Sahara Reporters*, 21 November 2011 http://saharareporters.com/news-page/boko-haram-detained-senator-admits-knowing-bh-spokesperson?page=1 and Ikechukwu Nnochiri, 'Danger alert: Al-Qaeda boss in West Africa lives in Kano', *Vanguard* 25 October 2010 http://odili.net/news/source/2012/apr/8/335.html
154. Interview with Muhammad Zubair, Kano, April 2013.
155. Taiwo Ogundipe, 'Tracking the sect's cash flow', *The Nation*, 29 January 2012 http://www.thenationonlineng.net/2011/index.php/mobile/sunday-magazine/cover/34867-tracking-the-sect%E2%80%99s-cash-flow.html
156. Ibrahim Shuaibu, 'Boko Haram: Shekarau Denies Monthly Donation',

This Day Live, 29 January 2012 http://www.thisdaylive.com/articles/boko-haram-shekarau-denies-monthly-donation/108119/

157. Ogundipe, 'Tracking the sect's cash flow'.
158. Onuoha, 'Countering the Financing of Boko Haram Extremism in Nigeria', p. 114.
159. Ibid., p. 115.
160. Chinedu Offor, Femi Ogbonnikan and Ekene Okoro, 'Nigeria: FBI Links Al-Qaeda to Abuja Blasts', *Daily Independent*, 6 January 2011 http://ibidapowhyteworld.blogspot.co.uk/2011/01/fbi-links-al-qaeda-to-abuja-blasts.html
161. Onuoha, 'Countering the Financing of Boko Haram Extremism in Nigeria', p. 116.
162. C. Nna-Emeka Okereke, 'Financing the Boko Haram: Some Informed Projections', p. 168.
163. Emmanuel Ogala, 'Boko Haram Gets N40million Donation From Algeria', *Premium Times*, 13 May 2012 http://saharareporters.com/news-page/boko-haram-gets-n40million-donation-algeria-premium-times?page=1
164. 'Priest freed in Cameroon arrives back in France', *BBC News*, 1 January 2014 http://www.bbc.co.uk/news/world-europe-25566473
165. 'Boko Haram makes $1 million on average for any abducted wealthy Nigerian', *Nigeria News*, 6 July 2014 http://news2.onlinenigeria.com/headline/363917-boko-haram-makes-1-million-on-average-for-any-abducted-wealthy-nigerian.html#ixzz36s4iaXER
166. Michael Olugbode, Tobi Soniyi and Adebiyi Adedapo, 'Shettima Ali-Monguno Abducted in Maiduguri', *This Day Live*, 4 May 2013 http://www.thisdaylive.com/articles/shettima-ali-monguno-abducted-in-maiduguri/146700/
167. Premium Times, 'Killed Boko Haram commander spearheaded kidnap of Ali Monguno, seven French citizens, others—Security sources', *Premium Times*, 14 August 2013 http://premiumtimesng.com/news/142757-killed-boko-haram-commander-spearheaded-kidnap-of-ali-monguno-seven-french-citizens-others-security-sources.html
168. ICG, 'Curbing Violence in Nigeria (II): The Boko Haram Insurgency', p. 29.
169. Beacham Publishing's TRAC (Terrorism Research & Analysis Consortium); *Boko Haram: Coffers and Coffins; A Pandora's Box—the Vast Financing Options for Boko Haram*; May 2014 http://www.trackingterrorism.org/article/boko-haram-coffers-and-coffins-pandoras-box-vast-financing-options-boko-haram
170. Malachy Uzendu and Ahmed Mari, 'Nigeria: How We Share Boko Haram Loot—Abdul Qaqa', *All Africa*, 14 February 2012 http://allafrica.com/stories/201202140935.html

171. Interview with senior Nigerian security officer, 13 April 2013.
172. C. Nna-Emeka Okereke, 'Financing the Boko Haram: Some Informed Projections', p. 169.
173. Daily Trust, 'Nigeria: Boko Haram 'Taking Over Northern Borno State', *Daily Trust*, 20 April 2013 http://allafrica.com/stories/201304200127.html
174. Ola' Audu, 'Despite State of Emergency, car snatching thrives in Maiduguri', *Premium Times*, 22 May 2013 http://premiumtimesng.com/news/135490-despite-state-of-emergency-car-snatching-thrives-in-maiduguri.html
175. *FAFT Report. Terrorist Financing in West Africa*, FATT/GIABA October 2013, p. 23
176. Ibid, p. 21.
177. Allwell Okpi, 'NDLEA probes drug barons for Boko Haram links', *Punch*, 30 June 2013 http://www.punchng.com/news/ndlea-probes-drug-barons-for-boko-haram-links/
178. Yonah Alexander, *Terrorism in North Africa & the Sahel in 2012: Global Reach & Implications* (Arlington VA: Inter-University Center for Terrorism Studies, February 2013) http://moroccoonthemove.com/wp-content/uploads/2013/08/AlexanderTerrorisminNASahel2012.pdf
179. Punch, 'NFIU probes banks, charities over Boko Haram funds', *Punch*, 23 March 2013 http://www.punchng.com/news/nfiu-probes-banks-charities-over-boko-haram-funds/ Later
180. Uduma Kalu, 'MP accuses UK trust fund of funding Boko Haram', *Vanguard*, 9 September 2012 http://www.vanguardngr.com/2012/09/mp-accuses-uk-trust-fund-of-funding-boko-haram/
181. Beacham Publishing's TRAC (Terrorism Research & Analysis Consortium); *Boko Haram: Coffers and Coffins; A Pandora's Box—the Vast Financing Options for Boko Haram.*
182. Jide Ajani, 'Boko Haram got N11bn to kill, maim', *Vanguard*, 4 May 2014 http://www.vanguardngr.com/2014/05/boko-haram-got-n11bn-kill-maim/

5. THE INTERNATIONALISATION OF BOKO HARAM

1. 'Nigerian Army states 1, 200 killed by Boko Haram in 2 years', *NGOLC*, 13 March 2012 http://ngonlinecommunity.blogspot.co.uk/2012/03/nigerian-army-states-1-200-killed-by.html
2. Jide Ajani, 'Nigeria: Trial of Mohammed Ashafa—the Making of Another Mohammed Yusuf, Boko Haram Leader', *Vanguard*, 11 March 2012 http://allafrica.com/stories/201203120553.html?viewall=1

3. Shehu Sani, 'BOKO HARAM: The Northern Nigeria (Hausaland)', *Newsdiary*, 3 August 2011 http://newsdiaryonline.com/shehu_boko_haram. htm

4. Shehu Sani, 'BOKO HARAM: The Northern Nigeria (Hausaland) (2)', *Vanguard*, 1 July 2011 http://www.vanguardngr.com/2011/07/boko-haram-the-northern-nigeria-hausaland-2/

5. Virginia Comolli and Jacob Zenn, 'Danger at Home: Boko Haram's Threat to Nigeria and The Limits of Its Strategic Expansion', *Terrorism Research & Analysis Consortium (TRAC)*, 30 July 2012 http://bit.ly/VM7CEr

6. Jacob Zenn, 'Northern Cameroon Under Threat from Boko Haram and Séléka Militants', *Terrorism Monitor* Volume: 12 Issue: 1, 9 January 2014 http://www.jamestown.org/regions/africa/single/?tx_ttnews%5Btt_news%5D=41804&tx_ttnews%5BbackPid%5D=55&cHash=fd64836810cf831f3d550e441958aeae#.U44hhnJdXVU

7. 'Boko Haram infiltrates Cameroon', *Cameroon Online*, 11 January 2012 https://beegeagle.wordpress.com/2012/01/11/boko-haram-infiltrates-cameroon-flee-nigerian-jstf-onslaught/

8. Divine Ntaryike Jr, 'Boko Haram menace: massive troop deployment in Cameroon's Far North', *Cameroon Postline*, 13 January 2012 http://beegeagle.wordpress.com/2012/01/14/boko-haram-menace-massive-troop-deployment-in-cameroons-far-north/

9. For details of attacks see 'Cameroon', *CrisisWatch Database* http://www.crisisgroup.org/en/publication-type/crisiswatch/crisiswatch-database. aspx?CountryIDs=%7b5C2283AD-398B-4CEB-8ED9-B322B29F7E9A%7d#results

10. Jon Gambrell, 'Video Claims Nigeria Sect Holds 7 French', *Associated Press*, 25 February 2013 http://news.yahoo.com/video-claims-nigeria-sect-holds-7-french-hostages-163759996.html

11. Haruna Umar and Sunday Alamba, 'Nigeria: French hostage and family in new video', *Associated Press*, 18 March 2013 http://news.yahoo.com/nigeria-french-hostage-family-video-171414745.html

12. Paul Cruickshank and Tim Lister, 'Boko Haram has kidnapped before—successfully', *CNN*, 12 May 2014 http://edition.cnn.com/2014/05/12/world/boko-haram-previous-abductions/

13. Nicholas Vinocur and Tiemoko Diallo, 'France says will not negotiate with Cameroon hostage-takers', *Reuters*, 26 February 2013 http://uk.reuters.com/article/2013/02/26/us-cameroon-kidnapping-idUSBRE91P0G220130226

14. 'Cameroon gunmen free French priest Georges Vandenbeusch', *BBC News*, 31 December 2013

15. 'Italian priests and Canadian nun 'freed in Cameroon'', *BBC News*, 1 June 2014 http://www.bbc.co.uk/news/world-africa-27655761

16. 'Suspected Boko Haram rebels attack Chinese plant in Cameroon', *France24*, 17 May 2014 http://www.france24.com/en/20140517-cameroon-boko-haram-attack-chinese/

17. 'Six arrested in Cameroon over Chinese worker abductions', *The Straits Times*, 4 June 2014 http://www.straitstimes.com/news/world/more-world-stories/story/six-arrested-cameroon-over-chinese-worker-abductions-20140604#sthash.AUPzDh4s.dpuf

18. 'Nigeria Ethno-Religious', *The Armed Conflict Database*, 20 December 2013

19. *OP RESTORE ORDER SITREP—Week Ending 25 January 2014*, 27 January 2014 http://peccaviconsulting.wordpress.com/2014/01/27/op-restore-order-sitrep-week-ending-25-january-2014/

20. 'Nigeria violence: Cameroon boosts anti-Boko Haram border forces', *BBC News*, 27 May 2014 http://www.bbc.co.uk/news/world-africa-27593163

21. Zenn, *Northern Nigeria's Boko Haram: The Prize in al-Qaeda's Africa Strategy*, p. 29.

22. David Lewis, 'Niger fears contagion from Nigeria's Boko Haram Islamists', *Reuters*, 19 March 2014 http://www.reuters.com/article/2014/03/19/us-niger-bokoharam-insight-idUSBREA2I16720140319

23. Emmanuel Grégoire, 'Islam and the identity of merchants in Maradi (Niger)' in Louis Brenner (ed.), *Muslim Identity and Social Change in Sub-Saharan Africa*, Bloomington and Indianapolis: Indiana University Press, 1993), p. 111.

24. Telephone interview with anonymous source #6, June 2013.

25. Ibid.

26. See 'Niger: Another Weak Link in the Sahel?', *Africa Report* N°20819 Sep 2013 http://www.crisisgroup.org/en/regions/africa/west-africa/niger/208-niger-another-weak-link-in-the-sahel.aspx

27. More details on Flintlock are provided in the next chapter on government responses.

28. 'Niger Gets New Planes and Trucks Through US Security Cooperation Programs', *United Stated African Command*, 16 July 2013 http://www.afri-com.mil/Newsroom/Article/11021/niger-gets-new-planes-and-trucks-through-us-security-cooperation-programs

29. 'Al-Mourabitoun threatens attacks against France over Mali intervention', *IHS Jane's Terrorism Watch Report—Daily Update*, 13 January 2014 http://www.janes.com/article/32393/al-mourabitoun-threatens-attacks-against-france-over-mali-intervention

30. 'Niger', *CrisisWatch Database* http://www.crisisgroup.org/en/publication-type/crisiswatch/crisiswatch-database.aspx?CountryIDs=%7bF26B8D94–91A6–4238-BEA8–0D07EF0D800D%7d#results

31. Bureau of Counterterrorism, US Department of State, 'Chapter 2. Country

Reports: Africa Overview', *Country Reports on Terrorism 2013*, 2014 http://www.state.gov/j/ct/rls/crt/2013/224820.htm

32. Adelani Adepegba, 'Boko Haram: Police arrest Chadian, Islamic teacher in Niger', *Punch*, 18 February 2012 http://www.punchng.com/news/boko-haram-police-arrest-chadian-islamic-teacher-in-niger/

33. Hakeem Onapajoa, Ufo Okeke Uzodikea and Ayo Whetho, 'Boko Haram terrorism in Nigeria: The international dimension', *South African Journal of International Affairs* Volume 19, Issue 3, 2012, p. 345.

34. Ifeanyi Okoli, 'Boko Haram: Police arrest 500 foreigners in Lagos', *Vanguard*, 23 March 2013 http://www.vanguardngr.com/2013/03/boko-haram-police-arrest-500-foreigners-in-lagos/

35. 'Chad', *CrisisWatch Database*, http://www.crisisgroup.org/en/publication-type/crisiswatch/crisiswatch-database.aspx?CountryIDs=%7b9C8A1AB3–7044–4ABE-904B-8D05DBFDC514%7d#results

36. Moki Edwin Kindzeka, 'Cameroon, Chad Finalize Boko Haram Security Talks', *Voice of America*, 23 May 2014 http://www.voanews.com/content/cameroon-chad-team-up-to-combat-boko-haram/1920228.html

37. 'Cameroon takes steps against Boko Haram', *IRIN*, 27 December 2013 http://www.irinnews.org/report/99396/cameroon-takes-steps-against-boko-haram

38. Anna Jefferys, 'Displaced by Boko Haram, Nigerians risk invisibility in Niger', *IRIN* 30 January 2014 http://www.irinnews.org/report/99558/displaced-by-boko-haram-nigerians-risk-invisibility-in-niger

39. Ibid.

40. Lisa Schlein, 'UNHCR Warns Against Forcibly Returning Nigerian Asylum Seekers', *Voice of America*, 29 October 2013 http://www.voanews.com/content/unhcr-warns-against-forcibly-reurning-nigerian-asylum-seekers/1779318.html

41. Nduka Nwosu, 'UN: 6, 000 Flee Nigeria over Boko Haram', *This Day*, 24 January 2014 http://www.thisdaylive.com/articles/un-6–000-flee-nigeria-over-boko-haram/169711/

42. 'NIGERIA-CHAD: Migrants fleeing Boko Haram violence await aid', *IRIN* 6 March 2012 http://www.irinnews.org/report/95014/nigeria-chad-migrants-fleeing-boko-haram-violence-await-aid

43. UNHCR, 'Nigerians flee from insurgent attacks into Chad', *UNHCR Briefing Notes* 5 August 2014 http://www.unhcr.org/53e0c0af149.html

44. Moki Kindzeka, 'Boko Haram threat harms Cameroon-Nigeria border trade', *Deutsche Welle*, 27 December 2012 http://www.dw.de/boko-haram-threat-harms-cameroon-nigeria-border-trade/a-16480155

45. Moki Edwin Kindzeka, 'Fear of Boko Haram Hits Food Prices in Cameroon During Ramadan', *Voice of America* 2 July 2014 http://www.voanews.com/author/23003.html

46. Interview with anonymous source #3, Nigeria 2013.

47. Waters are receding owing to the advance of the desert. Herders from Nigeria and Cameroon have therefore started to move southward resulting in tensions with local farming communities. See for instance: Elias Ntungwe Ngalame, 'Immigration surging in Cameroon as farmers and fishermen desert shrinking Lake Chad', *Thomson Reuters Foundation*, 5 October 2010 http://www.trust.org/item/20101005101300-nsmjp/?source=spotlight

48. Interview with Comrade Abba P. Moro, Minister of Interior, Abuja, 2013.

49. Interview with anonymoussource at the Ministry of Foreign Affairs, Abuja, 2013.

50. Benin does not currently have a Boko Haram problem but officials agree that the country should remain vigilant to avoid the possible setting up of cells.

51. Festus Owete, 'EXCLUSIVE: Nigeria, France, Cameroon, three other countries sign deal on massive, joint offensive against Boko Haram', *Premium Times*, 18 March 2014 http://www.premiumtimesng.com/news/156947-exclusive-nigeria-france-cameroon-three-other-countries-sign-deal-on-massive-joint-offensive-against-boko-haram.html

52. Moki Edwin Kindzeka, 'Lake Chad Countries Agree on Military Task Force Amid Insecurity', *Voice of America*, 18 March 2014 http://www.voanews.com/content/lake-chad-countries-agree-on-military-task-force-amid-insecurity/1873650.html

53. 'France sends troops to Central African Republic', *Deutsche Welle*, 24 March 2013 http://www.dw.de/france-sends-troops-to-central-african-republic/a-16695739

54. ICG, 'Central African Republic: Better Late than Never', *Africa Briefing* No. 96, 2 December 2013 http://www.crisisgroup.org/en/regions/africa/central-africa/central-african-republic/b096-central-african-republic-better-late-than-never.aspx

55. Alex Duval Smith, 'Central African Republic: 'seeds of genocide' being sown, warns UN', *The Guardian*, 16 January 2014 http://www.theguardian.com/global-development/2014/jan/16/central-african-republic-seeds-genocide-un

56. Hannah McNeish, 'Lawless CAR Attracting Terrorists' Attention', *Voice of America*, 22 November 2013 http://www.voanews.com/content/lawless-car-attracting-terrorists-attention/1795564.html

57. Jacob Zenn, 'Northern Cameroon Under Threat from Boko Haram and Séléka Militants', *Terrorism Monitor* 12(1) 9 January 2014 http://www.jamestown.org/programs/tm/single/?tx_ttnews[tt_news]=41804&tx_ttnews[backPid]=26&cHash=d4e4d12a549936b15fcc3042430485c2#.UurTcD1_vVV

58. NCTC, *2011 Report on Terrorism*, 2011 http://www.fas.org/irp/threat/nctc2011.pdf

59. The *2011 Report on Terrorism* compiled by the US government's National Counterterrorism Centre (NCTC) in spring 2012 indicated that global terrorist attacks had reached the lowest incidence level in years but also noted that, together with Latin America but rooted in different ideological positions, Africa was one of two regions of the world where violence at the hands of non-state groups had taken a turn for the worse.

60. START, *Despite fewer attacks in Western world, global terrorism increasing*, The National Consortium for the Study of Terrorism and Responses to Terrorism (START), 19 December 2013 http://www.start.umd.edu/start/announcements/announcement.asp?id=633

61. 'Sunni Rebels Declare New Islamic Caliphate', *Al Jazeera*, 30 June 2014 http://www.aljazeera.com/news/middleeast/2014/02/al-qaeda-disowns-isil-rebels-syria-20142385858351969.html

62. Interesting to note, in spite of his global ambitions bin Laden had discouraged Somalia's al-Shabaab, possibly for fear that such a move would have diluted the "prestige" al-Qaeda brand, from adopting the al-Qaeda name, and a formal alignment only happened after his death.

63. Pew Research, 'On Anniversary of bin Laden's Death, Little Backing of al Qaeda', *PewResearch Global Attitude Project* 30 April 2012 http://www.pewglobal.org/2012/04/30/on-anniversary-of-bin-ladens-death-little-backing-of-al-qaeda/

64. Vanguard. "Boko Haram Voices Support for Islamic State's Baghdadi, Al-Qaeda." *Vanguard*, July 13, 2014.

65. 'Nigeria rejects Boko Haram 'caliphate' claim', *Aljazeera* 25 August 2014 http://www.aljazeera.com/news/africa/2014/08/nigeria-rejects-boko-haram-caliphate-claim-20148251062176395.html

66. AQIM, previously known as the Salafist Group for Preaching and Combat (GSPC), it had earlier split from Algeria's Armed Islamic Group and re-branded itself in 2006 becoming part of the al-Qaeda franchise.

67. IISS, 'Extremism spreads across West Africa and the Sahel', *Strategic Comments* 18(40) 2012 http://www.iiss.org/publications/strategic-comments/past-issues/volume-18–2012/october/extremism-spreads-across-west-africa-and-the-sahel/

68. 'Quand le Boko haram se réclame d'el hadj Omar Tall, de Sekou Amadou et... La liste des principaux dirigeants du MNLA, D'ANÇAR-DINE, d'AQMI, du MUJAO..., des Katibas...', *Mali Web*, 5 February 2013 http://www.maliweb.net/la-situation-politique-et-securitaire-au-nord/quand-le-boko-haram-se-reclame-del-hadj-omar-tall-de-sekou-amadou-et-la-liste-des-principaux-dirigeants-du-mnla-dancar-dine-daqmi-du-mujao-des-katiba-124965.html

69. US Department of State, 'Abubakar Shekau. Up to $7 Million Reward', *Reward for Justice* 2013 http://www.rewardsforjustice.net/english/abubakar_shekau.html

70. More on the US stance on Boko Haram in the next chapter.

71. Carter Ham quoted in Karen Leigh, 'Nigeria's Boko Haram: Al-Qaeda's New Friend in Africa?', *Time*, 31 August 2011 http://content.time.com/time/world/article/0,8599,2091137,00.html

72. Ibid.

73. Beacham Publishing's TRAC (Terrorism Research & Analysis Consortium), *The Triad of Leaders in Boko Haram reflects it's Larger Transnational Aspirations*, accessed 7 June 2014 http://www.trackingterrorism.org/article/triad-leaders-boko-haram-reflects-its-larger-transnational-aspirations

74. Office of the Coordinator for Counterterrorism, US Department of State, 'Chapter 2. Country Reports: Africa Overview', *Country Reports on Terrorism 2010*, 18 August 2011 http://www.state.gov/j/ct/rls/crt/2010/170254.htm

75. See for instance Rob in Simcox, 'Boko Haram and defining the 'al-Qaeda network'', *Al Jazeera*, 6 June 2014 http://www.aljazeera.com/indepth/opinion/2014/06/boko-haram-al-qaeda-201463115816142554.html; or Jacob Zenn, 'Nigerian al-Qaedism', *Current Trends in Islamist Ideology* Vol 16, March 2014 http://www.hudson.org/research/10172-nigerian-al-qaedaism-

76. IISS, 'Extremism spreads across West Africa and the Sahel'.

77. Ibid.

78. Walker, 'What is Boko Haram?', p. 4.

79. 'How Boko Haram Leader, Tishau, Varnished from Custody—Chief Of defence Staff', *Point Blank News*, 28 September 2011 http://www.pointblanknews.com/News/os5639.html

80. 'The Punch Interview: "I Told The Inspector General Of Police In Advance That Abuja Would Be Bombed," Says Boko Haram Leader', *Sahara Reporters*, 20 September 2011 http://saharareporters.com/interview/punch-interview-i-told-inspector-general-police-advance-abuja-would-be-bombed-says-boko-ha

81. Shehu Sani, 'Boko Haram: History, Ideas and Revolt', *Newsdiaryonline*, 3 August 2011 http://newsdiaryonline.com/shehu_boko_haram.htm

82. Interview with anonymoussource #1, Nigeria, 2013.

83. Abu Qaqa quoted in Monica Mark, 'Boko Haram vows to fight until Nigeria establishes sharia law', *The Guardian*, 27 January 2013 http://www.theguardian.com/world/2012/jan/27/boko-haram-nigeria-sharia-law

84. Jason Burke, 'Bin Laden files show al-Qaida and Taliban leaders in close contact', *The Guardian*, 29 April 2012 http://www.theguardian.com/world/2012/apr/29/bin-laden-al-qaida-taliban-contact

85. *Strategic Survey 2013. The Annual review of world affairs*, (Abingdon: Routledge, 2013), pp. 248–51.

86. *Strategic Survey 2014. The Annual review of world affairs*, [Abingdon: Routledge, 2015].
87. 'Mali: Leader Warns of Jihadi Camps', *The New York Times*, 7 June 2012; *OP RESTORE ORDER SITREP—Week Ending 16 November 2013*, 20 November 2013 http://peccaviconsulting.wordpress.com/2013/11/20/op-restore-order-sitrep-week-ending-9-november-2013–2/
88. Peter Tinti, 'Understanding Algeria's Northern Mali Policy', *Think Africa Press*, 5 October 2012 http://thinkafricapress.com/mali/understanding-algeria-northern-mali-aqim-mujao-ansar-dine
89. See for instance 'Dozens of Boko Haram help Mali's rebel seize Gao', *Vanguard*, 9 April 2012 http://www.vanguardngr.com/2012/04/dozens-of-boko-haram-help-malis-rebel-seize-gao/
90. 'Boko Haram spreads terror campaign to Mali', *Punch*, 10 April 2012 http://www.punchng.com/news/boko-haram-spreads-terror-campaign-to-mali/
91. "La mythique Tombouctou sous le joug des islamistes", *Jeune Afrique*, 3 April 2012 http://www.jeuneafrique.com/actu/20120403T103318Z20120403T103316Z/
92. Jemal Oumar, 'Tuareg rebels vow terror crackdown', *Magharebia*, 22 November 2012 http://magharebia.com/en_GB/articles/awi/features/2012/11/22/feature-01
93. Issa Sikiti Da Silva, 'Mali Islamists seize town of Konna, advancing towards Sévaré, Mopti', *Moon of the South*, 11 January 2011 http://moonofthesouth.com/mali-islamists-seize-town-konna/
94. Colin Freeman, 'Boko Haram's Abubakar Shekau: The 'craziest commander of all", *The Telegraph*, 12 May 2014 http://www.telegraph.co.uk/news/worldnews/africaandindianocean/nigeria/10826012/Boko-Harams-Abubakar-Shekau-The-craziest-commander-of-all.html
95. 'Boko Haram leader Abubakar Shekau flees to Mali', *Elombah*, 28 January 2013 http://elombah.com/index.php/reports/14298-boko-haram-leader-abubakar-shekau-flees-to-mali
96. 'Boko Haram: Splinter group, Ansaru emerges', *Vanguard*, 1 February 2012 http://www.vanguardngr.com/2012/02/boko-haram-splinter-group-ansaru-emerges/
97. 'New Qaeda spin-off threatens West Africa', *Ahram Online*, 22 December 2011 http://english.ahram.org.eg/NewsContent/2/9/29968/World/International/New-Qaeda-spinoff-threatens-West-Africa.aspx
98. 'Nigeria: Islamist group Ansaru 'kidnapped' French man', *BBC News*, 24 December 2012 http://www.bbc.co.uk/news/world-africa-20833946
99. Tim Cocks, 'Islamists Ansaru claim attack on Mali-bound Nigeria troops: paper', *Reuters*, 20 January 2013 http://www.reuters.com/article/2013/01/20/us-nigeria-violence-idUSBRE90J0B520130120

100. Jacob Zenn, 'Cooperation or Competition: Boko Haram and Ansaru After the Mali Intervention', *CTC Sentinel* 27 March 2013 https://www.ctc. usma.edu/posts/cooperation-or-competition-boko-haram-and-ansaru-after-the-mali-intervention

101. Ibid.

102. For more on this issue see Raffaello Pantucci and A.R. Sayyid, 'Foreign Fighters in Somalia and al-Shabaab's Internal Purge', *Terrorism Monitor* Volume: 11 Issue: 22, 3 December 2013 http://www.jamestown.org/single/?no_cache=1&tx_ttnews%5Btt_news%5D=41705#.U5Ni8nKwLpg

103. AFP, 'Nigeria claims 'global terrorist' Kambar killed'.

104. 'Nigerian Islamists vow 'fiercer' attacks', *Agence France-Presse*, 16 June 2011 http://m.reliefweb.int/report/420355

105. Jacob Zenn, 'Boko Haram's international connections', *CTC Sentinel*, 14 January 2013 http://www.ctc.usma.edu/posts/boko-harams-international-connections

106. Cleophus Tres Thomas and Fuad Ahmed, 'Al-Shabaab support for Boko Haram reflects group's own sordid past with children', *Sabahi*, 16 May 2014 http://sabahionline.com/en_GB/articles/hoa/articles/features/2014/05/16/feature-01

107. Sean M. Gourley, 'Linkages between Boko Haram and al-Qaeda: a potential deadly synergy', *Global Security Studies* Volume 3, Issue 3, summer 2012, p. 9.

108. Telephone interview with anonymoussource #8, 2013.

109. Ibid.

110. Onapajoa, Uzodikea and Whetho, 'Boko Haram terrorism in Nigeria: The international dimension', p. 347.

111. Allwell Okpi, 'FG, Boko Haram hold secret talks in Senegal', *Punch*, 2 December 2012 http://www.punchng.com/news/fg-boko-haram-hold-secret-talks-in-senegal/ and 'Imam Ratib de la Grande mosquée de Bignona «Boko Haram est présent au Sénégal »', *SeneNews*, 23 August 2012 http://www.senenews.com/2012/08/23/imam-ratib-de-la-grande-mosquee-de-bignona-boko-haram-est-present-au-senegal_39852.html

6. GOVERNMENT RESPONSES

1. IISS, *The Military Balance 2014*, London: Routledge, 2014, p. 451.

2. Ibid., p. 415.

3. Bassey Udu, 'Jonathan signs Nigeria's 2014 budget as Defence gets 20 per cent', *Premium Times*, 24 May 2014 http://www.premiumtimesng.com/business/161390-jonathan-signs-nigerias-2014-budget-defence-gets-20-per-cent.html

4. Integrated Regional Information Networks (IRIN), *Nigeria: Timeline of Boko Haram activity*, 7 October 2011, http://www.refworld.org/cgi-bin/texis/vtx/rwmain?docid=4e93ffa02

5. Interview with senior police officer, Nigeria 2013.

6. Mohammed, *The Paradox of Boko Haram*, p. 81.

7. IISS, 'Boko Haram: Nigeria's growing new headache', *Strategic Comments* 17(42) November 2011.

8. Interview with anonymoussource #5, 2013.

9. Ibid.

10. Sagir Musa, 'Border Security, Arms Proliferation And Terrorism In Nigeria By Lt Col Sagir Musa', *Sahara Reporters*, 20 April 2013 http://saharareporters.com/article/border-security-arms-proliferation-and-terrorism-nigeria-lt-col-sagir-musa

11. Gbenga Omokhunu, 'Boko Haram menace is a temporary setback—Jonathan', *The Nation*, 10 November 2011 http://www.thenationonlineng.net/2011/index.php/news-update/25894-boko-haram-menace-is-a-temporary-setback-jonathan.html

12. Amnesty International, *Nigeria: Trapped in a cycle of violence*, London: Amnesty International, 2012, p. 8 http://www.amnesty.ca/sites/default/files/nigeriareport1november12.pdf

13. Hussein Solomon, 'Counter-Terrorism in Nigeria', *The RUSI Journal* 157(4) 2012, p. 7.

14. Tim Lister, 'Islamist militants in Nigeria warn Christians to leave north within 3 days', *CNN*, 2 January 2012 http://edition.cnn.com/2012/01/02/world/africa/nigeria-sectarian-divisions/index.html

15. See detailed list of attacks in Oftedal, *Boko Haram—An overview*.

16. Wole Oyetunji, 'US warns Boko Haram may be planning attacks in Abuja', *AFP*, 18 April 2012 http://www.google.com/hostednews/afp/article/ALeqM5irmUzsr9wBSbTol_OsZjjdfGAN2Q?docId=CNG.ef48bed6020889f8396c1f06d4203fc4.281

17. Lister, 'Islamist militants in Nigeria warn Christians to leave north within 3 days'.

18. Interview with CAN's General Secretary Reverend Dr Musa Asake, Nigeria 2013.

19. Interview with Dr Ustaz Aminu Igwegbe, Director of Administration, Nigerian Supreme Council of Islamic Affairs, Nigeria 2013.

20. 'Kaduna govt relaxes 24-hour curfew', *Channels Television*, 3 July 2012 http://www.channelstv.com/home/2012/07/03/kaduna-govt-relaxes-24-hour-curfew/

21. 'Nigeria: Ensuring Stability, Human Safety and Security', *Briefing Paper*, Open Society Initiative for West Africa, October 2012.

22. For a more detailed chronology of attacks see Manuel Reinert & Lou Garçon, 'Boko Haram: A chronology' in Marc-Antoine Pérouse de Montclos (ed.), *Boko Haram: Islamism, politics, security and the state in Nigeria*, West African Politics and Society Series, Vol. 2, 2014, pp. 237–245 file://iiss-ukfile03/home$/comolliv/Downloads/Boko_Haram_WAPOSO_2.pdf

23. 'Joint Task Force Declares Boko Haram Top Guns Wanted; N50m Bounty For Abubakar Shekau', *Sahara Reporters* 23 November 2012 http://saharareporters.com/news-page/joint-task-force-declares-boko-haram-top-guns-wanted-n50m-bounty-abubakar-shekau

24. Olalekan Adetayo, 'President not afraid to visit Maiduguri—Aide', *Punch* 2 March 2013 http://www.punchng.com/news/president-not-afraid-to-visit-maiduguri-aide/

25. Jide Ajani, Kingsley Omonobi & Ndahi Marama, 'Boko Haram: Plot to shoot down Joanthan's plane foiled', *Vanguard* 10 March 2013 http://www.vanguardngr.com/2013/03/boko-haram-plot-to-shoot-down-jonathans-plane-foiled/

26. Ibid.

27. 'NIGERIA: Why Boko Haram targets Lagos', *Nigeria News*, 4 April 2013 http://www.codewit.com/nigeria-news/7085-nigeria-why-boko-haram-targets-lagos

28. 'Boko Haram's Attack Threats Hit Lagos: Nigerian Immigration Service Deports Over 50 Illegal Immigrants From Chad, Niger & Mali', *Naija Gist*, 26 March 2013 http://naijagists.com/boko-haram-attack-threats-hit-lagos-nigerian-immigration-service-deports-over-50-illegal-immigrants-from-from-chad-niger-mali/

29. Jide Ajani, 'Why Obasanjo visited Mohammed Yusuf's family', *Vanguard*, 18 September 2011 http://www.vanguardngr.com/2011/09/the-scourge-of-boko-haram-why-obasanjo-visited-mohammed-yusuf%E2%80%99s-family/

30. Ruga Joe Omokaro and Maxwell Oditta, 'Nigeria: Boko Haram Kills Former President's Host, Rejects Peace Move', *The Moment*, 4 August 2012 http://allafrica.com/stories/201208050061.html?viewall=1

31. Ibid.

32. Etinosa Osayimwen, 'Internal Fighting in Boko Haram As Shekau Faction Insists on Cease Fire', *The Herald*, 25 February 2013 http://www.theheraldng.com/internal-fighting-in-boko-haram-as-shekau-faction-insists-on-cease-fire/

33. Abubakar Shekau quoted in Ndahi Marama, 'Boko Haram: Shekau denies ceasefire, dialogue with FG', *Vanguard* 3 March 2013 http://www.vanguardngr.com/2013/03/boko-haram-shekau-denies-ceasefire-dialogue-with-fg/ (emphasis added).

34. Stanley Mkwocha, 'Nigeria: Why Governor Shettima Advocates Amnesty for Boko Haram—Gusau', *Leadership*, 1 April 2013 http://allafrica.com/stories/201304010821.html?viewall=1

35. 'Nigeria: Boko Haram—Jonathan Sets up Amnesty Committee', Vanguard 5 April 2013 http://allafrica.com/stories/201304050714.html?viewall=1

36. The Committee consists of: Ahmed Lemu, Hakeem Baba Ahmed, Musa Shehu (rtd.), Abubakar Tureta, Abubakar Sodangi, Ahmed Makarfi, Mohammed Matawalle, Zakari Ibrahim, Naja'atu Mohammed, Adamu Ladan, Joseph Golwa, A.I. Shehu, R.I Nkemdirim, P. I. Leha, Nura Alkali, Salihu Abubakar, Abubakar Sani Lugga,Ibrahim Tahir, Ibrahim Sab, Baba Ahmed Jidda, Bilal Bulama, and Bolaji Akinyemi. Datti Ahmed and Shehu Sani, declined to serve on the committee, saying they were not sure of government's commitment to the process.

37. "Arewa" is Hausa for "Northern".

38. Interview with Interior Minister Abba Boro, Abuja, 2013.

39. Interview with security expert, National Defence College, Abuja 2013.

40. 'Nigeria: Boko Haram—Jonathan Sets up Amnesty Committee'.

41. Interview with civil society representative, Nigeria, 2013.

42. Interview with senior Army officer, Defence HQ, Abuja, 2013.

43. Interview with senior Army officer, Abuja, 2013

44. Interview with anonymous source #3, Nigeria 2013.

45. Ibid.

46. Interview with CAN's General Secretary Reverend Dr Musa Asake, Nigeria 2013.

47. BBC, 'Nigeria: Goodluck Jonathan declares emergency in states', *BBC News*, 15 May 2013 http://www.bbc.co.uk/news/world-africa-22533974

48. NSRP, *Conflict Briefing No. 14, 1 May–15 June 2013*, Nigeria Stability and Reconciliation Programme 2013 http://www.nsrp-nigeria.org/wp-content/uploads/2013/07/Conflict-Briefing-No-14–1-May-15-June-2013.pdf

49. Abubakar Sheakau, 'Nigeria's Boko Haram claims victories over military', Video via *AFP*, 29 May 2013 http://www.youtube.com/watch?v=XTMwqGtUyjQ

50. 'US drones spy on Boko Haram', *The Punch*, 25 May 2013 http://www.punchng.com/news/us-drones-spy-on-boko-haram/

51. Senator Iroegbu, 'DHQ: Over 1,000 Boko Haram Members Captured in Three Months', *This Day*, 9 August 2013 http://www.thisdaylive.com/articles/dhq-over-1–000-boko-haram-members-captured-in-three-months/155873/

52. Telephone interview with Nigerian journalist, June 2013.

53. Lanre Ola and Joe Brock, 'Nigeria lifts mobile phone blackout in militant stronghold', *Reuters*, 19 July 0213 http://uk.reuters.com/article/2013/07/19/nigeria-violence-idUKL6N0FP1AM20130719

54. BBC, 'Nigeria school massacre: Yobe secondary schools closed', *BBC News*, 7 July 2013 http://www.bbc.co.uk/news/world-africa-23221237
55. Telephone interview with anonymoussource #6, June 2013.
56. Maina Maina, 'Boko Haram: 3 killed, over 20,000 flee to Cameroun', Daily Post 3 July 2013 http://dailypost.ng/2013/07/03/boko-haram-13-killed-over-20000-flee-to-cameroun/
57. Chris Olukolade quoted in Senator Iroegbu, 'DHQ: Over 1,000 Boko Haram Members Captured in Three Months', *This Day* 9 August 2013 http://www.thisdaylive.com/articles/dhq-over-1–000-boko-haram-members-captured-in-three-months/155873/
58. Ola' Audu, 'Vigilantes going after Boko Haram; work under military supervision—JTF', *Premium Times* 30 June 2013 http://premiumtimesng.com/news/139944-vigilantes-going-after-boko-haram-work-under-military-supervision-jtf.html
59. Maina, 'Boko Haram: 3 killed, over 20,000 flee to Cameroon'.
60. 'Civilian JTF Commander Speaks On War Against Boko Haram In Maiduguri', *Naij* 2 April 2014 http://news.naij.com/63467.html
61. 'Boko Haram declares war on Borno, Yobe youth over vigilante activities', *Premium Times* 18 June 2013 http://www.premiumtimesng.com/news/139063-boko-haram-declares-war-on-borno-yobe-youth-over-vigilante-activities.html
62. 'Nigerian Boko Haram and vigilantes 'in deadly clashes'', *BBC News* 8 September 2013 http://www.bbc.co.uk/news/world-africa-24011745
63. Will Ross, 'Nigeria unrest: 'Boko Haram' gunmen kill 44 at mosque', *BBC News*, 13 August 2013 http://www.bbc.co.uk/news/world-africa-23676872
64. Abubajar Shekau quoted in Ola' Audu, 'Boko Haram: Shekau claims responsibility for attack on Giwa Barracks, threatens to attack universities, Civilian-JTF', *Premium Times*, 24 March 2014 http://www.premiumtimesng.com/news/157374-boko-haram-shekau-claims-responsibility-attack-giwa-barracks-threatens-attack-universities-civilian-jtf.html
65. Godwin Isenyo, 'Boko Haram Threatens to Kill Abducted School Girls', *Punch*, 22 April 2014 http://www.punchng.com/news/boko-haram-threatens-to-kill-parents-abducted-girls/
66. Nicolas Kristof, '"Bring Back Our Girls"', *International New York Times*, 3 May 2014 http://www.nytimes.com/2014/05/04/opinion/sunday/kristof-bring-back-our-girls.html?_r=0
67. Chuks Okocha et al, 'BOKO HARAM AMNESTY… Women, Children Detainees to be Released First, Says FG', *This Day Live*, 23 May 2013 http://www.thisdaylive.com/articles/boko-haram-amnesty-women-children-detainees-to-be-released-first-says-fg/148269/ and 'Nigeria Pardons 58 Boko

Haram Suspects', *Voice of America*, 31 May 2013 http://www.voanews.com/content/nigeria-military-pardons-58-boko-haram-suspects-women-children-yobe-borno/1672927.html

68. Ryan Cummings, 'Why Boko Haram may have kidnapped Chibok's schoolgirls', *Premium Times*, 3 May 2014 http://www.premiumtimesng.com/opinion/160044-why-boko-haram-may-have-kidnapped-chiboks-schoolgirls-by-ryan-cummings.html

69. Hamza Idris, 'Nigeria: Shekau's Wife, Others Freed', *Daily Trust*, 14 June 2013 http://allafrica.com/stories/201306140387.html

70. 'Amnesty committee, Boko Haram in secret meeting in Kaduna', *Osun Defender*, 25 May 2013 http://www.osundefender.org/?p=102035

71. Sani Takur, 'Presidential committee reaches ceasefire deal with Boko Haram—Minister', *Premium Times*, 9 July 2013 http://www.premiumtimesng.com/news/140523-presidential-committee-reaches-ceasefire-deal-with-boko-haram-minister.html

72. Peter Clottey, 'Boko Haram Tag Undermines Nigeria Peace Efforts, Say "Elders"', *Voice of America*, 5 June 2013 http://www.voanews.com/content/boko-haram-tag-undermines-nigeria-peace-efforts-say-elders/1676056.html

73. 'Nigeria: Reject Amnesty for Atrocities', *Human Rights Watch*, 2 July 2013 http://www.hrw.org/news/2013/07/02/nigeria-reject-amnesty-atrocities

74. Ibid.

75. Abubakar Shekau quoted in Okechukwu Uwaezuoke and Muhammad Bello, 'Shekau Denies Boko Haram Ceasefire', *This Day*, 14 July 2013 http://www.thisdaylive.com/articles/shekau-denies-boko-haram-ceasefire/153273/

76. Kingsley Omoboni, 'Boko Haram: New Army division takes over from JTF', *Vanguard*, 19 August 2013 http://www.vanguardngr.com/2013/08/boko-haram-new-army-division-takes-over-from-jtf/

77. Ibid.

78. Telephone interview with Nigerian military expert, 2013.

79. Lt. Gen. Azubuike Ihejirika quoted in Chiemelie Ezeobi, 'Nigeria, UK, US in Joint Exercise Against Piracy, Crude Oil Theft', *This Day Live*, 19 October 2013 http://www.thisdaylive.com/articles/nigeria-uk-us-in-joint-exercise-against-piracy-crude-oil-theft/162076/

80. Wale Odunsi, 'Women Civilian JTF emerges in Borno, targets female Boko Haram members', *Daily Post*, 24 August 2013 http://dailypost.com.ng/2013/08/24/women-civilian-jtf-emerges-in-borno-targets-female-boko-haram-members/

81. 'OP RESTORE ORDER SITREP—Week Ending 31 August 2013', *Vox*

Peccavi, 1 September 2013 http://peccaviconsulting.wordpress.com/2013/09/01/op-restore-order-sitrep-week-ending-31-august-2013/

82. 'OP RESTORE ORDER SITREP—Week Ending 26 October 2013', *Vox Peccavi*, 30 October 2013 http://peccaviconsulting.wordpress.com/2013/10/30/op-restore-order-sitrep-week-ending-26-october-2013/

83. 'Breaking News: Military declares 24 hour curfew as Harame Attack Borno airport', *Osun Defender*, 2 December 2013 http://www.osundefender.org/?p=134567

84. 'Northeast Nigeria: 2013 in Review', *Humanitarian Bulletin, Nigeria* issue 8, OCHA, December 2013 http://reliefweb.int/sites/reliefweb.int/files/resources/HB%20Nigeria%20December%20final.pdf

85. 'Death toll in Boko Haram attacks 'reach 1,500'', *BBC News*, 31 Match 2014 http://www.bbc.co.uk/news/world-africa-26816222

86. 'Nigeria: Jonathan Sacks Military Chiefs, Appoints Replacements', *Premium Times*, 16 January 2014 http://allafrica.com/stories/201401161379.html

87. Fidelis Soriwei and Sunday Aborisade, 'Boko Haram: Chief of Army Staff relocates to N'East', *Punch*, 10 March 2014 http://www.punchng.com/news/boko-haram-chief-of-army-staff-relocates-to-neast/

88. Fidelis Soriwai, 'Special forces capture B'Haram leader, kill 70 insurgents', *Punch*, 22 March 2014 http://www.punchng.com/news/special-forces-capture-bharam-leader-kill-70-insurgents/

89. See for instance 'Nigerian senator: "135 civilians killed' in attacks"', *BBC News*, 12 April 2014 http://www.bbc.co.uk/news/world-africa-27006876

90. 'Boko Haram Giwa barracks attack: Nigerian army 'killed hundreds'', *BBC News*, 31 March 2014 http://www.bbc.co.uk/news/world-africa-26819965

91. Will Ross, 'Nigeria violence: More than 70 killed in Abuja bus blast', *BBC News*, 14 April 2014 http://www.bbc.co.uk/news/world-africa-27018751

92. Kim Willsher, 'Boko Haram: African leaders agree joint action in rare show of unity', *The Guardian*, 17 May 2014 http://www.theguardian.com/world/2014/may/17/boko-haram-african-action-nigeria-schoolgirls

93. The north-south divide predates independence and has led to tensions and violence in the so-called Middle Belt making states such as Plateau infamous for spates of sectarian violence between indigene Berom and Muslim Hausa-Fulani settlers during the 2000s (ICG, 'Curbing Violence in Nigeria (I): The Jos Crisis', *Africa Report 96*, 17 December 2012 http://www.crisisgroup.org/~/media/Files/africa/west-africa/nigeria/196-curbing-violence-in-nigeria-i-the-jos-crisis.pdf.). This violence however goes beyond religious motivations and is symptomatic of the clash of opposing ways of life, i.e. sedentary agricultural and nomadic pastoral, and related tensions over land use or, as they are often described, the clash of indigenous vs. settler rights.

94. 'Nigerian army deploy more troops to North Central Nigeria; GOC 82 division relocates temporarily from Enugu to Benue', *Beegeagle's Blog*, 5 April 2014 https://beegeagle.wordpress.com/2014/04/05/nigerian-army-deploy-more-troops-to-north-central-nigeria-goc-82-division-relocates-temporarily-from-enugu-to-benue/

95. Isyaka Wakili, 'Turaki C'ttee submits report, recommends…"better equipment, pay for security agencies"', *Daily Trust*, 6 November 2013 http://dailytrust.info/index.php/top-stories/9381-turaki-c-ttee-submits-report-recommends-better-equipment-pay-for-security-agencies

96. 'OP RESTORE ORDER SITREP—Week Ending 9 November 2013', *Vox Peccavi*, 13 November 2013 http://peccaviconsulting.wordpress.com/2013/11/13/op-restore-order-sitrep-week-ending-9-november-2013/

97. Mohammed, *The Paradox of Boko Haram Nigeria*, pp. 122–3.

98. Amnesty International, *Nigeria: Trapped in the cycle of violence*, Amnesty International, 2012 http://www.amnesty.org/en/library/asset/AFR44/043/2012/en/04ab8b67–8969–4c86-bdea-0f82059dff28/afr44043 2012en.pdf

99. Amnesty International, *Nigeria. Human Rights Agenda 2011–2015*, Amnesty International, 2011, p. 30 http://www.amnesty.org/en/library/asset/AFR44/014/2011/en/5a1b7540–3afc-43ec-978c-3eab4c10d9ff/afr440142011en.pdf

100. 'Nigeria: Massive Destruction, Deaths From Military Raid', *Human Rights Watch*, 1 May 2013 http://www.hrw.org/news/2013/05/01/nigeria-massive-destruction-deaths-military-raid

101. NHRC, *The Baga Incident and the Situation in North-East Nigeria. An Interim Assessment and Report*, National Human Rights Commission, June 2013, p. 6 file://iiss-uk-file03/home$/comolliv/Downloads/NHRC%20 BAGA-NE%20EMERGENCY%20INTERIM%20RPT%20-%20 JUNE%202013.pdf

102. Interview with anonymous source #5, 2013.

103. Interviews with anonymous residents F1, F2, M1, Kano 2013.

104. Interview with anonymous resident M1, Kano 2013.

105. Interview with anonymous resident M2, Kano 2013.

106. Interview with anonymous source #8, Kano 2013.

107. Interview with Interior Minister Abba Moro, Abuja 2013.

108. Mohammed, *The Paradox of Boko Haram Nigeria*, pp. 151–2.

109. Ibid.

110. Ibid.

111. US Embassy Abuja, 'Nigeria: Terrorism Suspects Granted Bail', *Cable 08ABUJA538*, 20 March 2008 http://wikileaks.org/cable/2008/03/08 ABUJA538.html

112. Interview with Ijeoma Okwor, LEDAP, Abuja 2013.

113. Ibid.

114. 'Nigeria ethno-religious violence', *Armed Conflict Database*, IISS, October 2013 https://acd.iiss.org/

115. Interview with anonymous source #8, Kano 2013.

116. Amnesty International, *Nigeria: Trapped in the cycle of violence*, p. 40.

117. Telephone interview with anonymous source #6, 2013.

118. Amnesty International, *Nigeria: Trapped in the cycle of violence*, p. 42.

119. Will Ross, 'Boko Haram Giwa barracks attack: Nigerian army 'killed hundreds'', *BBC News*, 31 March 2104 http://www.bbc.co.uk/news/world-africa-26819965

120. Terrorism Prevention Act of 2011 (section 1A) cited by Mohammed Sambo Dasuki, 'Nigeria's Soft Approach to Countering Terrorism—NSA', *Press Release*, 19 March 2014 http://pressreleasenigeria.com/general/

121. United States Department of State, *Country Reports on Terrorism 2011—Nigeria*, 31 July 2012 http://www.refworld.org/docid/501fbca9c.html

122. 'Nigerian president sacks counter-terrorism chief', *Reuters*, 8 September 2011 http://af.reuters.com/article/topNews/idAFJOE7870FJ20110908?feedType=RSS&feedName=topNews

123. Interview with Dr Fatima Akilu, Abuja, April 2013. For the sake of completeness I note that earlier efforts to counter radicalisation and violent extremism had been launched by the Ministry of Foreign Affairs which, through its Institute for Peace and Conflict Resolution, had embarked on initiatives to detect early signs of violent extremism, had sent mediators to areas known for religious tensions, and so on. (United States Department of State, *Country Reports on Terrorism 2011—Nigeria*, 31 July 2012 http://www.refworld.org/docid/501fbca9c.html). Little however it is known of the effectiveness of such measures.

124. HM Government, *Prevent Strategy*, 2011. https://www.gov.uk/government/uploads/system/uploads/attachment_data/file/97976/prevent-strategy-review.pdf

125. Interview with Dr Fatima Akilu, Abuja, April 2013.

126. Ibid.

127. 'FG has convicted 40 Boko Haram members—ADOKE', *Vanguard*, 25 February 2014 http://www.vanguardngr.com/2014/02/fg-convicted-40-boko-haram-members-adoke/

128. United States Department of State, *Country Reports on Terrorism 2011—Nigeria*, 31 July 2012, http://www.refworld.org/docid/501fbca9c.html More details on the Act's provisions can be found here: Vera Ekundayo, 'Nigerian Terrorism Act: A right step forward', *Punch*, 24 January 2012 http://www.punchng.com/opinion/nigerian-terrorism-act-a-right-step-forward/

129. Interview with Interior Minister Abba Moro, Abuja, 2013.
130. Segun Adebowale, 'Nigeria's terrorism law is weak—US', *The Eagle*, 31 May 2013 http://theeagleonline.com.ng/nigerias-terrorism-law-is-weak-us/
131. BBC News, 'Nigeria: Jail terms to tackle Islamist militancy', *BBC News*, 5 June 2013 http://www.bbc.co.uk/news/world-africa-22779919
132. 'Nigeria to use 'soft' tactics to curb Boko Haram violence', *AFP*, 18 March 2014 http://news.yahoo.com/nigeria-soft-tactics-curb-boko-haram-violence-135229718.html
133. Mohammed Sambo Dasuki, 'Nigeria's Soft Approach to Countering Terrorism—NSA', *Press Release*, 19 March 2014 http://pressreleasenigeria.com/general/
134. 'Nigeria's Kano city hit by blasts targeting bars', *BBC News*, 30 July 2013 http://www.bbc.co.uk/news/world-africa-23498757
135. Telephone interview with anonymous source #7, March 2014.
136. Ibid.
137. '124 Almajiri schools to open in September', *Daily Trust*, 31 July 2013 http://dailytrust.info/index.php/news/2057–124-almajiri-schools-to-open-in-september
138. Segun Awofadeji, 'Sambo Inaugurates Tsangaya Model School, Other Projects in Bauchi', *This Day*, 3 November 2013 http://www.thisdaylive.com/articles/sambo-inaugurates-tsangaya-model-school-other-projects-in-bauchi/163328/
139. David J. Kilcullen, 'Three Pillars of Counterinsurgency', Remarks delivered at the US Government Counterinsurgency Conference, Washington D.C., 28 September 2006
140. Ibid.
141. Eric Chase, 'Defining Terrorism: A Strategic Imperative', *Small Wars Journal*, 24 January 2013 http://smallwarsjournal.com/jrnl/art/defining-terrorism-a-strategic-imperative
142. HMG, *Terrorism Act 2000*, http://www.legislation.gov.uk/ukpga/2000/11/pdfs/ukpga_20000011_en.pdf
143. 'Nigerian Air Force rejigs ops, get new combat command', *Beegeagle's Blog* 15 November 2010 http://beegeagle.wordpress.com/2010/11/15/nigerian-air-force-rejigs-ops-get-new-combat-command/
144. Bureau of African Affairs, *US Relations With Nigeria*, US Department of State, 28 August 2013 http://www.state.gov/r/pa/ei/bgn/2836.htm
145. Office of the Spokesman, 'U.S.–Nigeria Binational Commission', *Media Note*, US Department of State, 6 April 2010 http://www.state.gov/r/pa/prs/ps/2010/04/139562.htm
146. 'Nigerian army deploy first-ever wholly Special Forces Battalion', 24 April

2010 https://beegeagle.wordpress.com/2010/04/24/nigerian-army-deploy-first-ever-wholly-special-forces-battalion/

147. US Department of State, *Programs and Initiatives*, http://www.state.gov/j/ct/programs/index.htm#TSCTP

148. Lesley Anne Warner, *The Trans Sahara Counter Terrorism Partnership. Building Partner Capacity to Counter Terrorism and Violent Extremism*, CCO/CAN, 20 March 2014, pp. 1–2, 11, http://www.cna.org/sites/default/files/research/CRM-2014-U-007203-Final.pdf

149. Ibid., p. 27.

150. Ibid., pp. 37–8.

151. Ibid., pp. 42, 44–5, 47–8.

152. Ibid., p. 71.

153. 'Nigerian army deploy first-ever wholly Special Forces Battalion'.

154. Warner, *The Trans Sahara Counter Terrorism Partnership*, p. 75.

155. Ibid., p. 83.

156. There have been contrasting details emerging on the training provided to JTF elements as exemplified here: Fidelis Soriwei, Jude Owuamanam and Adelani Adepegba, 'Army deploys US-trained Nigerian commandos in the North', *Punch*, 13 November 2011 http://odili.net/news/source/2011/nov/13/806.html

157. Fidelis Soriwei, 'Nigerian Army establishes special command to tackle B'Haram', *Punch*, 14 January 2014 http://www.punchng.com/news/nigerian-army-establishes-special-command-to-tackle-bharam/

158. 'US offers to help hunt for abducted girls', *Reuters*, 2 May 2014 http://www.iol.co.za/news/africa/us-offers-to-help-hunt-for-abducted-girls-1.1682593#.U2ZLRoFdXAs

159. 'US experts join hunt for abducted Nigerian schoolgirls', *BBC News*, 7 May 2014 http://www.bbc.co.uk/news/world-africa-27304441

160. Linda Thomas-Greenfield, Assistant Secretary, Bureau of African Affairs, 'Countering the Threat Posed by Boko Haram', *Testimony to the House Foreign Affairs Subcommittees on Africa, Global Health, Human Rights, and International Organizations and Terrorism, Nonproliferation, and Trade*, Washington, DC, 13 November 2013 http://www.state.gov/p/af/rls/rm/2013/217653.htm

161. "The newly formed al-Murabitoun extremist group constitutes the greatest near-term threat to US and Western interests in the Sahel", claimed the US Department of State in December 2013 [Office of the Spokesperson, *Terrorist Designation of the al-Mulathamun Battalion*, US Department of State, 18 December 2013 http://www.state.gov/r/pa/prs/ps/2013/218880.htm]

162. Office of the Spokesperson, *Terrorist Designations of Boko Haram*

Commander Abubakar Shekau, Khalid al-Barnawi and Abubakar Adam Kambar, US Department of State, 21 June 2012 http://www.state.gov/r/pa/prs/ps/2012/06/193574.htm

163. 'JTF claims 'global terrorist' Kambar killed', *Vanguard*, 7 June 2013 http://www.vanguardngr.com/2013/06/jtf-claims-global-terrorist-kambar-killed/

164. Ibid.

165. 'US puts $7m bounty on Boko Haram leader, Abubakar Shekau', *Nigeria News*, 3 June 2013, http://news2.onlinenigeria.com/headline/290462-us-puts-7m-bounty-on-b%E2%80%99haram-leader%2C-shekau.html#ixzz2rKlmdhlZ

166. 'Wanted for Terrorism', *Rewards for Justice* http://www.rewardsforjustice.net/index.cfm?page=Wanted_Terrorist (accessed 22 April 2014)

167. Tobunko Adedoja, 'Nigeria: Designate Boko Haram As FTO, CAN Urges US', *All Africa*, 12 July 2012 http://allafrica.com/stories/201207120578.html

168. Zoe Flood, 'Top US General warns of coordination between al-Qaeda-linked African terror groups', *The Telegraph*, 1 March 2012 http://www.telegraph.co.uk/news/worldnews/al-qaeda/9116773/Top-US-General-warns-of-coordination-between-al-Qaeda-linked-African-terror-groups.html

169. Patrick Meehan and Jackie Speier, 'Boko Haram. Emerging Threat to the US Homeland', US House of Representatives, 30 November 2011 http://homeland.house.gov/hearing/subcommittee-hearing-boko-haram-emerging-threat-us-homeland

170. 'America, die with your fury', *Iol News*, 14 July 2010 http://www.iol.co.za/news/africa/america-die-with-your-fury-1.489783

171. 'Boko Haram Vows More Violence, Accuses Obama Of Waging War Against Islam', *The Times of Nigeria*, 28 January 2012 http://www.the-timesofnigeria.com/TON/Article.aspx?id=3552

172. Michael T. McCaul, Patrick Meehan and Peter T. King, 'Boko Haram. Growing Threat to the US Homeland', US House of Representatives, 13 September 2013, p. 3 http://homeland.house.gov/sites/homeland.house.gov/files/documents/09–13–13-Boko-Haram-Report.pdf

173. Ibid., p. 5.

174. Nduka Nwosu and Zacheaus Somorin, 'Nigeria: US Designates Boko Haram, Ansaru Terrorist Organisations', *This Day* 14 November 2013 http://allafrica.com/stories/201311140121.html

175. Office of the Spokesperson, *Terrorist Designation of Boko Haram and Ansaru*, US Department of State, 13 November 2013 http://www.state.gov/r/pa/prs/ps/2013/11/217509.htm

176. US Department of State, 'Background note: Nigeria', 20 October 2011 http://www.state.gov/r/pa/ei/bgn/2836.htm

177. *Nigeria*, US Energy Information Administration 30 December 2013 http://www.eia.gov/countries/analysisbriefs/Nigeria/nigeria.pdf

178. '"Niger Delta, you are in trouble"—Shekau says in new video', *The Herald*, 20 February 2014 http://www.theheraldng.com/niger-delta-trouble-shekau-says-new-video/

179. Virginia Comolli and Jacob Zenn, 'Danger at Home: Boko Haram's Threat to Nigeria and The Limits of Its Strategic Expansion', *Terrorism Research & Analysis Consortium (TRAC)*, 30 July 2012 http://bit.ly/VM7CEr

180. David Francis, 'Move over Boko Haram, Nigeria's MEND rebels set to restart oil war in Niger Delta', *The Christian Science Monitor*, 30 October 2011 http://news.yahoo.com/move-over-boko-haram-nigerias-mend-rebels-set-192800248.html

181. Donald G. McNeil, 'Gunmen Kill Nigerian Polio Vaccine Workers in Echo of Pakistan Attacks', *International New York Times*, 8 February 2013 http://www.nytimes.com/2013/02/09/world/africa/in-nigeria-polio-vaccine-workers-are-killed-by-gunmen.html?_r=0

182. Interview with US government officials, Abuja, April 2013.

183. See for instance 'PRESS NOTICE: UK trains an extra 17,000 Nigerian peacekeepers', Ministry of Defence 20 September 2005 http://webarchive.nationalarchives.gov.uk/+/http://www.operations.mod.uk/africa/newsItem_id=3565.htm

184. 'Deployments in Africa. Background', Ministry of Defence, 11 March 2005 http://webarchive.nationalarchives.gov.uk/+/http://www.operations.mod.uk/africa/bkgrnd.htm

185. Cooperation in the Niger Delta also comes under the rubric of the US-led Africa Partnership Station (APS). An example of APS efforts was a multinational three-week long exercise codenamed *African Winds* that was run in Nigerian waters in October 2013 including UK, US, Spanish, Dutch and Nigerian navies and armies [Chiemelie Ezeobi, 'Nigeria, UK, US in Joint Exercise Against Piracy, Crude Oil Theft', *This Day*, 19 October 2013 http://www.thisdaylive.com/articles/nigeria-uk-us-in-joint-exercise-against-piracy-crude-oil-theft/162076/]

186. Mark Lowe, 'Nigeria, UK Sign MoU On Security', *All Africa*, 8 March 2013 http://www.marsecreview.com/2013/03/15640/

187. Sarah Sharoka, 'ARMED EXTRACTION. The UK Military in Nigeria', *Platform*, April 2013 http://platformlondon.org/wp-content/uploads/2013/08/ArmedExtraction_web_final-4.pdf

188. Richard Norton-Taylor, 'UK intervention in Mali is strategy for future, says defence secretary', *The Guardian*, 29 January 2013 http://www.theguardian.com/world/2013/jan/29/uk-intervention-mali-strategy-future

189. AC Olukolade, *Press Release. Nigeria-UK deepen counter-terrorism collaboration*, Defence Headquarters, Abuja, 28 March 2013.

190. 'Nigeria and UK announce counter-terrorism co-operation agreement', *Jane's Intelligence Weekly*, 20 July 2011.

191. 'UK to fight Boko Haram', *The Nation* 14 March 2012 http://www.thenationonlineng.net/2011/index.php/news/39717-uk-to-fight-boko-haram.html

192. Home Office, *Proscribed terror groups or organisations*, updated on 8 April 214   https://www.gov.uk/government/publications/proscribed-terror-groups-or-organisations-2

193. Sharoka, 'ARMED EXTRACTION. The UK Military in Nigeria'.

194. 'Nigerians hit by UK ban', *Jane's Defence Weekly* 3 July 1993.

195. Foreign Affairs Committee, *Seventh Report. The UK's response to extremism and instability in North and West Africa*, March 2014 http://www.publications.parliament.uk/pa/cm201314/cmselect/cmfaff/86/8602.htm

196. *The UK's response to extremism and political instability in North and West Africa* [enquiry page], updated 21 March 2014 http://www.parliament.uk/business/committees/committees-a-z/commons-select/foreign-affairs-committee/inquiries1/parliament-2010/west-africa/

197. James Blitz, 'Cameron leads warnings on jihadi threat', *Financial Times*, 20 January 2013 http://www.ft.com/cms/s/0/546e45d6–6316–11e2–8497–00144feab49a.html

198. Dominic Casciani, 'Woolwich: How did Michael Adebolajo become a killer?', *BBC News*, 19 December 2013 http://www.bbc.co.uk/news/magazine-25424290

199. Virginia Comolli, 'Is Nigerian extremism really a threat to the UK?', *IISS Voices*, 8 July 2013 http://www.iiss.org/en/iiss%20voices/blogsections/iiss-voices-2013–1e35/july-2013-a513/nigeria-extremism-98b5

200. Ibid.

201. Jamie Grierson, 'Two extremist groups including Nigeria-based Boko Haram face UK membership and support ban', *The Independent*, 8 July 2013http://www.independent.co.uk/news/uk/crime/two-extremist-groups-including-nigeriabased-boko-haram-face-uk-membership-and-support-ban-8695492.html

202. Ibid.

203. UK Parliament, Debate, 10 July 2013, Column 455 http://www.publications.parliament.uk/pa/cm201314/cmhansrd/cm130710/debt-ext/130710–0003.htm

204. Tim Cocks, 'Nigeria Boko Haram leader urges global jihad in video', *Reuters*, 30 November 2012 http://uk.reuters.com/article/2012/11/30/uk-nigeria-bokoharam-idUKBRE8AT0S020121130

205. Foreign Affairs Committee, *Seventh Report*.
206. Toyosi Ogunseye, 'Boko Haram: Intelligence operatives investigate Nigerians in the UK, *Sunday Punch*, 5 February 2011 http://www.punchng.com/news/boko-haram-intelligence-operatives-investigate-nigerians-in-the-uk/; Robert Fox, 'Nigeria's dangerous Islamists are a potential threat to Olympics, *The Week*, 24 January 2012 http://www.theweek.co.uk/world-news/44630/nigerias-dangerous-islamists-are-potential-threat-olympics
207. 'Nigerians in the UK', Central Association of Nigerians in the United Kingdom http://www.canuk.org.uk/uknigerians.aspx
208. 'Nigerian tourists overtake Russians as UK's third biggest shoppers in new survey ', *Nigerian Watch*, 24 March 2014 http://www.nigerianwatch.com/news/4128-nigerian-tourists-overtake-russians-as-uks-third-biggest-shoppers-in-new-survey#sthash.JuEDRj8W.dpuf
209. Interview with NSRP staff, Abuja April 2013.
210. 'Canada designates Boko Haram as terror organisation', *Daily Trust*, 1 January 2014 http://dailytrust.info/index.php/news/13519-canada-designates-boko-haram-as-terror-organisation
211. 'Canada to assist Nigeria in fighting terrorism', *Vanguard*, 10 October 2012 http://www.naijafeed.com/2012/10/canada-to-assist-nigeria-in-fighting.html
212. AP, 'Gilberte Bussières, Canadian nun, and 2 priests abducted in Cameroon', *CBC News*, 5 April 2014 http://www.cbc.ca/news/world/gilberte-bussi%C3%A8res-canadian-nun-and-2-priests-abducted-in-cameroon-1.2599487

7. CONCLUSIONS

1. Interview with Dr Ustaz Aminu Igwegbe, Director of Administration, Nigerian Supreme Council of Islamic Affairs, Nigeria 2013.
2. Interview with senior Nigerian counter-terrorism officer, Nigeria 2013.
3. Interview with then Chief of Defence Staff Admiral Ola Sa'ad Ibrahim, Abuja 2013.
4. Ibid.
5. I have noted however an increase in the number of Nigerian troops that have undergone counterterrorism and counterinsurgency training which includes a better understanding of "winning hearts and minds".
6. Nigeria is ranked 144 out of 177 countries on Transparency International Corruption Index 2013 and corruption appears to be a pervasive feature of social interaction (Transparency International, *Corruption Perceptions Index 2013*, 2013 http://cpi.transparency.org/cpi2013/results/). Attempts have

been made to reform the political and banking sectors, to mention two, but this is a long process as too many interests benefit from a dysfunctional system. And it is also a dangerous process. Internationally respected Finance Minister Ngozi Okonjo-Iweala—who had embarked on a wide-ranging anti-corruption clean-up—has seen her own mother being kidnapped in 2012 (BBC News, Nigeria's Ngozi Okonjo-Iweala's mother freed by kidnappers, 14 December 2012, http://www.bbc.co.uk/news/world-africa-20725677). Many pages have been written on the issue of corruption in Nigeria and there is no need for me to go into a lengthy discussion on the subject. I would just make reference to 2014 events when the Governor of the Central Bank Lamido Sanusi was removed from office following his accusation that the Nigeria National Petroleum Corporation (NNPC) had failed to account for $20bn (out of $67bn) of oil revenues for the January 2012–July 2013 period (BBC News, 'Nigeria orders probe into 'missing $20bn' of oil money', 12 March 2014, http://www.bbc.co.uk/news/world-africa-26553388). Sanusi, who had claimed that over a 19 month period $1bn was disappearing on a monthly basis, later filed and won a harassment case against the government in March (BBC News, 'Nigeria's Lamido Sanusi wins damages case in Lagos court', 3 April 2014, http://www.bbc.co.uk/news/world-africa-26872357). A further insight into the years-long corruption problem was provided the same month when the US announced the freezing of $458m that former Nigerian dictator Sani Abacha had hidden around the world—part of the $3–5bn he is believed to have looted while in power between 1993 and 1998 (Reuters, 'US freezes $458m hidden by former Nigerian leader Sani Abacha', *The Telegraph*, 5 March 2014 http://www.telegraph.co.uk/news/worldnews/africaandindianocean/nigeria/10679487/US-freezes-458m-hidden-by-former-Nigerian-leader-Sani-Abacha.html).

7. The phenomenon of desertification whereby the Sahara desert is effectively expanding southward is forcing herdsmen to move south to feed their cattle contributing to the tensions alluded to above. In addition, and even more pertinent to the Boko Haram context, are the severe droughts experienced in Nigeria's neighbours Chad and Niger. Moreover, rising temperatures causing the evaporation of water and the shrinking of Lake Chad—whose basin is essential for the survival of approximately 30 million people from Nigeria, Chad, Niger and Cameroon—is affecting economic opportunities in the region (fishing above all) (Emmanuela Mayah, 'Climate change fuels Nigeria terrorism', *Africa Review*, 24 February 2012 http://www.africareview.com/News/Climate+change+fuels+Nigeria+terrorism/-/979180/1334472/-/xrkqw5z/-/index.html). A study by the Ahmadu Bello University Zaria titled *Ecological Crises and Social Conflict in Northern Nigeria's Dry Belt*, indicates that many of those who took part in the riots of the 1970s and 1980s, includ-

ing those of the Maitatstine, started in areas hosting refuges from ecological disasters, both farmers and pastoralists who had lost their livelihoods [ibid.]. More recently, in early 2012 Nigerian security forces indicated that some of the apprehended Boko Haram foot soldiers were likely to have been Nigerien nationals escaping a severe drought in Niger and joining the militants for economic rather than ideological reasons [ibid.].

8. NSRP 1 May–15 June 2013.
9. 'OP RESTORE ORDER SITREP—Week Ending 9 November 2013', *Vox Peccavi*, 13 November 2013 http://peccaviconsulting.wordpress.com/2013/11/13/op-restore-order-sitrep-week-ending-9-november-2013/
10. Interview with Borno State official, London March 2013.
11. 'OP RESTORE ORDER SITREP—Week Ending 25 January 2014', *Vox Peccavi*, 27 January 2014 http://peccaviconsulting.wordpress.com/2014/01/27/op-restore-order-sitrep-week-ending-25-january-2014/
12. David Hall, *Water and electricity in Nigeria*, Public Services International Research Unit (PSIRU), September 2006, p. 10.
13. Worth adding in the context of economic development, I was reminded during a field trip to Kano that the building of the Tiga dam in Kano state in the 1950s had significantly reduced the flow of water to Lake Chad and that this was a source of resentment for the Kanuri living in Borno state (bordering the lake) who no longer lived in a lush environment (Interview with Kano residents, Kano, 17 April 2013).
14. Post-independence from Great Britain in 1960, Nigeria emerged as a federation of 36 states and Abuja Federal Capital Territory but a period of military rule and coup d'etat meant that democracy was only restored in 1999 with the election of General Olusegun Obasanjo as President of the Nigerian Federation. From this point political unity between north and south was maintained by the application of an unwritten rule whereby presidents, entitled to serve only for two terms, would alternate between northern and southern candidates. This equilibrium was interrupted when President Umaru Yar'Adua, a Muslim from the north, died on 5 May 2010 during his first term. The then Vice President Goodluck Jonathan, a southern Christian, took over and served until the end of the four-year term in 2011. The 2011 presidential elections resulted in Jonathan's victory and became the first elections in the county not to be criticised by the international community for being flawed or unfair. Jonathan's current term is due to end in 2015 and the announcement that he would seek re-election has been met by strong criticism by those who believe that had it not been for Yar'Adua's death northerners would have been entitled to another presidential term. For this reason, much anticipation surrounds the 2015 election and an outbreak of violence should not be discounted.

EPILOGUE

1. 'Conflict Trends', Armed Conflict Location & Event Data Project's (ACLED), No. 33, January 2015, p. 8 http://www.acleddata.com/wp-content/uploads/2015/01/ACLED-Conflict-Trends-Report-No.-33-January-2015_updated.pdf

2. Fisayo Soyombo, 'Nigeria's 'fake' ceasefire with Boko Haram', Al Jazeera, 11 November 2014 http://www.aljazeera.com/indepth/opinion/2014/11/nigeria-fake-ceasefire-with-b-20141111103442243308.html

3. Rose Troup Buchanan, 'Scores killed and over 100 injured in suspected Boko Haram attack on Nigeria's Grand Mosque', *The Independent*, 29 November 2014 http://www.independent.co.uk/news/world/africa/scores-killed-and-over-100-injured-in-suspected-boko-haram-attack-on-nigerias-grand-mosque-9892476.html

4. Ibrahim Shuaibu, 'I'm Safe with Allah, Emir Sanusi Replies Boko Haram', ThisDayLive, 21 December 2014 http://www.thisdaylive.com/articles/i-m-safe-with-allah-emir-sanusi-replies-boko-haram/197316/

5. 'Nigeria's Boko Haram militants attack Chad for first time', BBC News, 13 February 2015 http://www.bbc.co.uk/news/world-africa-31453951

6. 'Boko Haram launches first attack in Niger', BBC News, 6 February 2015 http://www.bbc.co.uk/news/world-africa-31162979?ocid=socialflow_twitter Notably, only a few days earlier Boko Haram had vowed to retaliate against Niger if the country joined neighbours Cameroon and Chad in their counterinsurgency efforts [Dalatou Mamone and Edwin Kindzeka Moki, 'Boko Haram attacks town in Niger after assault on Cameroon', Associated Press, 6 February 2015 http://news.yahoo.com/boko-haram-attacks-town-inside-niger-cameroon-122511731.html]

7. Daveed Gartenstein-Ross and Laura Grossman, 'Boko Haram Did Not Declare a Caliphate', Foundation for Defense of Democracies, 4 September 2014

8. Alexander Smith, 'Nigeria's Boko Haram Violence Puts Maiduguri City on Edge', NBC News, 4 February 2015 http://www.nbcnews.com/storyline/missing-nigeria-schoolgirls/nigerias-boko-haram-violence-puts-maiduguri-city-edge-n299056

9. Charles Dickson, 'INVESTIGATION: Grim tales of rape, child trafficking in Nigeria's displaced persons camps', *Premium Times*, 31 January 2015 http://www.premiumtimesng.com/investigationspecial-reports/176005-investigation-grim-tales-rape-child-trafficking-nigerias-displaced-persons-camps.html

10. 'Boko Haram abducts Cameroon politician's wife', BBC News, 27 July 2014 http://www.bbc.co.uk/news/world-africa-28509530; 'Cameroon flies

freed Boko Haram hostages to capital', BBC News, 11 October 2014 http://www.bbc.co.uk/news/world-africa-29581495

11. Ejikeme Omenazu, 'Nigeria: Chad Deploys Troops to Fight Boko Haram', *Daily Independent*, 18 January 2015 http://allafrica.com/stories/2015011 90161.html

12. 'Chad military claims killing Boko Haram fighters', Al Jazeera, 4 February 2015 http://www.aljazeera.com/news/2015/02/chad-troops-kill-hundreds-boko-haram-fighters-150204091005115.html

13. 'Cameroon launches first air strikes against Boko Haram', France 24, 29 December 2014 http://www.france24.com/en/20141229-cameroon-launches-air-strikes-against-boko-haram-first-time/

14. Peter Clottey, 'African Union Hails Military Offensive Against Boko Haram', Voice of America, 5 February 2015 http://www.voanews.com/content/african-union-hails-military-offensive-against-boko-haram/2630375.html

15. Ibid.

16. 'Boko Haram crisis: UN 'not needed against Nigerian militants'', BBC News, 23 January 2015 http://www.bbc.co.uk/news/world-africa-30950 628

17. 'Angela Merkel: EU should fund force to fight Boko Haram—video', *The Guardian*, 19 January 2015 http://www.theguardian.com/world/video/2015/jan/19/angela-merkel-eu-should-fund-force-fight-boko-haram-video

18. 'Opération Barkhane', Ministère de la Défense [French Ministry of Defence], 11 August 2014 http://www.defense.gouv.fr/operations/sahel/dossier-de-presentation-de-l-operation-barkhane/operation-barkhane

19. John Irish and Marine Pennetier, 'France sends advisers to Nigeria border to coordinate Boko Haram fight'. Reuters, 6 February 2015 http://af.reuters.com/article/topNews/idAFKBN0LA0M720150206; Jack Moore, 'French Air Force Back Fight Against Boko Haram on Nigeria's Borders', *Newsweek*, 4 February 2015 http://www.newsweek.com/french-air-force-back-fight-against-boko-haram-nigerias-borders-304288

20. Interview with senior French security analyst, January 2015.

21. 'Nigeria elections: Security chief urges vote delay', BBC News, 22 January 2015 http://www.bbc.co.uk/news/world-africa-30938612

22. 'Nigeria's Elections: A Perilous Postponement', International Crisis Group, 12 February 2015 http://blog.crisisgroup.org/africa/2015/02/12/nigerias-elections-a-perilous-postponement/

23. 'Nigeria to postpone elections to fight Boko Haram', *The Guardian*, 7 February 2015 http://www.theguardian.com/world/2015/feb/07/nigeria-to-postpone-elections-to-fight-boko-haram

24. Karen Attiah, 'Nigeria's risky decision to postpone elections', *The Washington*

Post, 8 February 2015 http://www.washingtonpost.com/blogs/post-partisan/wp/2015/02/08/nigerias-risky-decision-to-postpone-elections/

25. Anne Look, 'Battle for Nigeria's Presidency Enters Courts', Voice of America, 11 February 2015 http://www.voanews.com/content/battle-for-nigeria-presidency-enters-courts/2639274.html

26. 'The least awful', *The Economist*, 7 February 2015 http://www.economist.com/news/leaders/21642168-former-dictator-better-choice-failed-president-least-awful

27. Uchenna Ekwo, 'The real reason Nigeria should delay elections', Al Jazeera, 5 February 2015 http://america.aljazeera.com/opinions/2015/2/the-real-reason-nigeria-should-delay-elections.html

28. 'Boko Haram attacks Gombe in Nigeria and calls for election boycott', *The Guardian*, 14 February 215 http://www.theguardian.com/world/2015/feb/14/boko-haram-launches-first-attack-in-chad

APPENDIX

1. Ahl al-Sunnah wal-Jama'ah, Ja'amutu Tajidmul Islami
2. Bauchi, Borno, Gombe, Jigawa, Kaduna, Kano, Katsina, Kebbi, Niger, Sokoto, Yobe, and Zamfara HRW, 'Political Shari'a?': Human Rights and Islamic Law in Northern Nigeria (2004) http://www.unhcr.org/refworld/country,,HRW,,NGA,,415c02ae4,0.html

INDEX

INDEX

INDEX

INDEX

INDEX

US Department of State: 98
US House of Representatives Committee on Homeland Security: 33
US Rewards for Justice Programme: 145

Vigilantes see Civilian Joint Task Force (C-JTF)

Wadoud, Abu Musab Abdel a.k.a. Abdelmalek Droukdel: 98
Wahhabism: 20, 47, 173(n)
Walker, Andrew: 33, 46, 50, 63, 65
Weapons: 115, 153; chemical: 54
Welfare: 52, 71
Wike, Minister of State for Education Ezenwo Nyesom: 140
Women: 3, 15, 21, 23, 50, 69, 92, 117–8, 122, 125–6, 128–9, 132, 161–2, 168; girls: 4–5, 69 71–2, 105, 125, 130, 144, 157, 162, 167–8
Woolwich attack (murder of Private Lee Rigby): 150
World Economic Forum: 157

Yakubu, Hassana: 126
Yan Tauri [street urchins]: 74, 141
Yaoundé (Cameroon): 89, 94
Yar'adua, President Umaru: 54, 162, 219(n)
Yobe: 20
Yoruba: 16, 18, 119
Yuguda, Governor Isa: 80
Yunfa, King: 15
Yusuf, Mohamed: 6, 27, 29–33, 41, 45–63, 65, 67–8, 71, 78–9, 86–7, 98, 100, 111, 116, 126, 131, 134, 151, 162–3, 179(n), 182–3(n)
Yusufyya: 30, 33, 41, 46, 68

Zakaria, Mohammed: 80
Zakzaky, Ibrahim: 27, 35–6
Zamfara: 14, 20–1, 220(n)
Zara, Malama: 126
Zaria: 114, 218(n)
Zenn, Jacob: 26, 28, 59, 63, 87, 95, 104
Zinder: 89–90
Zubair, Muhammed: 80; *Human Rights Research and Advocacy Centre* (Kano): 80